MW01681261

Experimental Pedagogy and the Psychology of the Child;

You are holding a reproduction of an original work that is in the public domain in the United States of America, and possibly other countries.You may freely copy and distribute this work as no entity (individual or corporate) has a copyright on the body of the work.This book may contain prior copyright references, and library stamps (as most of these works were scanned from library copies).These have been scanned and retained as part of the historical artifact.

This book may have occasional imperfections such as missing or blurred pages, poor pictures, errant marks, etc. that were either part of the original artifact, or were introduced by the scanning process. We believe this work is culturally important, and despite the imperfections, have elected to bring it back into print as part of our continuing commitment to the preservation of printed works worldwide. We appreciate your understanding of the imperfections in the preservation process, and hope you enjoy this valuable book.

Psych.
C588

EXPERIMENTAL PEDAGOGY

AND

THE PSYCHOLOGY OF THE CHILD

BY

DR. ED. CLAPARÈDE

PROF[E]SSOR OF EXPERIMENTAL PSYCHOLOGY AT THE GENEVA UNIVERSITY

Translated from the Fourth Edition of "Psychologie de l'Enfant et Pédagogie Expérimentale"

BY

MARY LOUCH

AND

HENRY HOLMAN

22156
6/5/12

LONDON
EDWARD ARNOLD
1911

(All rights reserved)

AUTHOR'S PREFACE TO THE FOURTH EDITION

This new edition differs from preceding editions by many alterations: the *Historical Sketch* is included for the first time, Chapters II., III., and V. have been completed and more or less remodelled; on the other hand, the chapter on *Mental Development* has been but little changed. The volume as a whole has been increased by nearly 200 pages, and the authors quoted now number 630 as against 250.

In some of the reviews of this work, regret has been expressed that it did not contain more practical advice for the pedagogue. But my aim in writing the book was not to compile a manual of pedagogy; I simply wished to introduce the educator to psychological science, and particularly to the psychology of the child. The first steps taken in learning a new science are always tiresome and difficult: time is lost in finding one's bearings, in understanding what exactly is the aim of the science, in discovering the problems which it tries to solve; therefore a guide is often very valuable. To be such a *guide* is the function of this book, at least a guide to the study of those problems which are here treated. And I should be glad if, into the bargain, it stimulated personal research, if it tempted some practical teacher to abandon the groove of ordinary routine, to ask himself from time to time some hard questions, which he would try to answer by reference to facts.

It may not be useless to mention here, in order to avoid misunderstanding, that when I speak of the *results* of experiments or inquiries, of statistics, curves, &c., these results are given chiefly by way of *example*, of illustration, of suggestion, for new researches, and not as the utterance of a truth already classified and definitely determined.

I have extensively used, and doubtless also abused, classification and marginal headings. . . . Is it necessary to say that I attach no intrinsic importance to all the divisions, subdivisions, and nomenclature that I have made use of: they are chiefly, to my mind, an expository device, a simple means of facilitating the reader's "apperception" of the subject-matter contained in this volume, which would have constituted an absolutely indigestible mass if it had not been classified and arranged under headings.

Such as it is, and in spite of its imperfections, this work has been judged capable of rendering some service, since there have been many requests for a translation: a Spanish and a Russian edition have already appeared, a German, an Italian, and an English edition will appear shortly. I wish to offer my very sincere thanks to the kind colleagues in foreign lands who have undertaken to make this book accessible to a larger circle of readers.

ED. C.

CHAMPEL, GENEVA,
September 15, 1910.

TRANSLATORS' NOTE

THE translators feel that if they had merely added another good book on Child-study to those already in existence—which are by no means too many—they would have had full justification, but in translating a work so simple, comprehensive, and scientific, and by an author with such a great reputation for his work in Experimental Psychology, they are convinced that they have attempted something that was well worth doing. There is, so far as the translators know, no book which covers the same ground in the same way; and, in their opinion, such a book has long been wanted, and will be eagerly welcomed by those who are concerned to know what Child-study really means, and how to take part in it. It is a book which should help teachers in the schoolroom, and parents in the home.

They wish to express their thanks to Professor Claparède for giving them the opportunity of translating his book, and for the help he has given them in the translation.

It will be noticed that the order of the words in the French title *Psychologie de l'Enfant et Pédagogie Expérimentale* has been changed. This was thought advisable so as to distinguish it from other books on Child-study.

MARY LOUCH.
HENRY HOLMAN.

July 1, 1911.

The titles of the periodicals frequently quoted in this work are generally abbreviated as follows :—

Am. J. Psy.	American Journal of Psychology.
An. Psy.	Année psychologique.
Ar. de Psy.	Archives de Psychologie.
Ar. f. g. Psy.	Archiv fur die gesamte Psychologie.
Ar. int. hyg. scol.	Archives internationales d'hygiène scolaire.
B. J. of Psy.	British Journal of Psychology.
Bull. S. psy. E.	Bulletin de la Société libre pour l'étude psychologique de l'enfant.
Ed. mod.	L'Educateur moderne.
Educ.	L'Education.
H. Sc.	L'Hygiène scolaire.
J. of ed. Ps.	Journal of Educational Psychology (U.S.A.).
Kf.	Kinderfehler (Zeitsch. f. Kinderforschung).
Ped. S.	Pedagogical Seminary (U.S.A.).
Ps. Arb.	Psychologische Arbeiten.
Ps. R.	Psychological Review.
R. di Psy.	Rivista di Psicologia.
Riv. Ped.	Rivista pedagogica.
Z. ang. Psy.	Zeitschrift fur angewandte Psychologie
Z. exp. Päd.	Zeitschrift fur experimentelle Padagogik.
Z. f. Psy.	Zeitschrift fur Psychologie.
Z. pad. P.	Zeitschrift fur pädagogische Psychologie.

CONTENTS

CHAPTER IV

CHAPTER V

EXPERIMENTAL PEDAGOGY

INTRODUCTION

PSYCHOLOGY AND PEDAGOGY

THAT pedagogy ought to be based upon the knowledge of the child, as horticulture is based upon the knowledge of plants, would seem to be an elementary truth. It is, nevertheless, entirely unrecognised by most teachers and nearly all educational authorities. To prove this, it is sufficient to point out that in most of the European training colleges for teachers no course in the psychology of the child is given. The young people who are sent out from these institutions, at the age of eighteen or nineteen, are placed by the State in primary or secondary schools; charged with the task of developing intelligences, forming characters, and restraining instincts; and yet no one has ever taught them what is the nature of intelligence, character, and instinct, and what are the laws of the development of these phenomena—laws which they certainly ought to know very thoroughly, so that they may adapt their methods of teaching to them.

Doubtless in the schools of horticulture there are, upon the time-table, at least a few hours set apart for botany and the knowledge of plants. In all times, as a matter of fact, people have given much more attention to the cultivation of flowers and fruit than to the education of children. They are also much more concerned about the raising of cattle. Herbert Spencer, in his book on *Education*, remarks on this in a very pungent manner, when he pictures to us the country gentleman making his daily visit to the stables and the pigsty, inspecting for himself the management of his horses and his hounds, but never appearing in the nursery to inquire as to the food which is given to his children, or to supervise their education.

More often still, we believe, the educational question resolves itself into a question of curriculum. We discuss, unendingly, the respective merits of "classical," "scientific," or "professional" education. But these discussions are in the air; they are based upon *à priori* assumptions, or upon class or party prejudices, and not upon exact observations. The arguments which we make use of are mostly arguments of sentiment, prompted by personal preferences and not by experiment. Besides, these questions of curriculum, however important they may be, are in reality secondary; by which I mean that they are subordinate to the methods of teaching. The very best and most judicious curriculum, on paper, will not bear fruit unless the teaching which springs from it is adapted to the mind, and to the mental type of the pupils.

But, to adapt the methods of teaching to this end, it is necessary to know at least a little of the psychology of the child.

The educational problem comprises, then, two things: the matter to be taught, and those to whom it has to be taught—the curriculum and the pupil. We have hitherto given all our attention to curricula, and to manuals; it is time that we concerned ourselves a little with those for whom these are supposed to be made. I do not forget that there is also a third thing, namely, the educator himself. But what he ought to be depends upon the manner in which it is desirable that the child should be treated and developed. The determination of the qualities which the educator ought to possess follows from the psychology of the child.

Many people consider that only the practice of teaching is able to form the teacher, and to give him the necessary experience. Certainly the value of practice is of the highest importance in the making of a specialist in any given art. But it is necessary to make every effort to reduce to a minimum the experiences which we demand of him, especially when it is human beings who have to suffer the consequences. The teacher who commences the practice of teaching without having the least knowledge of psychology is naturally reduced to mere gropings, *from which his pupils suffer.* He is obliged to make his experiments *in anima vili*; and sometimes these experiments are very long and very painful for the generations of scholars who undergo them. Without doubt practice is able, in a certain measure, to make up for an insufficiency of theoretical knowledge, but at the price of what détours, what errors! Without doubt, by force of making bridges which fall down, or machines which tumble to pieces, a mere mechanic without theoretical knowledge will finish by making a good job, because he discovers empirically the formulæ of construction, which he is incapable of calculating. But who would wish to be such an engineer?

A teacher without psychological education is placed in an exactly similar position; with this difference, however, that when a bridge happens to crack in the course of construction one immediately perceives it and repairs it, or builds a new bridge. But if it is intelligence or character which are being perverted in their development, one does not discover this until too late for it to be possible to remedy it; and in any case one is not able to reconstruct another.

It is the aim of theoretical studies, of science, to reduce to a minimum the vexatious experiments and gropings which always accompany the beginnings of the practice of no matter what art. For example, it is theoretical knowledge which distinguishes the doctor from the bonesetter—often very skilful—who has learnt his trade by handling . . . the leg or the arm of his patients. The teacher must have nothing whatever in common with the bonesetter!

It is true that psychological science is not yet very advanced. It has, however, made positive advances, and even if these are not sufficiently numerous to inspire all the educator's didactic methods, they are, nevertheless, sufficient to enable him to avoid certain errors; and this is worth a great deal. That which matters most of all is that psychology shall pervade pedagogy with its method and spirit.

All this seems self-evident. How comes it, then, that a man so clear-sighted as Professor William James, the celebrated American psychologist, refuses to subscribe to this? I do not jest. See the first chapter of his *Talks to Teachers*. He there affirms that though the educator ought to have a general knowledge of the mental mechanism, it is, nevertheless, not necessary that this knowledge should be very profound. "For the great majority of you," he says (in addressing himself to teachers), "a general view is enough, provided it be a true one; and such a general view, one may say, might almost be written on the palm of one's hand."[1] Further he reassures the teachers who believe that it is indispensable for them to cultivate experimental psychology, or add to their daily task personal researches into child mentality: "Avoid still more to consider that as a duty of education, the contribution to psychology of psychological observations methodically carried out. The worst thing that can happen to a good educator is to get a bad conscience about her profession because she feels herself hopeless as a psychologist. . . . I know that child-study and other pieces of psychology as well have been productive of bad conscience in many a really innocent pedagogic breast. I should indeed be glad if this passing word from me might tend to dispel such a bad conscience, if any of you have it."[2]

These words sound strangely in the countries of the old world, where there is certainly not any feeling of being "hopeless as a psychologist," which causes in the breast of the teacher the trouble of an unquiet conscience; where, on the contrary, too many educators have the greatest difficulty in understanding the necessity of even a very general knowledge of the psychology of the child; because of which they have the greatest fear of departing from the ordinary routine, and of seeming to be enthusiastic for innovations.

To understand the true sense of the whole of this

[1] James, *Talks to Teachers*, p. 12.
[2] Ibid., p. 14.

discourse of Professor James, it is necessary to carry our thoughts to the time and the place where they were spoken, and to read between the lines the allusions which are contained in it.

Under the impetus given by an accomplished scientist, Dr. Stanley Hall, the researches in child psychology, in America, became extraordinarily widespread, and created, at one time, a perfect rage for them. A large number of societies of "Paidology" were founded, and a multitude of periodicals were established for publishing documents collected in enormous quantity. They like to do everything on a grand scale over there. To get on more quickly, and to obtain a greater result, they proceeded by vast inquiries, of which the utility, not to speak of anything else, often remains problematic. Teachers were assailed by interminable "questionnaires" that the reviews of paidology sent forth; and those who did not engage in this new work were represented as old-fashioned. Amongst the inquiries of this kind, which have raised great criticism, may be quoted the work in 1896, by Dr. Hall himself, on *dolls*. In this it was endeavoured to discover, amongst other things, what were the preferences of children as to the material of which those toys, dear to the hearts of all young people, are composed. And when the statistics were completed, it was solemnly reported that out of 845 children, 191 preferred wax dolls, 163 paper, 153 porcelain, 144 rag, 11 papier mâché, and only 6 wood, &c.!

But a science cannot be built up as quickly as a town, even in America, and the faults of this feverish and artificial activity were soon apparent. A reaction arose against the infatuation for *Child-Study*—a reaction as exaggerated as was the movement which gave rise to it. Professor Münsterberg, a colleague of Professor James at Harvard, began the attack and, in an article in *The Educational Review* (1898) which made a great sensation, endeavoured to show that the teacher has no need to be a psychologist: that the purely scientific attitude, abstract and analytic, of the latter, was inconsistent with the concrete and living attitude which ought to be that of the educator towards the child. This without doubt was calculated to reassure the minds of the educators who felt themselves "useless as psychologists," as Professor James said, in 1899, in the words we have quoted above.

It is clear, nevertheless, that if we leave out of account the circumstances in which they were spoken, we shall not entirely accept the statements of Professor James. Without doubt pedagogy is an art which demands above everything tact, delicacy, and a self-sacrifice which have nothing to do with scientific knowledge; and, in this sense, it is quite certain that a knowledge of psychology does not *suffice* for one who is to be a good educator. But if it does not suffice, it is none the less necessary, for an art is nothing but the realisation of an end, an ideal, by appropriate means. It is, therefore, essential for the artisan to have a thorough knowledge of the material with which he works, and the way to set about his work, if he would get from it the desired effect.

Dare we deny, on the other hand, that a moderately deep knowledge of psychology enlarges the horizon of a teacher; enlightens his view of matters, while giving him a greater confidence in himself and a greater authority towards others, combined with an open-mindedness towards methods, the effects of which will make themselves felt in a happy manner in tact, patience, and kindness towards his pupils? To have taken part in some exact personal researches, even though they should in themselves be without practical utility, leaves, as a matter of fact, a beneficial trace. Even if the educator has forgotten his psychology, it is not superfluous that he should at some time, in the beginning of his career, have been a good psychologist. It is not only what we know which has an influence upon our conduct and upon our mentality, but what we have known. Professor James, in one of his talks, very justly remarks: "It is but a small part of our experience in life that we are ever able articulately to recall. And yet the whole of it has had its influence in shaping our character and defining our tendencies to judge and act."[1]

Let us consider the relations of physiology and of practical medicine, which are exactly comparable to those of psychology and education. From the fact that medicine is an art, and from the fact that the attitude—practical and sympathetic—of the doctor, who needs to take account in his treatment of a crowd of extra-scientific considerations, is entirely opposed to the calm and impartial attitude of the physiologist of the laboratory, it does not follow that experimental physiology ought to be cut out of the curriculum of medical studies. Even if a medical practitioner has no need to be a physiologist, every one will agree that

[1] James, *Talks to Teachers*, p. 142.

it is indispensable that he should have gone through a course of physiology in his apprenticeship.

I know, by the way, that a number of teachers and principals are the first to regret not having had the advantage, during their student days, of having their attention drawn to the psychological problems which daily present themselves. One may the better judge of this by the following lines, which I extract from a letter sent to me :—

"After five years' practice as a primary teacher in the canton of Neuchâtel, I feel compelled to confess that there is, between the efforts which the school demands and the results which they produce, a disproportion which becomes alarming when one stops to consider it seriously.

"Tormented by this very depressing discovery, I have brought my thoughts to bear upon this want of success which is even more real than apparent. I say more real, because it appears to me that nature itself is responsible, for the most part, for the progress which can be discovered in this domain. If the school were to add to this primary force a more suitable collaboration, it would meet with a clearer result.

"Take, not the young people going through the higher schools, though the same evil is apparent there, but the young people who have been taught only in the primary schools ; take them at the age of eighteen or twenty, interrogate them, and at once the scholastic fiasco reveals itself. Having become possessed of a superficial and very abstract word-knowledge, they have been regarded as having acquired a satisfactory amount of instruction at fourteen years of age ; but at twenty years of age there remains with them only a melancholy recollection of it, some very vague information, and, above all, an absolute indifference in relation to intellectual, artistic, or scientific questions. . . .

"After numerous observations and some reading upon the questions of psychology towards which these same observations drove me, I have come to the profound conviction that the fundamental cause of the non-success of the people's school proves that instruction pays no real attention to the physiological development of the nervous system.

"We work at the education of the child without knowing him! This is our fundamental mistake.

"I have submitted this plaint to my colleagues, and I have found that they echo it. Everywhere there was felt to be the same disproportion between conscientious work and its results."

The author of these very frank and loyal declarations afterwards asks me what are the works of psychology which he and his colleagues might consult with advantage. It seems clear, then, that the interest which one brings to bear upon the child does not suffice, by itself, to insure all the care which the child requires.

Professor James is, moreover, overwhelmingly in the right when he affirms that it is in no way the duty of the teacher to make contributions to the science of psychology, or personally make experimental researches upon his pupils. A doctor can assuredly be a good practitioner though he does not codify his personal observations, nor make them the subject of a scientific essay. To utilise the results of a science is one thing; to enrich that science is another matter. But one certainly does not see that in personally making some methodical observations, or some experiments upon his scholars, the teacher is likely to do harm to his calling.[1]

On the contrary, such a method should prove fruitful from a threefold point of view: first, in that it will bring a valuable contribution to paidology, since educators are in a much better position than any one else to study the mentality of the child. Such researches should have, moreover, an immediate utility for teaching, since, as we shall see later on, the majority of the experiments in school psychology furnish for the master useful didactic data, of which he is able to make immediate use.

I am certain, in the third place, that the fact of giving his attention to the solving of various problems will give to the head of an institution, to whom the task is often very laborious, a renewed interest in his teaching. He will see things with other eyes, and his conceptions will be enlarged; behind the manual, the time-table, and the examination he will more clearly see the pupil; and he will study with greater interest, when he is familiar with the problems which are connected with it, the development of each of the little individualities which are entrusted to him.

The following pages have as their aim to serve as a first guide to educators who desire to become acquainted with child psychology—not by giving a résumé of all that has been published, up to the present, upon the subject, for many volumes would be insufficient for this—but by indicating, through some examples taken here and there, the nature of the

[1] We notice that Professor Munsterberg in a recent book (*Psychology and the Teacher*, 1909) shows that he is completely converted from his former prejudices, and ranges himself as a decided partisan of experimental pedagogy. All's well that ends well!

problems which will present themselves to him, and the nature of the methods by which he ought to endeavour to solve them. I hope that this little sketch of the tendencies of the new pedagogy will show in what way we ought to direct our efforts so as to realise this ideal—still, alas, far distant—which is to establish teaching upon its natural basis: the knowledge of the child.

CHAPTER I

HISTORICAL SKETCH

THE first systematic observation of the mental development of a child dates from the year 1787; and was made by Tiedemann,[1] a German, whose work has remained almost entirely ignored. Towards the middle of the last century three important publications were devoted to the psychical evolution of the child: in 1851 the *Entwicklungsgeschichte der Seele des Kindes*, by Löbisch; in 1856, the *Kind und Welt*, by Sigismund; in 1859, the *Untersuchungen uber das Seelenleben des neugeborenen Menschen*, by Kussmaul. But these works have not received the attention which their merits deserved, and it was not until the appearance of the well-known work by Preyer on *The Mind of the Child* (1881) that there spread, amongst parents, the fashion of keeping a daily journal of the signs of progress in their babies; and not till then did they completely understand the importance of such observations, of which Taine, Egger, and Pérez in France, and Darwin and Pollock in England, had already set the example.

About the same time, Stanley Hall, in America, undertook a propaganda in favour of a reform of

[1] Tiedemann, *Beobachtungen uber die Entwicklung der Seelenfahigkeiten bei Kindern*, 1787; new edition published by Ufer, Altenburg, 1897. Some extracts from the 1787 edition were translated into French, by Pérez, Paris, 1881.

pedagogy, which he wished to see based upon child psychology. But the opposition to be overcome was very considerable, and it was not until ten years later that the impulse given by this pioneer resulted in a definite movement. Then appeared, on all sides and all at once, books, journals, and societies devoted to child-study. In 1893 Hall founded *The National Association for the Study of Children;* and in the following years similar societies were established in many provinces of the United States—in 1894, in Illinois and Iowa; in 1895, in Nebraska, Ontario; in 1896, in Minnesota and Kansas; &c. Their organ is *The Pedagogical Seminary*, of which Hall continues to be the editor, and which remains one of the best periodicals of child psychology. It has appeared since 1891.

It was in 1893—to be exact, on Wednesday morning, April 26, as he has related in an enthusiastic passage—that a pupil of Hall, Oscar Chrisman, invented the word "paidology" (from *paidos*, child, and *logos*, science) to designate this new branch of the science, having for its object the child regarded from every possible point of view. This new word proved a happy hit.

Since this time a considerable number of works and periodicals have appeared, one after another, and we are compelled to give up any idea of making a complete list of them. We will, however, mention the important works by Baldwin, *Mental Development in the Child and the Race* (1895); *Notes on the Development of a Child*, by Miss Shinn (1893–1907); *The Mental Development of a Child*, by Moore (1896); the collection of *Studies in Education* by Earl Barnes (1896–1902); *The Child and Childhood in Folk-Lore*, and *The Child, a Study in the Evolution of Man*, by Chamberlain (1896, 1900); and a number of periodicals: *The Educational Review*, from 1891, edited by Murray Butler; *The Child-Study Monthly*, published from 1895, edited by Krohn and Bayliss, and afterwards by Campbell; *Paidology*, edited by Chrisman, 1901 (only one volume appeared); *The Journal of Adolescence*, by Yoder, from 1900; *Investigations of the Department of Psychology and Education of the University of Colorado*, edited by Allin, from 1902; *The Psychological Clinic*, by Witmer, from 1908; finally, the quite recent *Journal of Educational Psychology*, devoted more especially to experimental pedagogy, edited by Bayley, Seashore, Bell, and Whipple, and published since 1910.

We must not forget to mention the names of Dewey (formerly of Chicago, now of New York); of his disciples De Garmo and King; also a multitude of psychologists or of physiologists, who have given themselves wholly or partly to the work of psycho-pedagogy: Burk, Burnham, Bryan, Elmer Brown, Dearborn, Dodge, Donaldson, Gilbert, Goddhard, Ellis, W. James, Johnson, Huey, Kirkpatrick, Lukens, Meyer, W. S. Monroe, O'Shea, Ogden, Pillsbury, Small, Starbuck, Partridge, Tracy, Thorndike, Tyler, Tylor, &c., &c. The reviews dealing with general psychology, such as *The American Journal of Psychology* (edited by Hall, Sanford, and Titchener), *The Psychological Review* (edited by Baldwin, Judd, and Watson), with its satellite *The Psychological Bulletin* (edited by Warren), and *The American Journal of Religious Psychology* (edited by Hall), have always given a large amount of space to the psychology of the child.

Most of the American psychological laboratories concern themselves with experimental pedagogy. A certain number of them specialise in the subject, notably those of Clark University, where Hall has just founded a fine *Children's Institute;* Pennsylvania University, where Witmer has instituted a psycho-pedagogical clinic; Cornell University, under the direction of Whipple; and The Teachers' College, of the Columbia University, where J. P. Monroe, Thorndike, and others teach.

All this activity has, naturally, had its echo in other countries.

England was one of the first countries to take up the work. In consequence of a visit to the International Congress on Education held at Chicago in 1893, where they were inspired by the words and work of Dr. Stanley Hall, some British teachers started *The British Child-Study Association* in 1894. Branches of this society were established in various large towns in England and Scotland, and they published a journal called *The Paidologist.* The members of this society consisted chiefly of teachers (the majority), parents, and doctors. There was also *The Childhood Society,* founded in 1894, the members of which were mostly doctors and scientists. In 1907 these two societies were amalgamated, under the title of *The Child-Study Society,* and the *Paidologist* was re-named *Child-Study,* and became the journal of the new society.

Before this, without going so far back as the masterly works of Spencer (1861) and Bain (1879), English paidology was indebted to important works by Dr. F. Warner, *The Children: how to study them* (1887), *Lectures on the Growth and Means of Training the Mental Faculty* (1890); to Romanes, *Mental Evolution in Man* (1889); and, above all, to Professor J. Sully, author of various essays (since 1880) on the development of the child, most of which have been collected in a volume under the title of *Studies of Childhood* (1896), and translated into several languages. More recently Messrs. Winch, M'Dougall, Wimms & Burt have published, in *The British Journal of Psychology*, some interesting essays dealing with psycho-pedagogy. Mention must also be made of works by Rivers on *Fatigue*, and the suggestive book by a London inspector, B. Branford, *A Study of Mathematical Education*. We must reserve a special place of honour for mention of the works of the illustrious Galton, and of his disciples Karl Pearson, Heron, Schuster, Elderton, Spearman, and W. Brown, upon heredity, individuality, and intelligence—works which open out the vast possibilities of applied psychology. In 1905 Galton and Pearson founded a *Eugenics Laboratory*, in London, where statistical researches designed to demonstrate the factors which influence the qualities of the race are made.

A committee, under the presidency of Professors Findlay and Green, have inquired into the present condition of experimental pedagogy in England. Their report appeared on the agenda of the 1910 meeting of the British Association for the Advancement of Science, for whom the inquiry was made.

In **France**, where the soil had already been prepared by Taine, Pérez, Compayré, and Queyrat, a vigorous impulse has been given to the new pedagogy by A. Binet, director of the psychological laboratory at the Sorbonne, whose important writings appear in *L'Année Psychologique*, founded in 1896; and to him we owe some books of the first rank, *e.g.* *La Suggestibilité* (1900), *L'Étude expérimentale de l'intelligence* (1903), and *Les Idées modernes sur les Enfants* (1909). In 1900 M. F. Buisson founded *La Société libre pour*

L'Étude psychologique de L'Enfant, which is now under the management of MM. Ribot, professor of the College of France, and Bédorez, Director of Primary Education. M. Binet is the present president and scientific director of the society. The society is mainly composed of teachers, who meet at stated times to exchange notes as to their experiments, and to arrange for carrying on researches upon some definite part of school psychology. Their observations and their studies are recorded in the *Bulletin* of their society, and one appreciates in reading them the multiplicity of pedagogic problems which may be attacked by the experimental method. Mention may be made of the works of A. Belot, an inspector of wide views and an open mind; of Malapert, Clavière, Roussel, and Cousinet; of Mmes. Fuster and Kergomard; and the work of Duprat on *Le Mensonge* (1903). In 1905 Binet had the happy idea of founding—in a primary school in Paris, with the permission of the Director of Primary Education—a laboratory of normal pedagogy. This School-laboratory, installed in a little room of the school in the Grange-aux-Belles street, had for its aim the organising, according to scientific methods, the study of the physical, intellectual, and moral aptitudes of children, and also the study of methods of teaching. A great number of researches have already been carried out by Binet himself, with the collaboration of M. Vaney (the director of the school), Dr. Simon, and some teachers who have thus made themselves familiar with the systems of measurement.

An offshoot of this *Société libre* has just been established at Lyons (1909), through the initiative of MM. Chabot and Goblot. There has also been instituted in the same town, by the municipality, a course of "psychology applied to education"—a course for popularising the subject, conducted by M. Nayrac.

At Bordeaux, too, a movement, also aiming at the popularising of paidology, has been started by the efforts of MM. Persigout and Thamin, and Drs. Régis and Cruchet.

In 1902 there was constituted in Paris a *Ligue des médecins et des familles pour l'hygiène Scolaire,* on the initiative of Drs. Le Gendre and Mathieu. This association, which is very active, naturally lays stress upon the study of the physical and mental development of the child: development to which teaching ought rigorously to adapt itself, if overpressure is to be avoided. It publishes a quarterly paper, *L'Hygiène Scolaire,* and has organised two conferences, which were held in Paris in 1903 and 1905. One of its members, Dr. M. de Fleury, is the author of a very useful work, *Le corps et l'âme de l'enfant* (2 vols., 1900 and 1905); another member, Dr. Dinet, has set forth in a thesis, *Physiologie et Pathologie de l'éducation* (1903), the reforms desired. One interesting result of the efforts of this *Ligue* is the construction (1908), in Gay-Lussac Street, Paris, of a laboratory of school hygiene for the use of the students of the Higher Normal School, of which the director, M. Ernest Lavisse, is the ardent champion of a pedagogical reform based upon a knowledge of the bodily and moral needs of children.

In spite, however, of the movement begun by Binet, we are obliged to recognise that, in France, paidology is but little studied. The pedagogic problem has some difficulty in getting out of the traditional rut of either abstraction or phraseology, and placing itself upon the solid ground of exact observation and experiment: Nevertheless we are able to mention a number of works which, although they do not strictly come within the limits of experimental pedagogy, nevertheless contain some suggestive remarks or very judicious counsels, and mark a tendency more or less clear to take psychology as the basis of the educative art, *e.g. L'enseignement des langues*, by Bréal (1891); *L'éducation de la volonté*, by Payot (1893); *La suggestion dans l'éducation*, by Thomas (1895); *L'esquisse d'un enseignement basé sur la psychologie de l'enfant*, by Lacombe; *La psychologie de l'éducation*, by Le Bon; *L'éducation des filles*, by Marion (1902); *L'art et l'enfant*, by Braunschvicg (1907); *Comment former un esprit*, by Dr. Toulouse; *L'éducation de la petite enfance*, by Mme. Girard (1908); the publications by Tissié on fatigue and impulse, &c.—he has also for twenty years been publishing a *Revue des jeux scolaires*. The works of psychologists like Ribot, Féré, Janet, Dumas, Piéron, Bourdon, Dugas, B. Leroy, &c., have also contributed, one need hardly say, to the progress of psycho-pedagogy. Cramaussel, in 1908, collected into one volume observations which he had made on *Le premier éveil intellectuel de l'enfant*; and, in the work entitled *L'esprit et le cœur de l'enfant* (1909), Lindet has collected a number of the words used by a child. There remain to be mentioned two good reviews, which contribute largely to the new movement: *L'Education moderne*, founded in 1906 by Drs. Philippe and Paul Boncour, and edited since 1909 by Compayré; and *L'Education*, issued by Bertier from 1909.

Germany, as one can well understand, has not lagged behind. Some important periodical publications bear witness to this: *Die Kinderfehler*, a journal originally devoted to abnormal children, to-day, under the title of *Zeitschrift für Kinderforschung*, embraces the whole of paidology: this was established in 1896 by Trüper, Koch, and Ufer, who have since been joined by Anton and Martinak; the *Sammlung*, by Schiller, Ziegler, and Ziehen, a collection of writings relating to pedagogical psychology (from 1897); the *Zeitschrift für padagogische Psychologie* (from 1899), founded by Kemsies, and edited since 1910 by Brahn, Deuchler, and Scheibner; the *Padagogisch-psychologische Studien* (from 1900), edited by Brahn and afterwards by Seyfarth; and finally, more recently, a review of experimental pedagogy, *Die Experimentelle Padagogik*, founded in 1905 by Lay and Meumann, and at present edited by Meumann. It is to be noted that the numerous periodicals on physiological psychology which appear in Germany also contain essays having a direct bearing on pedagogy. In 1899 the *Verein fur Kinderpsychologie* was founded in Berlin, its first president being the eminent Professor Stumpf. And in 1906 a congress on paidology, conducted in German (*Congress fur Kinderforschung und Jugendfursorge*), met in the same capital. At Jena and at Mannheim there are also *Vereine fur Kinderforschung*.

Among the "epoch-making" contemporary works on paidology produced in Germany, we may mention, as being in the first rank, those of Karl Groos dealing with *The Play of Animals* (1896) and *The Play of Man* (1899); and we shall see later on with what new light they illuminate the psychology of the child and the pedagogical problem. Lay has vigorously drawn attention to *Experimentelle Didaktik*, through a large work bearing that title (issued in 1903). In

1898, in a book entitled *Führer durch den Rechenunterrich der Unterstufe,* he had previously shown the possibility of founding teaching methods upon experimentation. Meumann has given a general view of researches made in this direction in his splendid *Vorlesungen zur Einfuhrung in die experimentelle Padagogik* (1907). We must also mention the observations of C. and W. Stern upon the development of language in the child, *Die Kindersprache* (1907), and the two books of Levinstein and Kerschensteiner, issued simultaneously in 1905, upon the drawings of children.

Neither ought we to pass over the works of Griesbach, Ebbinghaus, G. E. Müller, Kemsies, Lobsien, Kräpelin and his pupils, and Ament, who have given a strong impetus to psycho-pedagogy. Griesbach founded, in 1905, in collaboration with Drs. Mathieu (Paris), Brunton (London), Johannessen (Christiania), the *Archives internationales d'hygiène scolaire.* In 1888 Kotelmann had already brought out the *Zeitschrift für Schulgesundheitspflege.*

One might still cite a crowd of names. In no country has psychology been studied so much as in Germany, and during the last five or six years a large number of experimental researches have had for their object problems of paidology or of practical pedagogy —see the works of Baade, Cohn, Dürr, Elsenhans, Ephrussi, Erdmann, Friedrich, Mme. Hösch-Ernst, Hopfner, Krüger, Laser, Mayer, Offner, Pfeiffer, Pilzecker, Pohlmann, Schmidt, Schulze, Schäfer, Schumann, Sommer, Wagner, Winteler, Ziehen, &c.; to which must be added those of doctors like Baginsky, Strümpell, and of educators like K. Lange, Münch, Rein, Gaudig, Barth, and Th. Ziegler. Good manuals for the popularisation of paidology have been recently issued by Adèle Schreiber, *Das Buch vom Kind;* Gaupp, *Psychologie des Kindes*, 1908; and Lipmann, *Grundriss de Psychologie für Pädagogen* (1909). The work by Ostwald, *Grosse Männer* (1909), contains a number of most valuable suggestions and documents for educators.

The teaching body itself is being won over to the cause of experimental pedagogy; or at any rate there are some favourable signs in this direction. In June 1908 the *Deutscher Lehrerverein*—being of opinion that "it is not the curriculum which ought to be the chief guide in pedagogy, but the psychological evolution of the child"—decided to establish a central bureau, *Pädagogische Zentralstelle*, for the purpose of co-ordinating efforts made with a view to educative reform. This bureau has already under consideration the project of creating a Pedagogical Academy: a sort of superior normal college designed for the training of members of the teaching body. The *Berliner Lehrerverein* also constituted, in September 1909, amongst its own members, a committee of empirical pedagogy; and it hopes to be able to create a psycho-pedagogical institute, similar to that which the *Leipziger Lehrerverein*, through the initiative of Schulze, has possessed since 1906. The *Lehrerverein* of Munich, following in the movement, has decided, in its turn, to found an institute of this kind.

Finally, a number of educators and psychologists have just laid the foundations (October 1909) of a *Bund für Schulreform*, at the head of which we find Cordsen, of Hamburg, supported by Meumann, Stern, Kräpelin, Trüper, and other savants. This league will seek to bring the school into touch with reality and life; and will base its projects of reform upon the knowledge of the child, as is indicated in the significant device *Reform vom Kinde aus.* It has a good programme, which deserves unstinted praise.

Before finishing with Germany, we must not forget that *The Institute of Applied Psychology*, founded in 1906 at Berlin by G. E. Müller, Stern, and Lipmann, is actively working in the domain of paidology.

In **Belgium** experimental pedagogy is pursued with ardour by Schuyten, who in 1899 established in Antwerp a department of paidology, with a laboratory, in connection with the communal schools. The numerous studies which have emanated from this department have been published in the *Paedologisch Jaarboek*, a periodical written in Flemish, with résumés in French. A Paidological Society came into existence, in the same town, in 1902. It issues a *Bulletin*, which is also written in Flemish, but unfortunately has no résumés in French. In Brussels abnormal children have, from the first, been the object of the solicitude of doctors and educators—Demoor, Decroly, Ley, Jonckheere (author of a little outline of paidology, *La science de l'enfant*, 2nd edition, 1909), Rouma, Herlin, Marquebreucq, Querton, Mlle. Degand. And the psychology of the abnormal very much concerns that of the normal also. A course of paidology was introduced, in 1905, at the normal school of Brussels, where there is a laboratory, and, in 1906, in the provincial normal schools at Charleroi and Mons. Mlle. Ioteyko, who teaches in the two last-named towns, has published, since 1908, a *Revue psychologique*, devoted almost exclusively to psycho-pedagogy; and she opened, in 1909, a *Séminaire de pédologie* in Brussels. In 1906, Nyns, Decroly,

Ley, and others founded, at Brussels, a *Société de pedotechnie,* which publishes a small bulletin, and which has organised a new thing, and one which deserves to be imitated—free paidotechnical consultations, having for their object the supplying to parents directions and advice concerning the physical and moral culture of their children. These consultations are held every Sunday morning at Brussels.

In 1909 M. van Biervliet, of Gand, was engaged by the Belgian Government to give a course of lectures on psychology applied to education, and he has, moreover, just founded an *Institut de pédologie,* which will publish *Annales.* We may mention also the efforts of Eddy (pseudonym of Edw. Peeters) of Ostend, and of Varendonck of Ghent The two reviews, *L'Education familiale* and *L'Ecole nationale,* started ten years ago, give an ever-increasing space to the new paidology. Since 1907 there has also been published, under the direction of Mlle. Poelemans, a little bulletin devoted to the abnormal, *L'Enfance anormale.*

In **Holland** there is no marked paidological movement. Paidology is, however, represented in the Amsterdam University, by van Wayenburg; at Utrecht by Breukink and van der Torren; and at Groningen the work of Heymans and Wiersma on psychical correlations and on heredity of characteristics will be most helpful to the cause of education. In 1887 Dr. Guye, of Amsterdam, rendered signal service to practical pedagogy in drawing attention to *aprosexie nasale,* that psychical ailment which accompanies adenoid growths in children.

Italy, the home of anthropology, ought to have been one of the first to take up child-study. As a matter of fact there have appeared, from 1879, some works upon the psychological evolution of babies, by Luigi Ferri, Marro, and Garbini; in 1887, the short study, still a classic, by Ricci, *L'arte nei bambini;* afterwards, in 1893, *Saggi pedagogici,* by Vecchia; in 1894, *Saggi di psicologia del bambino,* by Paola Lombroso; in 1895, the study of Colozza, on the pedagogy of children's plays; later the works of Sanctis, on the difficulties of the measurement of attention; in 1897, the famous work by Marro, *La puberta;* and in 1899, *L'antropologia pedagogica,* by Melzi.

C. Melzi, now inspector of schools at Alexandria, founded in 1897, at Arona, a bureau of pedagogical anthropology; the first institution of its kind in Italy, and probably in Europe. His work was continued, in 1899 at Crevalcore, by U. Pizzoli, by whom the institute of experimental pedagogy was removed to Milan in 1904. This institute was purchased by the town of Milan in 1909, and was under the direction of Z. Treves till his death in April 1911.

Abnormal children have been specially studied by de Sanctis, Ferreri, and Ferrari. The last named founded, in 1905, an excellent periodical, the *Revista di psicologia applicata.* Sanctis and Ferreri publish a *Bollettino* devoted to the pedagogy of abnormals; and, in connection with the abnormals, we may mention the *Rivista di pedagogia correttiva,* edited by Carrara.

In 1904 a distinguished educator, L. Credaro, then Minister of Public Instruction, established in the universities a *Scuola pedagogica,* that is to say, finishing courses for future teachers. To these courses are added, at Rome, lessons in experimental psychology, given by Professors de Sanctis and Chiarini. Credaro started, in 1908, an important *Rivista pedagogica,* edited since 1910 by Vecchia and Raulich. In January 1910 appeared the first number of another paidological journal, the *Vita infantile*, edited by Comba and Loreta.

It would be unjust not to mention, further, the names of numerous psychologists, doctors, and philosophers who have made useful contributions to paidology: Assagioli, Badaloni, Bellei, Billia, Castagnola, Colucci, Consoni, Cozzolino, Mlle. Faggiani, Ferrai, Gerini, Guidi, Kiesow, Martinazzoli, Montesano, Morselli, Mosso—whose famous work on fatigue appeared in 1891, and gave rise to many researches—Neyroz, Obici, Patini, Patrizi, Pennazza, Pistolesi, Renda, Romano, de Sarlo, Sergi, Tamburini, Vidari, Villa, &c.

Austria-Hungary has some paidological societies: *Oesterreichische Gesellschaft für Kinderforschung*, at Vienna, since 1906; and *Komitee für Kinderforschung*, at Budapest, from 1903, transformed in 1906 into *Ungarische Gesellschaft fur Kinderforschung*, with a laboratory of paidology, installed in a school building and directed by Rauschburg. As special reviews devoted to child psychology we have *Gyermek* (The Child)—written in Hungarian and with résumés in French—which has appeared at Budapest for four years, under the direction of M. Nagy; *Eos*, founded in 1905 at Vienna, edited by Druschba, Krenberger, Mell, and Schlöss, and treating of the anomalies of childhood.

Burgerstein published, in 1895, a treatise on school hygiene, which is classical; Heller is the author of the fine *Grundriss der Heilpadagogik* (1904); Freud, the famous Viennese neurologist, has drawn attention to the importance of sexual phenomena in the child, and to the part they play in the ultimate development of his mentality. We must also mention the names of Martinak, Blažek, Pékar, Weszely, and Witasek, to whom paidology is indebted for various contributions.

Russia possesses in Sikorsky, of Kiew, one of the pioneers of experimental pedagogy; for it is he who, by his famous study upon the means of measuring intellectual fatigue in scholars—published, in 1879, in the *Annales d'hygiène publique* (Paris), but remaining unnoticed for a long time—was the initiator of experimenting in the schools.

In 1900 the *Musée pédagogique* of St. Petersburg instituted courses in experimental psychology which were conducted by Netschajeff—the energetic worker and author of important and much-appreciated works and manuals of school psychology. In 1904 this institution was enriched by a laboratory of experimental pedagogy and a course in paidology, given by Netschajeff himself, Lasursky, Krogius, Lapschin, and others. It issued, from 1905, the *Cahiers des psychologie pédagogique;* and was eventually, in 1908, transformed into an independent *Académie pédagogique.* Among the initiators of this experimental paidological movement, we must mention, as being in the front rank, Bechterew, director of the laboratory of psychology of the medical-military academy, and editor of a journal of psychology, founded in 1904. There still exists in St Petersburg an *Institut psychopédologique,* opened in 1906, and designed for the bringing up of children, who are maintained there from their birth till the age of twenty-one years.

Moscow was not slow to follow the example of the capital. In 1906, Bernstein, with the collaboration of Baltalon, Ignatieff, Rossolimo, and Bogdanoff, founded a *Société pédagogique*, which opened a laboratory in 1908. Professor Tchelpanoff took part in the work by conducting a laboratory of psychology at the university. At Odessa paidology is represented by N. Lange—the author of the work on *L'âme de l'enfant* (1893)—and at Kasan by Iwanovsky. In 1897 Teliatnik made a study of mental fatigue; in 1900 Lesgaft published a work upon types of scholars; and, in 1910, Roumanzieff published a general work on paidology.

In 1906, and in 1909, two *Conférences russes de psychopédagogie* were held at St. Petersburg, and they contributed much to the extension of the new science. In June 1909 a *Société russe de pédagogie expérimentale* was constituted, under the presidency of Netschajeff.

In **Poland** also we find that a *Société polonaise pour l'étude de l'enfant* was founded in 1897, by Mlle. Szyc, MM. Weryho, Chodecki, and Bogdanowicz. Since 1887 there have appeared, in Polish, various paidological studies, carried out by Dawid and A. Szyc.

In **Bulgaria** paidology is represented, at Sofia, by Professors Gheorgov—author of important works upon the evolution of language in children—Noïcow, and Dr. Bonoff; and in the provinces by E. Ivanoff. At Schumna a little journal of empirical pedagogy has appeared, since 1909, under the direction of Zoneff and Gineff.

In **Servia** there was founded, in 1906, a *Société pour la psychologie de l'enfant*, of which the headquarters is at Belgrade. It publishes a *Bulletin*, conducted by S. Yevritsch, a teacher.

In **Roumania** there are Mme. Conta-Kernbach—

author of works on pedagogy—Radulescu-Motru—professor at Bucharest and director of the *Studii filosofice*—and Vaschide (who died in 1907).

In Scandinavia the name of **Sweden** is closely associated, in the minds of educators, with that of Ling, the originator of Swedish gymnastics, who, a century ago, tried to establish physical education upon a rational basis, such as we are endeavouring to-day to make for psychical education. In 1889 Axel Key, the hygienist, published his celebrated researches on puberty. In 1901 Mme. Ellen Key brought out her book *Le Siècle de l'enfant*, which achieved a far-reaching and deserved success. Psycho-pedagogy, properly so called, is cultivated by Alrutz, editor of the journal *Psyke* (founded in 1906), Scheele, editor of the pedagogical journal *Manhem* (1905–1907), Geijer, Hammer, Larsson, Beckman, Herrlin, Bergqvist, &c.

For **Norway** we may cite the names of the psychologists Aall and Aars.

For **Denmark** we may mention the psychologists Höffding and Lehmann, and Drs. Malling-Hansen and Ingerslev.

Spain has possessed, since 1882, a *Musée pédagogique national*, at Madrid; which was established with the view of bringing together all that concerns teaching, and organising conferences, meetings, excursions, &c. This museum has had, since 1894, a laboratory of psychology, directed by Professor Simarro, and with the paidological teaching in the charge of MM. Cossio, D. Barnès (director and secretary of the museum), and Rubio. Various works dealing with our science have been published in the course of the last few years: anthropometric researches on children, by Rufino Blanco and Luis de Hoyos Sainz; the language of children, by Machado; the psychology of children, by Sanz del Rioz and Giner de los Rios; and child-culture, by Professor Vargas (of Barcelona). Many of these works have been published in *La Evolucion pedagogica*, a journal published at Barcelona; and others in the *Boletin de la Institucion libre de Ensenanza*—this institution, founded in 1876, is a free, non-sectarian school, which endeavours, with success, so I am assured, to instil new pedagogical ideas. Abnormal children are the objects of the devoted care of F. Pereira—who has published, since 1907, a small review, *La Infancia anormal*, at Madrid.

We cannot permit ourselves to finish with Spain without having done honour to the memory of Francisco Ferrer, the apostle-pedagogue, shot at Montjuich on October 13, 1909, in the odious circumstances that are well known. He conducted, since 1908, a journal, *L'Ecole rénovée*, published in Paris, having for its aim—as its name indicates—the reforming of the school. The executioners of Ferrer, in making him the martyr of free thought, have magnified his name immeasurably; they have taken his life, but they have made him immortal.

From the **Argentine Republic** have come, during the last few years, some interesting works on child psychology and pedagogy, due, amongst others, to Dr. Senet, Pinero, Ducceschi, and above all to V. Mercante—formerly director of a training college at Buenos Ayres, at present director of the pedagogical department of the University of La Plata. He is also the author of a large work on the development of the mathematical capacity of the child; and he founded, in 1906, the *Archivos de Pedagogia y ciencias afines*.

Japan possesses, at Tokio, a *Société de pédologie*,

which has been established twenty years, and has more than a thousand members. It is presided over by Professor Motora, publishes a journal, *Jido Kenkyu*, and organises annual conferences. Sakaki, professor of psychiatry at Fukuoka, is well known for his researches on school fatigue.

Switzerland, divided into twenty-two autonomous cantons for all that concerns public education, does not offer very favourable ground for the propagation of great scientific movements. School hygiene is represented by a large society, *Schweizerische Gesellschaft fur Schulgesundheitspflege*, which publishes a *Jahrbuch*. Abnormal children are also the objects of close study by educators; and every two years a small congress of those interested in the lot of these unfortunate ones meets—*Konferenz fur das Idiotenwesen*. The first was held in Zurich in 1889. But paidology, as such, has not, in Switzerland, a medium which centralises or co-ordinates isolated efforts.

At Zurich pedagogy is represented by F. W. Fœrster, whose book *L'Ecole et le caractère* has obtained a well-deserved success. Dr. Schwarz, in *Schule und Leben* (1910), demands that pedagogy should proceed along more psychological lines. Pastor Pfister, inspired by the new and much-discussed theories of Freud—which are represented in Zurich by Bleuler and Jung—shows by striking examples, drawn from his personal experience, the invaluable help that psycho-analysis can give to those who have the care of souls, and lays the foundations of an *Experimentelle Moralpadagogik*. Dr. Zollinger, Secretary of Public Instruction, edits the *Feuilles Suisses d'hygiène scolaire et de protection de l'enfance*. Ebert, a teacher, has studied, in collaboration with Meumann, the education of the memory.

Among others we may mention O. Messmer, of Rorschach, the author of a work on the psychology of reading.

At Berne Dr. Vannod carried through, in 1896, some researches on the measurement of mental fatigue among scholars. At Lausanne Dr. Combe has collected a number of anthropometric records from the schools (1886), and Larguier des Bancels has studied methods of memorising. At Neuchâtel Professor P. Bovet has founded a *Collection d'actualités pédagogiques* (edited by the "Foyer solidariste"), which was started with the translation of a work by Foerster, mentioned above, and with the *Vie mentale de l'adolescent* of Lemaitre.

At Geneva, the home of Rousseau and of Mme. Necker de Saussure, we doubtless do not do all that we should, for the honour of these great ancestors. We are, however, able to mention some paidological studies—by Boubier on the plays of children during lessons; of Lemaître, professor at our college, on various phenomena discovered among his pupils (internal language, synopses, mental dissociations, &c.); by A. Ferrière on the new education. Mlle. Borst published in 1904 some *Recherches sur l'éducabilité du témoignage;* Katzaroff, in 1908, some *Expériences sur la Mémorisation.* Most of these essays have appeared in the *Archives de Psychologie,* founded in 1901. The *Société pédagogique Genevoise* established four years ago, at my suggestion, a *Section pour l'étude psychologique de l'enfant.* It has produced some interesting works, of which I will mention only that of Mlle. Métral, on the memory of spelling—the only one which has been published. This section, however, is far from having made the progress that it merits.

The reorganisation of the special teaching of backward children, which has just been accomplished, will doubtless give an impetus to researches in school paidology. From 1903 I have conducted at the University a course in child psychology, inspired by the new methods. At various times, also—through the enlightened interest of the Chief of our Public Instruction—courses, conferences, or seminaires, on pedagogical psychology, designed specially for all teachers in the primary schools, or for candidates for primary teaching, have been organised at our laboratory of psychology at the University.

The world of teachers appears also to feel the necessity for a closer touch with psychology and its methods. Their principal organs, in Switzerland, *L'Educateur*, edited by Professor Guex, director of the normal schools of the canton Vaud, and the *Schweizerische Lehrerzeitung*, edited by Fritschi and Conrad, both give more and more prominence to questions of school psychology. At its last triennial assembly, held at Geneva in 1907, the *Société pédagogique romande* discussed the grave question of how the school ought to proceed, so as to secure the normal development of pupils in accordance with their individual aptitudes. This is a happy sign of the times.

In 1907 I proposed to Swiss teachers a collective experiment upon children's drawings. By means of the generous support of M. Guex, this experiment produced brilliant results, which have been fully set forth by M. Ivanoff.

Thus we see that, to-day, the pedagogical question is pre-eminently "the question of the day." The large number of international congresses devoted to questions of education or of paidology suffice to prove the need that is felt of revising the old pedagogical conceptions, and infusing into them some positive methods—International Congress on School Hygiene, Nuremberg 1904, London 1907, Paris 1910; Congress on Home Education, Liège 1905, Milan 1906, Brussels 1910; Congress on Moral Education, London 1908; International Congress on the Teaching of Drawing, Paris 1900, Berne 1904, London 1908; Congresses on General Psychology have also given an important place to pedagogical psychology.

In the month of August 1909 various paidologists, gathered at Geneva on the occasion of the sixth International Congress on Psychology, took steps to form a committee for organising some future International Congresses on Paidology. A fresh meeting, which was arranged at Paris on the 27th of the following December, definitely constituted this committee, and appointed Schuyten as its president. As a result of a very striking coincidence there was founded on the same day, and also at Paris, a similar committee at the instigation of MM. Binet and van Biervliet. This second committee, which took the name of "The International Committee of Pedagogical Psychology," has for its principal object the co-ordination of the efforts of paidologists, and the endeavour to introduce into the practice of education "the definite and useful conclusions resulting from researches in pedagogical psychology." Let us hope that these two committees, composed partly of the same persons, will lose no time in amalgamating.

All this activity has already begun to bear fruit. Some educators have realised the necessity of organising school life in a fashion more in accord with the needs of the child. In 1898 Dr. Lietz founded in the Hartz a *Landerziehungsheim*, or country school, to enable the developing of children to take place in conditions less artificial, and less removed from the reality of life, than town schools. His example has been followed, and to-day we find these "new schools" not only in Germany, but also in England, France, Poland, Denmark, and in Russia. In Switzerland there are half-a-dozen: at Glarisegg (Thurgovie), Oberkirch (St. Gall), Chailly sur Lausanne, Châtaigneraie near Coppet, and Grünau near Berne.

There are also boarding-houses due to private initiative. Shall we ever be able to let the public school benefit by this new conception of school life? Efforts have been made in this direction; and different towns have already organised some "forest schools" (*Waldschulen*)—in Germany, at Charlottenburg, from 1904, since at Mulhouse, Gladbach, Elberfeld, Kiel, Lübeck, Munich, &c.; in Switzerland, at Hessigkofen (Soleure) and Lausanne; in England, at London, Bradford, and Halifax; in France, at Lyons; in the United States, at Providence and Boston.

And even more, the town of Mannheim, through the efforts of Sickinger and Dr. Moses, introduced in its schools, in 1905, a system of organisation based upon the fact of the diverse capacities of pupils. Each class has been divided into three subdivisions: one for intelligent pupils, a second for the weak, and the third for the very weak. What may be the value of this organisation, considered in its detail, we need not discuss here, but it is devoted to the great principle of adapting the teaching to the mental nature of the scholar. The Mannheim System stands in the history of pedagogy as the first administrative application of a principle consciously deduced from child psychology.

Truth would seem to be on the march.

BIBLIOGRAPHY

There does not exist, to my knowledge, any work setting forth in detail the history of the modern paidological movement. Some information, more or less detailed, will be found in the following works :—

The Paidological Movement in General.—FRITZSCH, *Die Anfange der Kinderpsychologie und die Vorlaufer des Versuchs in der Padagogik*, Z. päd. P. XI., 1910. CHRISMAN, *Paidologie, Entwurf einer Wissenschaft des Kindes*, Diss Jena, 1896; *Evolution of Paidology*, Paidol. I., 1900. KEMSIES, *Entwickelung der pad.-Psychol. im 19. Jahrhundert*, Z. pad. P. IV. ROUMA, *Le mouvement moderne en faveur de l'étude scient. de l'enfant*, Ed. mod., Jan. 1910.

America—STIMPFL, Z. päd. P. I. MONROE, MACDONALD, ibid.; HALL, ibid. V., p. 112. MEYER, Z. ang. Ps I., 471. CAMERON, *Wissench. Padagogik in Amerika*, Z. exp. Päd. X. HALL, *General Outline of the new Child Study Work at Clark University*, Ped. Sem., June 1910.

Europe.—MONROE, Ped. Sem. VI., and various articles in Z. ang. Ps. I.

Germany.—On the *Institut de péd. exp. de Leipzig*, SCHLAGER, Z. exp. Pad. VIII.; Z. pad P. XI. On the aims of other Teachers' Societies, *cf.* Z. exp. Pad. X., and Z. pad. P. XI. MEUMANN and CORDSEN, *Der Bund f. Schulreform*, Z. exp Pad X. On the schools of *Mannheim*, DEUCHLER, Z. päd. P. X. (where will be found a bibliography). The meetings of the *Vereine fur Kinderpsychologie* of Berlin and Jena are summarised in the Z. pad. P.

Belgium.—SCHUYTEN, Z. ang. Ps. I., 278. JONCKHEERE, Z. exp. Pad. V., 105. **France.**—On the *Laboratoire-école*, BINET, An. psy. XII., 233. **Hungary**—RANSCHBURG, Z. exp. Päd. II., 121. Italy.—LOMBROSO, Kf I., 24; CONSONI, Ar de Ps. IX., 147; CREDARO, *La scuola pedagogica*, Rome, 1907; SAFFIOTTI, *Das Stadtische Lab. f. exp Padag.*, Z. ang Ps III, 1910. **Russia**—JURGENS, Z. exp. Pad. III., GRETCHOULEVITCH, Ar. de Psy. IX.; EPHRUSSI, Z. ang. Ps. II., 301; NETCHAJEFF, *Padag. Akademie in St. Petersburg*, ibid III., 315.

Some general information will also be found in the articles published periodically by BLUM in the *Rev. philos.*; by COMPAYRÉ in

L'Ed. mod. on the paidological movement; by AMENT, *Fortschritte der Kinderseelenkunde* (1895–1903), Leipzic, 1906; also in the *Arch. intern. d'hygiène scolaire* and other paidological periodicals, which frequently publish reports on the progress of hygiene or school psychology, in various countries.

On the **New Schools**.—LIETZ, *Emlohstobba, Roman oder Wirklichkeit*, Berlin, 1897; *Die deutschen Landerziehungsheime*, Leipsic, 1910; *Principes fondamentaux des Landerz.*, Educ., March 1903. FERRIÈRE, *Hermann Lietz*, Biblioth. Univers., 1909; *Projet d'école nouvelle*, St Blaise, 1909; *L'école nouvelle, methodologie et applications*, Rev. psy. 1910. BADLEY (head of the Bedales School), Educ., December 1909

On **Open Air Schools**.—BAGINSKY, *Ueber Waldschulen*, Z. pad. P. VIII., 1906. ROUMA, *L'école en forêt*, extr. de la Vie. Intell., Brussels, 1908. SCHOEN, *Les nouvelles écoles sous bois*, Educ., Sept. 1909. CURTIS, *Out-door Schools*, Ped. Sem., June 1909 (with a bibliography).

CHAPTER II

THE PROBLEMS

WHAT are the problems to which *Child Psychology* and *Experimental Pedagogy* have to furnish solutions?

They are very different in kind according to the point of view from which we look at them.

Before setting forth the data, it is necessary to put very clearly the meaning of each of these two terms, as well as the relations which unite them, both to each other and also to *Paidology* and *Pedagogy*. Since these two terms are often used the one for the other, it will be useful to give them a definite and fixed meaning.

1. THEORETICAL PROBLEMS, AND PROBLEMS OF APPLICATION

The science of the child embraces all those positive branches of knowledge which have to do with the child and his development—including the methods enabling us to attain to these branches of knowledge. This science of the child, like all science, may be *pure* or *applied*. As pure science it has for its object the determining of all the physical, physiological, or psychological phenomena which relate to the child, and the impartial search for the laws of these phenomena. As applied science it endeavours to discover the practical means for arriving at certain given ends.

Paidology and Paidotechny.—To distinguish more easily between these two terms we shall restrict the name of Paidology [1] to the pure science, and that of Paidotechny [2] to the applied.

Paidology includes within its limits a whole series of sciences: *Child Psychology*, *Child Pathology*, *Child Physiology*, &c.—in a word, all the sciences which may of directly concern the child.

Paidotechny has as many ramifications as there are ends to which the knowledge of the child may be applied. These ends are manifold: we want to know the child so that we may cure him if he is ill; and this medical section of paidotechny is called *Paidiatry*. We wish to know the child so that we may be able to judge if he is guilty of a crime, and to regenerate him. This is *Judicial Paidotechny*. We desire also to know the child so that we may educate him. This is *Experimental Pedagogy*.

In fact, I believe that these three branches are the only ones which have sprung from the trunk of paidotechny—and, further, judicial paidotechny is best looked upon as simply a branch of experimental pedagogy. But we can easily imagine other

[1] It may be objected that since "paidology" signifies "science of the child," it is an error in logic to restrict its use to the pure science, at the same time as we extend the appellation of "science of the child" to all that is included in the term. But what would be the use of Greek translations of French words, if it were not precisely that it enables us to vary and to enrich the nomenclature, by setting apart a special name for a certain category of objects which the French word does not expressly designate? For example, "bible," though it is an exact translation of the word "book," none the less retains a special meaning, which we find it very convenient to use; similarly, "lithography" is but one definite kind of "writing on stone," &c

[2] This word has been suggested by Persigout, *Ed. mod.*, 1907, p. 243.

branches :—Cannibals might, and doubtless do, apply a knowledge of the child to the culinary art; manufacturers might ask of child physiology if it is more economical to use the child rather than the adult for certain manual work. . . . But it matters little to us how numerous may be the possible number of sections in paidotechny, since we have to consider here only one of them, viz. experimental pedagogy.

Experimental Pedagogy is the knowledge of, or the inquiry into, the circumstances favourable to the development of the child,[1] and the means of educating him towards a given end. Hence it includes *Psycho-pedagogy* and *School Hygiene*, and, if it has to do with the education of abnormal children, *Medico-pedagogy* or *Orthophreny* (the putting right of mental deformities: Greek *orthos*, right, *phren*, mind). But, of this total, Psycho-pedagogy is so large a part—not only because the formation of the mental functions assumes a wide field of knowledge, but, above all, because it is to that formation that all other educative means ought to be subordinated—that it is often it alone that we understand by the term experimental pedagogy.

Experimental Pedagogy and General Pedagogy.—The definition of experimental pedagogy which has just been given marks it off from pedagogy in general, of which it is also a part. Experimental pedagogy works with a certain end in view, but *this end is given to it*; that is to say, that it takes it such as it is, without discussing it, and without consider-

[1] Experimental pedagogy pushes its roots also into adult and animal psychology. It is none the less true, however, that the laws derived from the study of adults or animals will be of use to pedagogy only in so far as we have reason for supposing that these laws also govern the psychic phenomena of the child.

ing its *value*. "Being given such and such an end, by what means can we attain it?" "It being given that we wish to make a child an honest worker, or on the contrary a pickpocket, how can we bring it about?" Such is the kind of problem which it has to solve. But it has not to give a decision upon the question if this particular child *should* embrace one rather than the other of these professions.

This study of ends belongs to another part of pedagogy: to *Dogmatic* (or *Teleologic*) *Pedagogy*, which will borrow from morals, philosophy, æsthetics, religion, sociology, and politics, an ideal, more or less remote, or more or less immediate, towards which it should direct the educative action.

We sometimes pretend that science is able to furnish us with this ideal. But this is an error, and we ought to be quite convinced that it is. Science explains the course of phenomena, but it never lays it down that phenomena *ought* to follow one course rather than another. Chemistry teaches us about the explosive power of dynamite, but it does not tell us what use we ought to make of this explosive power: whether we ought to employ it to blow up a mine or a potentate. Physiology teaches us what are the effects of morphia, but it does not tell us whether we ought to make use of it to relieve rather than to kill the sick: it simply says, "*If* you wish to relieve, then take such and such a dose; *if* you wish to kill, go up to this dose." And that is all it does, its recipe given, it is not concerned in the use made of it.

Science being blind in regard to the end we propose to ourselves, as a Daltonian[1] is blind to red colour, it is not able, therefore, to point out to us

[1] So named after the discoverer (Dalton) of colour-blindness.

what we ought to make of a child: towards what destiny to embark him. Ought he to become an atheist, or a bigot; a patriot, or an internationalist; a blacksmith, a solicitor, or a sailor? Science never answers questions of this sort; all that it is able to do is to show that the child is more likely to succeed in one career rather than in another—it predicts, for example, that a very agile and adroit child will be a good pickpocket; but it never tells us whether we ought to encourage or, on the other hand, counteract these natural dispositions. It does not even tell us that it is necessary to make anything whatever of the child; and it declines to have anything whatever to do with the serious question as to the knowledge of what are "the rights of the child": whether the child belongs to itself, or whether it belongs to its parents.[1]

Similarly, when purely physical education, or hygiene, is in question, we find that the verdicts of science remain subordinate to the philosophical aspirations of those who deal with the problem. Here is a striking example of this: Ought, or ought not, the

[1] Compare this portion of the report of the meeting, on March 17, 1903, of the Chamber of Deputies, at Paris:—

M. Reille. That concerns only the parents

M. Ferdinand Buisson. The child does not belong to the parents. (*Strong protests from the right and the centre.*)

M. Lasies. To whom does it belong?

M. F. Buisson. To whom does the child belong? To himself He is a human being. If I were to speak in the terms of those who interrupt me, I should say that he is a creature of God, and does not belong to any other creature.

On this question of the rights of the child, see Daubresse, *L'émancipation de l'enfant*, Revue bleue, Mar. 21, 1903; and Tauro, *Fondamento e limiti del diritto di educare*, Cœnobium, April 1910 child to be fed on meat? This seems to be a wholly scientific question. But if you consult the doctors, you will find that moral considerations are by no means omitted from their prescriptions. Dr. de Fleury, for example, condemns vegetarianism as enervating to both body and mind, disposing to sedentary professions, and extinguishing the spirit of adventure and conquest. On the other hand, his colleague, Professor Armand Gautier, affirms that vegetarianism ought to be adopted, "because it tends to make us pacific, and not aggressive and violent"; because it forms "kindly, intelligent, and artistic races, who are, nevertheless, prolific, vigorous, and active."[1] It is certainly not biological chemistry or physiology which enjoins us to be, or not to be, a people given up to sedentary occupations, to conquests, or to anything whatever. Biology itself, the science of life, ascertains what are the circumstances most favourable to life, but it does not say that we must live. It teaches us how to perpetuate races, but it does not tell us whether we ought to perpetuate our own race: whether we ought to be celibate or to have many children.

Pedagogy, then, is marked off from experimental pedagogy in that it implies the study of the ends of education. It includes also other departments: *The history of pedagogical theories*; the study of *school organisations*, considered from the material or administrative point of view; and finally, and above all, *Propaideutics*, that is to say, the art itself of education, the technical apprenticeship of teaching. It is not sufficient, in fact, to be a good educator, to know the end to be attained, and the means to attain it;

[1] De Fleury, *Le corps et l'âme de l'enfant*, Paris, 1900, p. 47, A. Gautier, *L'alimentation et les régimes*, Paris, 1904, p. 397.

it is also necessary to be personally trained in the art of applying these means, just as a violinist trains himself to carry out the movements which theory has taught him. We shall not concern ourselves here with these various departments.

PSYCHO-PAIDOLOGY AND PSYCHO-PEDAGOGY.—Let us now return to the psychology of the child and consider it in its two forms: 1st, *pure* child psychology (Psycho-paidology), which has for its object the **explanation** of the processes and of the psychic activity of the child, that is to say, the determination of laws as general as possible. 2nd, the psychology of the child as *applied to pedagogy* (Psycho-pedagogy), of which the problems, being all of a practical nature, divide themselves into two classes, according as they concern the appraising of a certain given psychical state (psychodiagnostics), or the obtaining of a certain desired resultant (psychotechnics).

An example will easily make clear to us the difference between these three sorts of problems. Let us take the question of intellectual fatigue. Pure psychology will ask, What is fatigue; what is its nature; what are its physiological conditions; its variations according to age, sex, the nature and duration of the work; and what are the laws which synthesise its various manifestations? Psychodiagnostics, on the other hand, concerns itself only with the discovery of practical methods for estimating, and diagnosing the presence or the degree of fatigue in a given case.

As to psychotechnics, this is the sort of question that it puts: How can we fight against fatigue? Given a piece of work to do, how can we carry it through with the least possible fatigue? At what point should we interrupt the work so that the pauses may be most profitable? Of what duration ought an interval of recreation to be, in order to counteract the fatigue resulting from forty-five minutes of work? &c.

If, instead of fatigue, we consider memory, the three different points of view present themselves anew. *Pure psychology:* What are the laws of memory; its factors; its evolution? *Psychodiagnostics:* How can we measure memory, the faculty of acquisition, the conservation of recollections in an individual or in a given case? *Psychotechnics:* What is the best way in which to memorise a passage in a given time? How can we educate memory? &c.

We see that these three points of view exactly correspond to those under which the problems of medicine present themselves: pure psychology being analogous to physiology and general pathology; psychodiagnostics corresponding to clinical diagnostics; and psychotechnics to therapeutics.

Psychodiagnostics may have for its object the estimation of a present character or, on the other hand, of a future aptitude or condition. We may, in fact, be interested in asking not only if, to-day, Paul is overworked or not, and what his power of attention may be; but, especially, if he risks overworking himself by undertaking such and such work; and if he shows such aptitudes that we ought to direct his attention to the exact sciences, or to the fine arts, or to commerce and industry. This diagnosis for a long time ahead, which deserves the name of *psychoprognostics,* certainly constitutes a problem of first-rate importance. What life failures, disillusions, and ruin would be spared us if only, in the choice of a career, more account were taken of the natural aptitudes of

Table showing the Relation between the Science of the Child and Pedagogy

SCIENCE OF THE CHILD.								
PURE:— **Paidology.**	APPLIED:— **Paidotechny.**							
	In Medicine. PAIDIATRY.	In Law. JUDICIAL PAIDOTECHNY.	In Education. EXPERIMENTAL PEDAGOGY.					
Child psychology (or Psychopaidology).	Child Psychiatry.		Psycho-pedagogy.	*Final Ends:*— Morality, metaphysics, religion, æsthetics, and theory of the ideal.	History of Pedagogy.	Training in the Art of Education.	School Systems, &c.
		Child Criminology, &c.		*Approximate Ends:*— Sociology; Contingencies.			
Child pathology.	Child Clinic.	....	Medico-pedagogy; Orthophreny.				
Child physiology, &c.	Child Hygiene, &c.	....	School Hygiene.				
			EXPERIMENTAL.	DOGMATIC.	HISTORICAL.	PROPÆDEUTIC.	ADMINISTRATIVE.

young people.[1] This is, it is true, a question of the future, which assumes a very accurate knowledge of the laws of heredity, and an enormous quantity of exact records, examined by the help of rigorous methods. To-day, however, we are able to begin the gathering in of such documents, and the problems which present themselves to us are as follows: (1) This man of whom we know the character and aptitudes, what was he as a child? (2) This child, who is endowed in such and such a manner, who shows such and such an interest for work, what will he do later on in life?

Such are the problems which can only be solved by many observations, each extending over a long period. Old schoolmasters who have retained an exact recollection of their former pupils might be able to furnish useful hints as to what became of the pupils later. And young teachers ought, henceforward, to begin to take accurate notes about those of their pupils whom, it is probable, they will not lose sight of when they are grown up. By systematically comparing the school records of pupils who have attended the same college for six or seven years consecutively, we may, even now, obtain some useful data.

Among the psychotechnic problems, there is one category which, from the point of view of practical pedagogy, has a special importance, viz. that which concerns the processes of teaching, and which we have grouped under the term **Experimental Didactics**.

[1] Jonckheere has shown, particularly, that the profession of teacher is but rarely undertaken because of a vocation for it (Jonckheere, *Contribution à l'étude de la vocation*, Arch. de Psy. VIII, 1909, p. 55).

This in its turn includes problems of methodology, technics, and economics. *Methodological Didactics* determines the best methods for initiating the pupil into new knowledge, and for instructing him in that branch of knowledge. What is the best method for learning to read? for learning geometry? for learning to speak a foreign language? for learning to translate into good English? to ride a horse?—such is the form in which its problems present themselves. *Technical and Economical Didactics* seeks, once the method of teaching is determined, to find the technical procedure which enables us to apply this method in developing to the greatest possible extent the natural aptitudes of the pupil; in placing him in the most favourable conditions for work; and in making him accomplish his task in the most economical manner, that is to say, by the expenditure of the least possible energy and time.

Let us take as an example the teaching of the English language. We will assume that proper experiments have shown that one way of training pupils to speak this language well is to make them learn by heart passages from good authors. Here we have a method belonging to methodological didactics. But which will be the better process, to memorise passages of prose or of poetry? This is a problem which comes within the province of technical-economical didactics.

A problem which belongs to didactics is that of the *Educator*. Given a group of children to bring up, to instruct, what is the attitude that it is desirable that the teacher should take on coming face to face with them; and what ought to be the character of the teacher? What are the temperaments which are most suitable for the pedagogic vocation? The

Psychology of the Master certainly appears to belong to psychotechnics.

We still have to describe, as a new-comer into this group of problems, **Eugenics.** This new department, created by Galton (see p. 17), and which has for its object "the study of the natural social elements which improve or debase the native qualities, both physical and mental, of the race," is certainly an applied science, since it pursues a very definite object, that of indicating the practical means of making future generations as healthy as possible. That part of eugenics which is only concerned with the improvement of mental characteristics may be given the name of *Psycho-Eugenics.*

THE RATIONAL METHOD AND THE EMPIRICAL METHOD.—For the finding of the solution of the various problems which present themselves, two methods offer themselves to psycho-pedagogy—the rational method (theoretical deduction), and the empirical method (gropings).

If it be possible, psycho-pedagogy will choose the rational method, that is to say, it will derive its sources of information from pure science. From the psycho-physiological laws of mental life it will *deduce* the data which will enable it to act upon the psychical functions of the child, or to estimate their quality and strength. It is in this way that the general laws of mental development point out the line of action which should be followed in education and in instruction; the manner in which, for example, the idea of number is developed in the race or in the child suggests useful ideas as to the beginnings of instruction in arithmetic; and it is thus also, that, from the laws of memorisation or of forgetfulness, we are able to derive practical

CHILD PSYCHOLOGY.			
Pure :—PSYCHO-PAIDOLOGY.		Applied to **Education** :—PSYCHO-PEDAGOGY.	
The mental processes, considered :—		Methods discovered :—	
1. In themselves	**Structural Psychology.**		**Psychodiagnosis** (and **psychoprognosis**).
2. In their relation to the needs of the subject	**Functional Psychology.**	*Rationally* (by theoretical deduction).	
3. In their relation to growth	**Genetic Psychology.**	*Empirically* (by gropings).	**Psychotechnics.** Action upon :— The race, **Psycho-Eugenics.**
4. In their individual varieties	**Individual Psychology.**		The child, **Education and Instruction.**
			Methods of teaching, **Experimental Didactics.**
5. In their modifications under social influence	**Collective Psychology.**		The Master, **Psychology of the Master.**

guidance as to the manner of presenting to the child the things which it ought to learn; so, again, from the laws governing suicide amongst scholars we may deduce the means of preventing it, &c. Or, yet again, to give an example derived from psychodiagnosis: a knowledge of the normal development of certain functions enables us, up to a certain point, to diagnose the amount of backwardness of a child in whom the function has not shown itself, &c.

But pure psychology is too little advanced to furnish precise answers to a thousand questions which present themselves to the educator. And, on the other hand, reality is so complex, and such a large number of factors intersect, that it will often be practically impossible to disentangle the action of a single process, even if we knew its laws. Also, it will very often be necessary that applied psychology should go on ahead, flying, as it were, with its own wings. It will then have recourse to empiricism; it will proceed by gropings; and, in default of general laws, it will search for *signs*, for *recipes*. Thus, not being able to discover anything from the laws of the mechanism of fatigue as to the practical manner of diagnosing this condition and estimating its degree, it will seek to find, by gropings,[1] what are the signs of

[1] This word "groping," which is used here for definitely indicating the empirical method, does not exclude, it must be clearly understood, an absolute strictness in the inquiry. The inquiry will always be founded upon observation and experiment. "Gropings" signifies that the problem consists not in the determination of the nature (resolving) of a given phenomenon, but in the *inquiry* as to what is the phenomenon which best suits the proposed end. Thus one will explore the various sensorial and motor processes *until* he finds one which, varying in a fashion sufficiently closely with fatigue, will serve in the estimating of its amount.

fatigue, and by what certain and convenient means they may be registered. Similarly, not being able to deduce from the laws of memory, insufficiently established, any positive indication as to the best processes of teaching orthography, psycho-pedagogy will test, empirically, what are—among the various possible processes for teaching this subject (spelling, transcription, &c.)—those which succeed best.

In medicine it is just the same. Medical clinic is nearly always in advance of physiopathological theories. It employs many medicaments, because experience has shown that they succeeded, although we do not at all know how they act. What is, for example, the mode of action of salicylate of soda in rheumatism? We do not know. Though many theories try to give an account of it, not one is definitive. Diagnostic signs, like the means of treatment, are also far more often empirical than rational. The "white tongue" is an excellent sign of gastric disorder. But why does gastric disorder blanch the tongue? Nobody knows anything about this.

Like medicine, psycho-pedagogy will more often be empirical than rational. But that in no wise lessens its practical value. Empirical formulæ, if they are founded upon sound experience, are quite as definite as derived laws; from which they are only distinguished by their lesser generality, and by the different practical part which they play: we take them for their own worth, and not so much for their explanatory value. But we must not forget that it is the accumulation of empirical formulæ which leads to the discovery of rational laws. Applied science is thus in its turn most useful to pure science: each lends to the other a mutual support. Between child psychology and psycho-pedagogy there will, in consequence, be set up a constant exchange of give and take.

2. Pedagogical Problems

Since experimental pedagogy is, as we have just seen, the science which is destined to furnish the means whereby the educator can reach the end which he proposes, the first thing to do is to make quite clear what is the end which he tries to attain.

What is the aim of education? Very few agree upon this point. So many persons, so many points of view. Each, naturally, wishes that education should be taken in the sense of his preferences, social or political, philosophical or religious. If we make up our minds to wait until the whole world is agreed upon the end to be sought, the science of education would never be founded.

Fortunately the problem is by no means so desperate as it seems. In the same way as the kneading of the paste is quite independent of the form which will be given to the pastry, so the *manner* of teaching is, up to a certain point, independent of the *matter* of teaching. The rules of harmony and the musical advice which a professor of singing gives, and the technical exercises which he makes his pupil perform, serve equally well for the execution of a patriotic or religious song as for a revolutionary hymn.

On the other hand, instruction—especially primary instruction, and a good part of secondary—is an immediate end which is almost entirely independent of the final end of education. Many branches of study are entirely independent of the use which will be made of them, and remain the same whatever may be the final aims of the educator—arithmetic, orthography, physics, geography, &c. There is not a spiritualistic arithmetic and a materialistic arithmetic, no more than there is a citizen physics and an anarchist physics.

Education, by which I mean the education of the heart, the character, and the will—the education which ought to dominate the whole of our school system, where instruction actually reigns alone—education can hardly be carried on at all unless we have before us a clearly defined ideal. It is not necessary here to discuss what this ideal ought to be. We need only remark that, in spite of inevitable individual divergencies, educators are agreed in recognising that it is proper to make of the child an honest and healthy man, independent in mind, and a lover of the good, the true, and the beautiful, and that his physical and intellectual potentialities should be developed with due regard to his personality.

The pursuit of this aim brings the educator face to face with a certain number of problems of practical pedagogy, which may be grouped under the following four heads: the preservation of health, intellectual and physical gymnastics, memory furnishing, and education proper. Each of these aims admits of its own special problems.[1]

1. **Health Preservation.**—The first duty of the educator, every one will agree, is to do no harm. The *primo non nocere* (firstly not to harm) is as much in its place here as in medical practice. Certainly, it is impossible to conform literally to this requirement,

[1] The problems referred to here are those previously included under the name of *psychotechnics*; but they will now be looked at from the point of view of their educational function.

for all school education is harmful in some way to the normal development of the child, if it only be that the child is obliged to remain seated the whole day in a close atmosphere, and with bent back, instead of being allowed to run about freely.

But the constant care of the educator ought to be to reduce the injury as much as possible: he ought never to do such harm to a child, under the pretext of instructing him, that it outweighs the good that results to him from the instruction. What is the good of storing the memory of an individual, and teaching him the art of thinking, if this teaching results in overworking him, enfeebling his vital energies, and wearying him with effort; that is to say, to keep him far away from precisely those situations in which he might be able to profit by his knowledge and his judgment?

The problem of health preservation includes, before all, the questions of fatigue and overpressure; of overcrowding of syllabuses; of the arrangement of time-tables (so as not to put too many exhausting lessons following each other); of the allotment of rest periods; and of intellectual hygiene in general; in a word, all the measures taken in order that the growth and development of the child may be hindered in nothing.

Among the problems of health preservation there enters also the question of *economy of work.* Given that the forces of a pupil are limited, and that it is desirable to take from him the least possible amount of time, we set ourselves to find out what are the means which enable us to accomplish a piece of work with the minimum of effort, and in the best time. By *the best* time we do not mean the absolute minimum, but the most favourable length of time for the realisation of the proposed end, without expenditure of any superfluous time or strength. For example: A piece of poetry has to be learned; what is the process of study which will enable it to be learned by heart, while giving to it the least possible time and energy?

2. **Gymnastics** (mental and physical).—Before learning anything it is necessary *to learn how to learn.* The problems which enter into this category relate to the education of the senses, of movements, of the power of observation, of attention, of judgment, of reasoning, and of natural aptitudes. They also have for their object the conditions most favourable to the stimulation or to the play of mental functions. For example: What is the normal order of the development of these faculties? What is the value of such and such a study (the dead languages, mathematics, &c.) as a means of exercising such and such a faculty? At what age ought a certain subject to be taught so that its gymnastic value may be the greatest? What is the function of object-lessons, or manual work, or play, or physical exercise, in the development of intelligence? Is the memory developed by exercise? Is it better that the pupil should work by himself, or, on the other hand, in common with his comrades? For what kind of work is isolation most (or least) profitable?

3. **Acquiring Information** (instruction proper).—Important as it is that we should learn how to learn, and however much we may lament the fact that the gymnastics of the mind are too often sacrificed to the loading of the memory, it is none the less true that the acquisition of a solid capital of knowledge is, in fact, indispensable. It is necessary to furnish the

memory, to make the nervous centres take on certain settled modes, and to create fixed habits; and consequently questions arise which demand a knowledge of: at what age the mind is most apt for acquiring a given category of knowledge—through which memory (visual, auditive, verbal, or motor) impressions are best retained; if we cannot facilitate the retention of facts by presenting them, and associating them, in a certain manner; whether interest or repetition constitutes the best condition for the fixation of information; at what time in the day the fixation of recollections is most easy (for example, before or after a meal, evening or morning), &c.

4. **Education proper.**—Here it is not merely a question of exercising the intelligence or furnishing the memory, but rather of directing the character aright, of stimulating zeal, and of developing the will and personality. This task, the most delicate and difficult of all, includes alike the exercise or the inhibition of certain instincts, the cultivation of certain ideals, and the acquisition of certain habits; it implies, therefore, both gymnastics and furnishing; it is a synthesis. The problems which it raises are numerous. For example: What are the elements of character, and how can we bring influence to bear on them? What are the causes of idleness, and how can we act on them? What are the conditions for will, and how can we strengthen it? What is "zeal"? Is the zeal that a scholar shows in his work the cause or the effect of his aptitude for that branch of his studies? Has the development of the æsthetic tastes a re-echo in that of the moral qualities? What are the psychological foundations of lying? How can we remedy fear, and timidity? What is the influence of sports on the

education of the will? What are the psychological effects of punishments? &c.

We could multiply to infinity questions of this kind. It is important that we should convince ourselves that not one of them can be resolved *à priori* or by theoretical discussions. Only EXPERIENCE is able to furnish the solution of them. But it is *à priori*, or by starting from preconceived dogmatic ideas, that the ordinary pedagogy—which I should like to be allowed to call the "old pedagogy"—has always decided them, or daily decides them, as if they were the easiest things in the world, when the least of them is bristling with difficulties.[1]

3. General, Individual, and Collective Psychology

Having considered the problems of child psychology from the point of view of their intrinsic form

[1] We may mention here an interesting classification given by Baade of the effects of teaching This writer distinguishes those effects which are *primary*, belonging to instruction proper, and the effects which are *secondary*, arising unexpectedly and accidentally, without having been contemplated beforehand. These secondary effects are sub-divisible into three groups—1st, *Useful effects*, pedagogically, such as that exercise of memory which takes place when we learn something; 2nd, *Effects upon the receptivity* of the scholar: those influences which are able to further (as does interest) or to hinder (as does fatigue) the primary effects; 3rd, *Indifferent effects*, but those which must be taken into account, simply because they exist and are liable to absorb energy uselessly, *e g.* unmethodical repetitions in memorising. (Baade, *Exp. und krit. Beitrage z. Frage nach den sekundaren Wirkungen des Unterrichts*, Dissertation, Göttingen, 1906.) These various categories of effects each raise problems connected with the four classes I have distinguished: the obtaining of the primary effects implies the problems of memory-furnishing and education; and the secondary effects suggest the problems of gymnastics or the preservation of health

(diagnostics or technics), and under that of their practical bearing, it remains for us to differentiate them according to their universality. Sometimes, in fact, these problems only seek for averages, *general* results, the discovery of laws valid, broadly speaking, for all children of the same age: sometimes, on the other hand, they have for their object the individual in his concrete and personal reality, and they then aim to determine the *individual differences* which exist among children; the various mental types; that special constitution of each which makes John to be John and not Peter; and sometimes they refer to children considered *collectively*.

INDIVIDUAL PSYCHOLOGY.—The questions belonging to the second group, which constitutes what we have called individual psychology, are, we take it, of very great importance for the educator, whose action always affects, in the final result, individuals, each of whom has his own psychical character, his own personal manner of behaving, thinking, and feeling.

Individual psychology includes four different problems.—

1. What are the individual varieties of the various psychical processes, considered in themselves?
2. What are the various types of individuals? What is it that characterises an individual? What is individuality?
3. What are the relations existing among the functions or psychical processes of the same individual? Are there any processes of greater importance on which others depend?
4. Do the different functions which exist in the same individual reciprocally influence each other, and to what extent?

1. **Individual Varieties of Processes.**—This problem includes the study of the various types, quantitative and qualitative, of memory (strong, feeble), imagination (visual, auditory, &c.), attention (synthetic, analytic, concentrated, diffused, &c.), judgment, reactivity, aptitudes (literary, scientific, &c.), &c.

2. **Individuality.**—What is it that characterises an individual? How do the various mental functions (sensibility, memory, reactivity, &c.) reflect the peculiar character of the individual? This is how the problem first presented itself. If it were solvable in this form, it would be very convenient, for in experimentally determining the nature or the capacity of certain mental functions we might arrive at the diagnosis of the individual type. Suppose, for example, that the individuality was completely reflected in tactile sensibility: then we should simply have to measure this sensibility by means of Weber's compasses, and we should be able to recognise whether we had to do with a man of intelligence, an idiot, or a criminal—Lombroso, we know, has observed that criminals have a very blunt tactile sensibility.

For the last twenty years various psychologists have set themselves to the task of determining the mental processes susceptible of revealing individual aptitude or character (Cattell in America, 1890; Kraepelin in Germany, 1895; Binet in France, 1896). The numerous tests which they have formulated to this end are well known under the name of *mental tests.*

This method of mental tests, however, is too simple. It rests upon a hypothesis which is not proven, viz. that the essence of individuality ought necessarily to be found in a certain number of functions considered separately. But it is only after a theoretic study of the structure of individuality that we shall be able to know just how far this is the case, and what are the tests which have a diagnostic value. This study ought itself to be based upon a knowledge of the *correlations* of various functions or aptitudes.

This is how the preliminary questions present themselves for solution :—

How far are the various mental functions able to be independent of each other, or, on the other hand, how far do they reciprocally influence each other ? For example, to what extent can an intelligent individual be divested of memory ? To what extent may it be possible for a pupil strong in arithmetic to be weak in orthography ? Or : to what extent ought an individual having a strong memory to show a fixed degree of sensibility ? &c.

If the correlation of various functions, of diverse mental characters, was absolute and invariable, it is evident that these questions would not present themselves. There would then be no *individuality,* but only identical beings, as though they came out of the same mould ; for individuality is only the result of variation in the proportion of the characteristics of the race among its various representatives. But there are individuals ; for all animals, even all vegetables, and still more all men, diverge more or less from the average type of the race. This proves, then, that the correlation of divers characteristics is not rigid, but presents a certain flexibility, a margin more or less large for individual caprices.

Among the divers characteristics or aptitudes, certain are more closely associated among themselves, and form as it were correlative constellations relatively stable. Others, on the contrary, remain more independent; that is to say, their presence is not necessarily responsible for the presence of other aptitudes. These independent aptitudes, or, as we call them, aptitudes "of high variability," are evidently those which contribute most to the *characterising* of an individual; the others representing, on the other hand, the commonplace and those common to all.

The problem of individuality then returns to the search for those characteristics or fundamental aptitudes which most distinguish individuals from one another, and which may serve to classify them into a certain number of definite types. We shall also ask ourselves what repercussion these fundamental aptitudes have upon the other psychical functions, and what is the form which the total correlative constellation takes under their influence. This being determined, we shall then be in a position to set up the various tests enabling us to diagnose the general type to which an individual belongs, and we shall understand in what the specific nature of an individual consists.

A special problem of individual psychology is that of the psychology of the *sexes:* What are the distinctive psychological traits of boys and of girls?

3. The Relations of the various Processes in the same Individual.—The problem here consists in determining the correlations of which we have just spoken. We shall learn also what are the functions or aptitudes which are conjoined. This has also a practical interest. If, for example, a child has a strong memory, what other faculty ought we to be able to expect that he also probably possesses in a high degree? If there be an anomaly in a function, will that anomaly entail anomalies in other faculties?

The problem is a delicate one, for, as a fact, there are neither psychophysiological aptitudes which are always conjoint, nor others which are absolutely independent. There are only some aptitudes which we find *more often* associated than others. To measure the degree of rigidity or flexibility of the correlation of two or many mental qualities or attributes, is to determine how great is the chance of meeting a certain aptitude associated with another given aptitude (or many others), in such a way that, if it is shown that in a subject a certain function A has a value *a*, we are immediately able to infer that the value *b* is most probably in this subject from another function B. As one might anticipate, this kind of problem is very delicate, for the calculation of the degree of correlation is a calculation of probability: "What probability is there that such a union of functions may be due to a fixed cause and not to chance?" Such is the problem to be solved for each given correlation. The formulæ suggested for arriving at its solution are at the present moment engaging the attention of mathematicians and biometricians (notably Pearson); and some psychologists (Spearman, Krüger, Thorndike, Brown, and Burt) are also engaged in the study of this question.

4. **The Reciprocal Influence of various Functions.**—When we educate a certain function, are we acting upon others at the same time? What are they? This problem is very akin to the preceding, to which it is a sort of psychotechnical pendant. It is not, however, entirely involved in it. It is conceivable that the functions may be correlative without there existing between them a relation of direct influence: the cause of the observed relation may indeed be

mediate; that is to say, the functions may both depend upon a certain common factor, without depending directly upon each other. Thus we show that certain scholars are, at the same time, strong in drawing and history. This does not prove that there exists between these aptitudes a direct relation which implies a mastery of these two branches of study; for the aptitude for the one or the other may result from a common factor, such as application to work. The question of the direct dependence of two, or many, aptitudes certainly constitutes, therefore, a special problem.

To solve the various problems of individuality it is first of all necessary to collect a considerable number of records enabling us to set forth a list of characteristics met with in various individuals. Two methods of procedure have been employed to this end:—

First, a direct study of living persons, whom we subject to a detailed psychological examination; or, second, analysing the published biographies of historical personages, or others (principally of great men). The first of these has been used, on many occasions, by Binet, who has made out the psychological portraits of some dramatic authors, and recently of a young artist. The second has been carried out with remarkable care and patience by Heymans and Wiersma. But it would be better if the enumeration of the characteristics of an individual were still more systematic than even in this case; and, to make uniform and facilitate this enumeration, it would be useful to proceed according to a formulary laying down in advance all the points upon which information is desired. Stern, Lipmann, and Baade have recently elaborated one of these schematic formularies. These authors have given the name of *Psychography* to this methodical description of the characteristics of an individual, and *Psychogram* to the descriptive form on which this description is entered.

It would also be very interesting to determine to what degree the correlations vary according to age. Are individual differences greater among children or among adults? Do the links of affinity between two given faculties, for example, memory and reactivity, become closer or looser when the child grows up? We can easily multiply questions of this kind. We will confine ourselves to remarking how extremely well placed the teacher is for furnishing to psychologists those documents useful for the solution of the problems of correlation; since he has occasion to follow simultaneously the condition and progress of a great number of different aptitudes: aptitudes for calculation, memory, will-power, attention, &c. He should find a quantity of material already in the notes which he has taken of his pupils. in the course of the year, with regard to the various branches of study.

COLLECTIVE PSYCHOLOGY.—It has long been observed that individuals, when they are part of a group, a society, or an excited mob, think and act in a different manner from what they would if each of them was isolated. Beside general psychology and individual psychology it is, therefore, necessary to reserve a place for collective psychology, the object of which is the study of that collective mind which emanates from the communion of individual minds, and which is a new product presenting characteristics markedly different from those possessed by each of the units which compose it (in the same way as water is very different from oxygen and hydrogen).

Is there a collective psycho-paidology ? Assuredly : though the groupings of children may be more rare, less permanent, and less varied than those of adults. Do not children of the same school, and the same class, form a homogeneous and autonomous grouping ? Outside the school, or in their games, do they not frequently unite in bands, and societies, which occasionally contend with rival bands, or societies, and which submit to the authority of leaders ?

It is not without interest for the master, whose teaching addresses itself precisely to this well-marked collectivity which a class of pupils constitutes, to know the psychological characteristics of groupings of children. What are the laws of the collective psychology of the child ? What modifications or deformations of psychism induce in the child the fact of being a member of a definite collectivity ? What are the faculties, sentiments, and functions which the participation in a collectivity develops ? What are the respective advantages of individual and of collective teaching ? These are the problems of collective psycho-paidology.

4. The Genetico-Functional Problem

There still remains one category of problems to be considered, namely, those which concern the nature of the psychical processes and their mechanism. For example, What is perception ? What is a sentiment ? What are their causes, their effects, &c. ? These problems are proper to pure psychology, and we need not enumerate them here. I should only wish to show in what sense most of these problems should be taken, when the child is in question. First of all let us recall the two tendencies which are manifested in contemporary psychology as to the manner of viewing the mental life. Some lay stress upon the *description* of elements which analysis distinguishes in the psychic life; they consider the various processes in a state of isolation, so to say. This is *structural psychology*. Others, on the contrary, start from the fact of the psychical *life* itself, of the unity of the individual, and inquire, before all else, what are the relations of the various processes with this psychical life; what are their rôles, function, and significance; why do they appear; and how do they accomplish their task? This is the point of view of *functional psychology*.

These two points of view, far from excluding each other, ought to be reconciled. But, if they are equally legitimate, they are not equally valuable, for the functional problem alone really interests the practician, the structural problem having only a transitory interest, and its value consists in its giving rise to the functional problem or in making its terms precise. For example: what constitutes the psychical process of the perception of a tree? It is structural psychology which teaches us this; by submitting this perception to a close analysis we shall discover that all the details of the tree which are impressed upon the retina of the subject are not the only ones to be found in it, but that, on the contrary, a certain number of images, of recollections, and of feelings, foreign to the physical impression, make an integral part of this perception, in such a way that we may define it thus: "an impression of the senses accompanied by an escort of images." But why have only certain outside impressions been seized upon by the consciousness of the subject; and what is it that has determined that certain mental images have mixed themselves up with the sense impressions? What does all this mean? Here it is functional psychology which will reply; and it will show us that it is the actual dispositions and needs of the subject which have brought about a selection among the impressions or the images constituting his perception of the tree, and that this selection is made in accordance with his interest at the moment. Thus the perception of a tree differs according to whether it is seen with the eye of an artist, a botanist, or a woodcutter.[1]

During the course of the last thirty years structural psychology has been almost exclusively cultivated, and this need not be regretted, since it has had for its result the raising of many problems. But it is indispensable that we should adopt the functional point of view when, leaving pure theory, we wish to acquire such knowledge as will enable us to act upon human beings; for they are wholes, unities, and each of their activities is governed by the total needs and interests which constitute their personality, at a given moment. We are only able, therefore, to grasp the significance of the psychophysiological processes of which they are the seat, by referring to the organic whole of which these processes form an integral part.

[1] With the structural problem, which is concerned to show how the psychical processes are *constituted*, and the functional problem, which endeavours to find out *what use they are*, should also be mentioned the *problem of mechanism*, which seeks, by taking account of the structural facts, to show *how the functional result is attained*. But, in most cases, the problem of mechanism evades psychological investigation, and it then becomes necessary, in order to find a solution, to have recourse to physiological hypotheses.

When it refers to a child the functional problem takes a special form and importance.

A child is a being which develops and grows. Its various mental functions are not in a state of equilibrium, but show a constant progress. This phenomenon of growth necessarily influences all the activities of the child, and gives them a special form and manner. It will be an ever-present factor, and one of which we must, therefore, always take account. The problem, then, will not only be to determine what is the significance of a psychological problem, in relation to the circumstances of the moment, but also the detaching of this significance, having regard to the necessities and needs of growth.

This taking into consideration of the circumstances of growth is what we characterise as the **genetico-functional problem.** This problem is a double one, for in the case of a given process there will be occasion, as a matter of fact, to ask :—

1st. *What are the conditions of its production ?*

2nd. *What is its genetic function ;* that is to say, what part does it play in the formation of future functions ? The appearance of a phenomenon may, in fact, be as necessary to form, or cause the production of, subsequent phenomena, as the presence of antecedent phenomena were necessary to its own production.

This genetic problem is of first-rate importance for the educator. To guide the development of the child, he ought to know how this development is effected ; what favours and what hinders it ; so as to be able to determine the correlations of growth. It is from the point of view of this creative utility that he ought to consider the mental phenomena.

This point of view, which has been strikingly emphasised by Professor Dewey of Chicago, and his pupil Irving King, has been but little regarded, so far, even by those who are engaged in child psychology. Most writers have believed that it was sufficient to draw up a list of the various faculties exhibited by a child at certain ages; as if the problem consisted solely in the determination of the date and order of the appearance of these various faculties—see, for example, Preyer. His work contains numerous records; but, on the whole, these records are of very little value for the educator, because Preyer has never set himself the question as to *what part* a certain process, or a certain activity, plays in the general development of the individual; *how* and *why*, at such and such a period, such and such a form of activity disappeared (*e.g.* impulses), to make place for some other form (*e.g.* inhibitions).[1]

. . . . . .

The various problems which we have just enumerated have not engrossed paidologists to the same degree in different countries. Whilst the Americans are pre-eminently attached to the biological point of view, and have made prominent the problem of growth, Europeans have preferred to pursue the experimental analysis of the various psychical functions, considered separately—some, with Binet, principally attack the study of the complex and higher phenomena, such as intelligence, suggestibility, and intellectual types; others, with the German school, confine their investigations to elementary phenomena, such as sensibility, reaction, memory, and association.

[1] *Cf.* King, *The Psychology of Child Development*, Chicago, 1903; and the introduction to this work by Professor Dewey.

But these different schools tend towards uniformity nowadays. All these forms of research have, however, their justification; but the biological points of view, both genetic and functional, ought to dominate all others, and it is to it that we must have recourse for the co-ordinating and interpreting of them.

BIBLIOGRAPHY

Applied Psychology.—STERN, *Angewandte Psychologie*, Beitr. zur Psychol. der Aussage, I., 1903, p. 4. WUNDT, *Ueber reine und angew. Psychologie*, Psych. Stud., V., 1909, p. 1. COHN, *Was kann die Psychol von der Padag. lernen*, Z. pad P., 1899.

Subdivisions of Pedagogy.—PERSIGOUT, *Essais de pédologie générale*, Paris, Paulin, 1909.

Pedagogy, its aim and its position.—DURKHEIM, *Pédagogie et sociologie*, Rev. de métaph. et de morale, Jan. 1903. CELLÉRIER, *Esquisse d'une science pédagogique*, Paris, 1910. LECLÈRE, *L'éducation morale rationnelle*, Paris, 1909. GAULTIER, *La vraie éducation*, Paris, 1910. MARCERON, *L'art de l'éducation*, Rev. phil., Feb. 1910. MARCHAND, *Un levier puissant dans l'éducation*, Porrentruy, 1907. LAISANT, *L'éducation fondée sur la science*, Paris, 1904. DURR, *Einfuhrung in die Padagogik*, Leipsic, 1908. BAUMGARTEN, *Ueber Kindererziehung*, Tubingen, 1905. OSTWALD, *Wieder das Schulelend*, Leipsic, 1909; &c., &c. (see also the works of LACOMBE, LE BON, EL. KEY, FORSTER, SCHWARZ, cited on pp. 20, 29, 32).

Pedagogy and Experimental Didactics.—KEMSIES, *Fragen u. Aufgaben der pad. psych.*, Z. pad. P., 1899. LAY, *Experimentelle Didaktik*, Wiesbaden, 1903 (3rd ed., Leipsic, 1910). MEUMANN, *Vorlesungen zur Einfuhrung in die exp. Padagogik*, Leipsic, 1907, II, p. 143 *seq.* On the concept of economy and of technique in work: MEUMANN, ibid. II., p. 12, and *Œkonomie und Tecknik des Gedachtnisses*, Leipsic, 1908. MEUMANN and LAY, Z. exp. Pad. I. (Introduction).

Eugenics.—PEARSON, *The Problem of Practical Eugenics*, London, 1909; and *The Groundwork of Eugenics*, ibid.; *The Scope and Importance of the State of the Science of National Eugenics*, ibid.

Individual Psychology.—GALTON, *Inquiries into Human Faculty*, London, 1883. BINET, An. ps. II., 1896, p. 411. KRAEPELIN, Psy. Arb. I., 1895. *Oehrn*, ibid. SHARP, *Individual Psychology*, Amer. Jour. Psy., 1899. STERN, *Ueber Psychologie der individuellen*

Differenzen, Leipsic, 1900. DEL GRECO, *Il problema fondamentale della etologia*, Report of the International Congress of Psy., Geneva, 1909, p. 638. PERSIGOUT, C. R., ibid., p 403.

Psychography and psychographic formulary.—STERN, BAADE, LIPMANN, Z. ang. Psy. III., 1909, p. 163. *Mental Tests* Cattell, Mind (the Magazine), 1890; JASTROW, BALDWIN, and CATTELL, Psy. Rev., 1898; &c. LUCKA, *Problem einer Charakterologie*, Ar. f. ges. Ps. XI. WHIPPLE, *Manual of Mental Tests*, Baltimore, 1910.

Correlations.—PEARSON, KARL, *The Grammar of Science*, London, 1900. BINET and VASCHIDE, *Corrélations des épreuves physiques*, An. psy. IV., 143, 236. BINET, *Corrélation des mesures céphaliques*, An. psy. VIII., 363. SEE, Bull. S. psy. Enf., July 1904, p. 492. SPEARMAN, Amer. J. Psy. XV., 1904. KRUGER and SPEARMAN, *Die Korrelation zwischen verschiedenen geistigen Leistungsfahigkeiten*, Z f Psy., vol. 44. HEYMANS, *Ueber einige psychische Korrelationen*, Z. f. ang. Psy. I., 1907. THORNDIKE, *Empirical Studies of the Theory of Measurements*, New York, 1907. IVANOFF, Ar. de Psy. VIII., 1908 THORNDIKE, *Educational Psychology*, New York, 1910. BROWN, *The Use of the Theory of Correlation in Psychology*, Cambridge, 1910. DUBOIS, *Le problème pédagogique*, thèse, Genève, 1910. ROEHRICH, *Philos. d. l'éducation*, Paris, 1910. MLLE. DUGARD, *L'evolution contre l'éducation*, Paris, 1910.

Structural and Functional Psychology.—TITCHENER, *The Postulates of a Structural Psychology*, Philos. Rev. 1898, 1899. CALDWELL, Psy Rev. 1899. ANGELL, *The Province of Functional Psychology*, Psy. Rev. 1907.

Genetic Psychology —KING, see p. 71 STERN, *Grundfragen der Psychogenesis*, Report of the Congress of Child-Study, Berlin, 1906, p. 100. KIRKPATRICK, *The Point of View of Genetic Psychology*, J. of Ed. Psy., Feb. 1910.

CHAPTER III

METHODS

How are the problems mentioned in the preceding chapter to be solved ? By intuition ? By theoretical discussions ? No ; nothing but the study of *facts* and of actual experience can lead to the desired solution.

This is obvious. Yet teachers have found and still find it very hard to understand. Open some pedagogical treatise and see if you can find any really definite directions as to the education of the senses, the power of observation, or memory ; as to fatigue, or to the teaching of spelling or arithmetic. You will see how feeble is the treatment of these subjects. What strikes one most is that the author never has recourse to *facts*, but always to *opinions ;* he quotes the teaching of Rousseau, Herbart, Spencer, of this, that, and the other person ; often he cites the opinion of literati, but never does he make it his business to know whether these different writers have based their opinions on facts, and whether these facts have been observed by sufficiently careful methods.

Nor does one ever find an author avowing quite simply that, in the present state of knowledge, it is impossible to decide between the opinions advanced, and that more experience is necessary in order that the question may be settled. On the contrary, the pedagogue appears to think that he possesses some sort of innate instinct, the pedagogic instinct, which renders him omniscient and infallible. No one would deny that this state of mind does not tend to research, for doubt alone leads to experimental inquiry. And that is why "pedant," which originally meant "teacher," has unhappily become a term of contempt, which is applied only to those who do not know how to doubt.

Binet, in the preface to his book on *Intellectual Fatigue*, has severely, but on the whole justly, characterised traditional pedagogy as follows: "The pedagogy of the past, in spite of certain good points of detail, ought to be completely suppressed, for it is permeated with one radical defect, it is all founded upon 'knack,' the result of preconceived ideas, it is based on gratuitous assumptions, it confuses exact demonstration with literary quotations, it answers the most serious questions by reference to authorities like Quintillian and Bossuet, it substitutes exhortations and sermons for facts; it is mere *verbiage*."

For this dogmatic method, the worthlessness of which is always in evidence, must be substituted the experimental method, which consists in interrogating facts. In order that the desired answer may be obtained, these facts must be collected, compared, and investigated as to cause and effect. That is the object of special methods of research. But when it is a question of special research connected with beings on a different mental level from our own (animals or children) the crude results must in some cases be interpreted. We shall therefore add to the explanation of methods of research a few words on methods of interpretation.

1. Methods of Research

The various methods of child psychology, which for that matter are nearly the same as those of general psychology, should be regarded from different standpoints which do not exclude each other but intersect: (1) Kind of phenomena collected; (2) general conditions of investigation; (3) collection of facts; (4) nature of the subject investigated; (5) means of investigation employed.

This appears very complicated. But these distinctions are necessary if one does not wish to risk—as is often done and is a constant source of confusion to beginners—regarding as opposite methods which are not opposed, but simply come under another heading.[1]

(1) NATURE OF PHENOMENA COLLECTED. — The methods used in collecting phenomena are **Introspection** and **Extrospection.**

The introspective method, which consists in the direct observation of the facts of consciousness by the thinking subject himself, can only be used with great circumspection in the case of children: firstly, because introspection is a very delicate operation, next, because the child, being very suggestible, has a tendency to answer in the manner suggested by the question put to him; lastly, because any verification of the

[1] Certain manuals of psychology, for example, subdivide psychological methods into Introspective and Experimental; but it is possible to have introspective experiment! Others classify as follows: Experimental Method; Genetic Method; Pathological Method; but the genetic and pathological methods can make use of experiment, and the pathological method can itself be genetic! It is as though one classified men as fair men, workmen, and invalids; a man could come under one, two, or even all three headings.

evidence given is impossible. It is therefore necessary, whenever possible, to arrange things in such a manner that the state of mind experienced may be translated into some external, tangible manifestation which can be objectively recorded. One might, nevertheless, find valuable introspective records in letters, or above all in diaries, written by children (*e.g.* the journal of Marie Bashkirtseff), provided, of course, that they were written in all good faith. But private diaries containing genuine confidences are just what is most difficult to get. Was there ever a young girl, says Stumpf, who did not register a solemn vow on the first page of her journal that no mortal eye should ever behold its contents ?

If introspection cannot be practised by the child, it can be performed by the adult who can recall what he thought and felt about such or such a thing when he was himself a child. This retrospective method is always uncertain, and it is impracticable or dangerous when it has to do with reminiscences of early childhood ; for not only are such reminiscences very incomplete, but they may have undergone transformation in the course of years, as one may easily prove to oneself.[1]

Yet it is hardly necessary to say that useful information or interesting remarks can be obtained from certain autobiographies, such as those of Goethe, Darwin, Renan, or Tolstoi, and even from such literature as *The Story of a Child* by Pierre Loti.[2]

[1] For reminiscences of childhood, see V. and C. Henri, An. Ps. 3, p 184, and Dumesnil, Bull S. p. Enf. 1903, p. 300 Yet retrospection may be used efficaciously in the interpretation of children's mental states, as Barnes rightly observes (see below, p. 96, *note*).

[2] Mmes. Bäumer and Droescher have made an anthology of extracts relating to child-life, gathered from biographies and other literary works (*Von der Kinderseele*, Leipsic, 1906).

The *objective method*, or *extrospection*, is a study of psychic states as expressed objectively. These objective manifestations are of four kinds :—

(*a*) By physical expression : we judge of a child's suffering by its cries or pallor ; and we judge of his æsthetic enjoyment by his gestures, &c.[1]

(*b*) By conduct (including play).

(*c*) By his work : we judge of a child's attention or memory by his drawings or other productions, &c.

(*d*) By physical structure : we judge of the psychological development of a child of a certain age by the anatomical study of the brains of children of that age (*the anatomical method*), or by the size of his head (*the anthropological method*), and by his physiognomy, or even by his hands (*physiognomical method*[2]).

(2) General Conditions of Investigation.—We adopt here the established distinction between observation and experiment. The most simple method is that of the observation of children during their daily life, in a free state when they are at liberty to do as they like, and not suspecting that they are the object of attentive curiosity. But the greater part of research work cannot adapt itself to this kind of procedure, and experiment becomes necessary, by means of which more varied and more exact results can be obtained.

(3) Methods of Procedure in Collecting Facts.—The methods differ according to whether a subject

[1] *Cf.* the interesting observations of Schultze, *Die Mimik der Kinder beim kunstler Geniessen*, Leipsic, 1906.

[2] For the method of estimating by physiognomy or by hands, *cf.* Rousson, *Lecture d'une physionomie d'enfant*, Bull. S p Enf., June 1906 ; Borel, *La Méthode des majorités* (discussing Rousson's observations), An. ps. XIV., p. 125 ; Binet, *Les signes physiques de l'intelligence*, An. ps. XVI., 1910, pp. 23, 27.

is studied individually or collectively. Individual experiment is carried on at home, in the laboratory, or in some private part of the school. Collective experiment can be carried on in the class-room itself. Each of these methods has its advantages and disadvantages according to the end in view. In the laboratory the child can undergo deeper and closer investigation; he is not distracted by companions; and more exact apparatus can be used. Experiment in the class-room has other advantages: the experiment being collective, the number of the subjects examined is much larger, and consequently the results have wider value; moreover, pupils take more seriously an experiment made in the class-room, and which is given to them as school work; lastly, and above all, the conditions of the experiment are not artificial, the child is in his natural surroundings, and the experiment to which he is subjected does not differ from ordinary school work; the conclusions drawn from such experiments have therefore more value for the science of education.

If, instead of an experiment on some particular or limited topic, it were a question of studying mental development in general, we should still use these two ways of getting information: sometimes, indeed, one traces the development of a single child, *i.e.*, builds up his biography (*biographical method*); and sometimes, on the other hand, in order to reconstruct the history of mental development, material is collected which relates to different children (*bio-statistical method* [1]). In fact, the former of these

[1] Miss Shinn (*Notes on the Development of a Child*, 1907, p. 3) calls this latter method "the comparative method" This nomenclature seems to me unfortunate; first, because the name is already

methods has been employed, and is specially fitted to be employed, in the study of infants, the second being more appropriate to the study of older children.

The collecting of material differs, again, according to whether the inquirer is working personally and directly, or whether he is having recourse to impersonal, indirect collaboration, more or less widely extended and sometimes anonymous. It is the latter case only which requires special mention.

As it is necessary to work on a certain quantity of material in order to obtain sufficiently definite results, the *Method of Inquiry* is often used in psychology; a questionnaire is sent to a large number of parents or teachers, who are asked to return it after having filled it up in the manner desired.

Thus at one stroke can be obtained thousands of observations of a given phenomenon. Stanley Hall, who, as we have seen, has used and abused this method, has brought out questionnaires on a multitude of topics: on fear, on honour, on the earliest manifestations of personality, on faults, &c. Many inquiries have also been organised by the Society for the Psychological Study of the Child, in Paris, which have led to very instructive results, notably the inquiries on fear, lying, scolded children, and anger.[1]

The questionnaire method has been much criticised;

in use to designate another kind of method (see below, p. 83); next, because there is not really any comparison in the process in question. It is for this reason that I substitute for it the term "bio-statistical" until a better can be found. One might also make use of the terms "mono-biographical" and "poly-biographical" to denote the two methods.

[1] See, for example, Binet, *La peur chez les Enfants*, An. ps., II.; Duprat, *Le Mensonge*, Paris, 1903, Malapert, *La Colère chez les Enfants*, An. ps., IX.

chiefly on account of the impossibility of verifying the statements made by those who answer them; the questions also are often little understood and are answered carelessly. These criticisms are very sound, but they are not sufficient to condemn completely the system of inquiry, which in certain cases brings out truths as no other method can. Naturally this method must always be used with discretion.

A method which is like that of the questionnaire without its disadvantages was inaugurated by the Society for the Psychological Study of the Child, and called "Work Commissions." A certain number of teachers undertake simultaneously the same research, each in his own class. They have previously discussed the question together, have arrived at an understanding with regard to methods, and then proceed concurrently. Later on they bring their observations together, these observations being naturally much more numerous than they would have been had they been furnished by one person only, and much more exact than if they had been obtained by means of the questionnaire. The *Society for Child Psychology* and the *Institute for General Psychology* in Berlin have also started similar commissions; one for the study of untruthfulness in children, and the other for the study of the development of language.[1]

(4) Methods relative to the Nature of the Subject.—Let us first of all examine these methods from the point of view of *general psychology* and then from the point of view of the particular case of child psychology.

To study a mental process, *e.g.* attention, investiga-

[1] See Z. päd. P. VII–VIII., and Z. ang. Ps. II., 1908, pp. 313, 397.

tion may be directed to the process as displayed by a normal adult **(normal method)**. More often, however, it will be better to make use of the methods by which an analysis may be effected which the normal method would not accomplish. For example, one perceives more clearly the constituent elements of mind when studying mind in the process of *evolution*, or of *dissolution*. The method which is designed for the study of psycho-physiological phenomena in process of evolution, in such a manner that the successive phases of their development, and their increasing complexity, may be grasped, is called the **genetic method.** The evolution of a function may be traced either in the individual (in a child, by growth), which is called *ontogeny*, or in the race (or animals) through all the stages it has passed through, when it is called *phylogeny*.

The method which makes use of decadence as a means of study is the **pathological method.** This method, held in high estimation by Ribot and Charcot more than a quarter of a century ago, is a valuable auxiliary to psychology; disease, abnormality, decadence, by making clear what is abnormal in mental mechanism, cause us to realise all the better what normal function is, and by ascertaining the disturbance that is introduced into the economy of mind by the loss of a power, we learn the better to understand its use in the healthy individual, in whom its working is apt to be lost sight of in the general activity.

One can also get valuable information about mental processes by comparing the way in which these processes are manifested in different types of individuals, those on different mental level, *e.g.* the man and the child, human beings and animals, the civilised man and the savage, the virtuous man and the criminal.

Comparison causes certain characteristics in phenomena to stand out in relief; it is therefore an extremely valuable factor in analysis **(comparative method).** This method has a more extensive range than the preceding two; indeed, comparison has its part in the genetic and pathological methods; the object of these methods being, after all, so far as general psychology is concerned, to help us to understand normal processes in the adult, it is essential to compare the stages in the evolution or dissolution of a function with its normal condition.

The genetic and pathological methods can also be combined; this is done when one studies the development of an abnormal person or that of an animal from which some portion of the cerebral centres was removed at birth, in order to see what change such a removal would bring about in development. Another form of genetico-pathological combination is found in the method lately proposed by Binet, which consists in arranging in order of intelligence a certain number of backward children (idiots, imbeciles, &c.) and of studying some particular phenomenon, such as attention, through each step in the scale in order to see how the particular power in question evolves, and what are the stages it goes through in its development.[1] Binet calls this method by the name of "psychogenic"; the less ambiguous name of *patho-psychogenic* would suit it better.

Let us now take up the special point of view of child psychology, and let us remark, to begin with, that the psychology of the child has a twofold position in relation to general psychology: it is at once a means by which general psychology is studied, and

[1] Binet, An. ps. XIV., 1908, p. 284, and XV., p. 2.

also a study by itself having its own methods. When one studies the child with the idea of making the knowledge gained serve in the elucidation of some law of general psychology, one is making use of the genetic method; and when one carries out the same study for the sake of getting to know the child himself, one is engaged with child psychology. It is a question of point of view.

The methods used in child psychology are the same as those of general psychology, with the exception of that method which applies to adults only, which we have called the *normal method.* But we now come to a method of child psychology which takes precedence of all others, viz. the *genetic method.* The child being always in a condition of growth, it is impossible to make any observations or any series of experiments on him, without taking into account this fact of growth, which will modify the results from one day to another. Therefore, in spite of oneself, the genetic method is always more or less used in studying children.[1]

In child psychology, the *pathological method* consists specially of the study of backward and abnormal children; the investigation of their minds and of the means of developing them sometimes provides valuable material for paidology and normal pedagogy.

The *comparative method* will make comparisons be-

[1] In certain cases, it is true, the observations (or experiments) made may be exactly similar to those of the normal method; it is possible that one may be interested in studying for its own sake, and in its present state, a certain function of the child, *e.g.* the sense of touch, without having any regard to the evolution of the function. Nevertheless, one will not be able to ignore this fact of evolution if, after an interval of some months, one has to compare the tests made on the same child.

tween children of various classes, social and otherwise; between children and imbecile adults; between children and savages or aborigines; between children and animals. In the last two cases the comparative method will be closely allied to the genetic method, for the comparisons made will be chiefly comparison of the evolution of processes; *e.g.* one will try to find out if the evolution of language, of drawing, &c., is the same in the child as in the human race; or if the way of forming a habit is the same in the animal and the child, &c. Such genetic comparisons will be very helpful in understanding the child; for instance, the succession of developmental phases is sometimes so rapid in the child that the study of aborigines or of animals in whom, on the contrary, these phases succeed each other more clearly, will be of assistance in the analysis of the phase; and, again, the differences that we shall detect between the development of the child and that of animals or of the race will help us to grasp the special characteristics of the mental evolution of the child.

(5) Technical Method.—Under this heading come **qualitative** or **descriptive** methods, and **quantitative** methods.

The qualitative methods, which may be called *psycholexy*, play a very important part, for in psychology there are many psychic phenomena which are only interesting on account of their quality, or even by the mere fact of their presence; *e g.* the visual or auditory nature of mental images, the phenomena of language or of reasoning, &c.

The quantitative methods (*psychometry*) have for their aim the measurement of various mental functions; for example, memory, sensibility, &c. Measurement, when it is possible, constitutes a valuable means of analysis and of comparison ; it is never an end in itself : for we do not measure for the sake of measuring, but because a knowledge of the quantity of a phenomenon enables us the better to detect its variations and consequently the conditions of its existence.

As one cannot measure psychic functions by direct means, one has recourse to divers expedients : thus one sometimes measures a psychological phenomenon by measuring the physical cause which produced it (*psycho-physical* process) ; sometimes by measuring its duration (*psycho-chronometrical* process) ; sometimes by measuring its dynamic effect, or its physiological concomitants (*psycho-dynamic* process) ; and sometimes by computing the percentage of individuals in whom the particular phenomenon is found (*psycho-statistical* process). It is not possible to enter here into more detail as to these various processes. Later on we shall have an opportunity of giving examples of several of them.

In concluding this rapid review of methods, let us note that psychological investigation, like all scientific investigation, may assume the two forms of *analysis* and *synthesis*. As an example of the analytic process, one might cite *mental tests*, which have as their aim the determination of the various characteristics, mental or physical, of an individual : his stature, sense-perceptions, reaction time, memory power, &c. As an example of the synthetic process one might point to the *training* or *educative* method ; the way in which an educative process succeeds or fails gives us insight into the minds of the children with whom it has succeeded or failed. No one is in a better position to apply this method than the educator himself.

Let us take an example in order to better understand the distinction between the method of *tests* and the method of *education*, which, by the way, supplement each other. Here is a child who appears backward and abnormal. One can find out whether this child is really mentally defective, and what the nature of the defect may be, either by tests, when one would examine one function after the other, hearing, sight, memory, &c., or by the method of education, when one would try to find out if the child could be developed by the ordinary school methods which succeed with normal children of that age ; and if that is not the case, the deficiencies in the educational results allow of our inferring with a certain degree of accuracy the nature of his mental defectiveness.

2. Methods of Interpretation

When observation and experiment have provided the psychologist with a certain amount of material, he still has to interpret it.

There are many kinds of interpretation. First there is the **logical** interpretation of experiment, which consists in tracing the relation of cause and effect between the ascertained phenomena, and for that purpose one will have recourse to the four well-known methods of *agreement, difference, concomitant variations,* and *residues.* I need not speak of them here, since they are to be found in text-books of logic. How useful it would be to teachers if they would saturate themselves with these methods, instead of, as they so often do, taking as proven the results of a certain school method without having previously eliminated causes of error arising from other factors acting simultaneously !

Another kind of interpretation, with which also we need not here occupy ourselves, is the **physiological** interpretation: a mental process having been ascertained, it may be profitable to consider what are the physiological foundations. Most psychologists admit that to every mental phenomenon there is a corresponding physical change; to this postulate has been given the name of *Law of psycho-physical parallelism.*

The **psychological** interpretation is the kind of interpretation which most concerns the paidologist; it is necessary when investigation is directed to beings sufficiently different from ourselves for us to be unable to infer with any degree of certainty that the feelings, thoughts, and motives which cause them to act are the same which we should ourselves experience in the same circumstances. It is especially the actions of animals which call for this kind of interpretation; it has even been claimed that animals are so different from men that all idea of making out their psychology must be abandoned, and that we must confine ourselves to studying such of their manifestations as can be directly apprehended through the sense-organs of the observer, that is to say, organic and physiological phenomena.

When it is a question of children the matter is much less difficult than in the case of animals, for children are much nearer to ourselves, and quickly, by word of mouth, do they inform us of what they experience or wish. But just for this very reason psychological interpretation is particularly delicate and insidious, for, even more than when one has to do with animals, one is tempted to make use of, not anthropomorphism —that word is not suitable here—but *teleiomorphism,* if I may be permitted that new word, indicating the tendency to think of the child-soul in terms of the adult-soul (Greek *teleios*, complete, adult, and *morphe*, form). The first thing, indeed, which it is necessary to be quite clear about, when one begins paidological research, is that the child is not, as one often fancies, a man in miniature. His mind is not only different in quantity but also in quality; it is not only less, it is *different*. One must always guard against drawing hasty conclusions from adult psychology about the psychology of the child.

The questions relating to the psychological interpretation of a process can be reduced to three: (1) *The question of mentality:* Is the phenomenon observed really accompanied by consciousness? (2) *The question of complexity:* What is the nature of the mental process with which one has to do? On what plane is it? (3) *The question of function:* What is the exact function of the process?

There is really no question of mentality in the case of the child. One may wonder whether crystals, plants, and worms have mental life; but I do not know that any one has ever doubted its existence in children.[1]

[1] It is true that some writers would limit the study of children to objective manifestations (reflex movements, secretions, circulatory or other reactions) without trying to interpret them, and without paying attention to the psychic process which these may reveal (*e.g.* Bechterew in his recent article, *Objektive Untersuchung der neuropsychischen Sphäre im Kindesalter*, Zeits. f. Psychotherapie, 1910, p. 129). Legitimate as this method may be for those who, like the eminent psychologist of St. Petersburg (M. Bechterew), have pre-eminently in view the physiology and anatomy of the nervous centres, it would not suffice for the psycho-pedagogue who desires a much deeper analysis of the motives of a child's actions than that which is made possible at the present day by the rough drafts and vague concepts of the physiology of the nervous system.

The problem of complexity, on the other hand, is constantly coming in. One has to judge of the structure of a phenomenon, whether it is simple and inferior, or more complex and superior, in the mental hierarchy. For instance, does a certain act show judgment and reasoning, or is it simply the result of mere consecutiveness of ideas? Is it instinctive, or is it acquired? Does this child repeat like a parrot what it has heard said, or does he understand the meaning of his words? It is said that young children give a particular name to a whole class of objects; does that indicate that they generalise? Here is a young rascal who has cured himself of some bad fault; is that the result of fear of punishment, or a sign that his moral sense has developed? &c.

Unhappily there is no absolutely certain means of solving this problem of complexity. But we must bear in mind the *law of economy*, a law which applies to all scientific interpretation, which is a safeguard against superfluous hypotheses, and which the English psychologist, Lloyd Morgan, has expressed in the following rule, drawn up for psycho-zoologists: "In no case may we interpret an action as the outcome of the exercise of a higher psychical faculty, if it can be interpreted as the outcome of the exercise of one which stands lower in the psychological scale." [1]

This rule, which I have called "Morgan's Principle," certainly deserves to be taken into account by the psycho-paidologist. But its application is beset with difficulties, for we do not always know whether one faculty is "higher" than another; neither do we know whether that which appears to us simpler and more

[1] Lloyd Morgan, *Introduction to Comparative Psychology*, London, 1894, p. 53, Chaparède, Ar. de Psy., V., 1905, p. 15.

economical has also been more economical for nature. For instance, is a hereditary, instinctive act more, or less, economical than an acquired act ? It is impossible to say. Moreover, it is not always the process which we conceive to be the simplest which is the simplest in reality. If it is legitimate to try to account for the mental life of the child on the most economical principle, one must nevertheless make sure that the simplicity involved in the explanation squares well with the facts.

Another principle of interpretation, which will prove more serviceable than the foregoing, consists in judging of the degree of advancement of a child's action by the level of his general conduct. Thus one would not assume that the words of a young child have a general and abstract meaning if the child does not show in other ways a capacity for abstraction, or if his general conduct reveals a lack of power of abstraction. This might be called Descartes' principle : for it is known that the great philosopher refused to consider that the industrial instincts of animals revealed intelligence, on the ground of the lack of intelligence evinced in their behaviour in other domains.[1] This "Descartes's Principle," which we instinctively make use of in ordinary affairs, furnishes only problematical help when it is a question of interpreting the first beginnings of a new activity which are manifest only at distant intervals.

[1] "Although there are several animals that display more industry than ourselves in some of their actions, it is also evident that the same animals show none in many other actions ; so that it cannot be inferred from those of their actions in which they excel us that they have intelligence, for in that case they would have more than any of us, and would do better in everything." (Descartes, *Discours de la méthode.*)

Let us mention finally a third method, which we will call "Meumann's Principle," that writer having propounded it for the interpretation of the phenomena of language;[1] but which certainly has a wider bearing. It consists in judging *retrospectively* of the nature of a process according to observations made of the nature of the *subsequent* development of the individual in whom it has been observed. If, for example, it is certain that abstraction has been lacking during the years which follow the time when it was considered that abstraction had been observed, one would conclude retrospectively that it had been absent on the former occasion. In this way a deeper study of a child five or six years old helps us to understand better the mentality of the same child when younger. Meumann would have us remark that this principle is purely *negative;* it only shows what principles of explanation to exclude.

Helpful as these various methods may be, there is a rock upon which we might make shipwreck and from which they do not protect us, and which it is absolutely necessary to avoid when one wants to interpret a psychic process in a child; it is to this rock that I alluded just now under the barbaric name of "teleiomorphism." To describe the processes of a child according to adult standards, or to apply to them the criteria of adult psychology, is for science barren in results, and for pedagogical practice dangerous; for by forcing ourselves to make the phenomena fit into a framework not made for them, one runs the risk of a double mishap: either, not finding in the child such and such a process corresponding to one

[1] *Die Entstehung der ersten Wortbedeutungen beim Kinde* (2nd ed.), Leipsic, 1908, p. 5.

of the categories of an adult, we shall declare that the child does not possess a function of the kind; or, on the other hand, we shall pronounce processes alike which are in reality different, and consider the infantile process identical with that of the adult.

Let us suppose that we have to describe a hamlet by making use of the terminology and concepts suitable to the description of a capital. We should be in danger either of giving the name "Cathedral" to the modest chapel by the roadside, of calling the miserable erection which does duty for the mayor's office the "Town-hall," and the little den in which the police lock up thieves the "Central Prison"; or, on the other hand, of declaring that this hamlet possesses neither cathedral, town-hall, nor prison; and in both cases we should be wrong in accepting such a superficial statement. For if a hamlet has no prison, it has nevertheless something which takes its place, and which in its way plays a like part to that of the central prison in the life of a great city.

This somewhat rough comparison helps us to understand on what lines the interpretation of the mental processes of a child should proceed: we have not to ascertain whether a child does or does not possess certain faculties belonging to the adult, but "The child must be interpreted in terms of himself," as has been so truly said by I. King, and after him by another disciple of Dewey, viz. I. E. Miller.[1]

To quote an example from the latter writer: do young children think? "Evidently," will say those who have based their ideas of the child-mind on the pattern of that of the adult; "and since they think,

[1] King, *op. cit.*, p. 7; Miller, *The Psychology of Thinking*, New York, 1909, p. 111.

and to think is to reason, therefore children reason." "Not at all," others will reply; "children do not reason, therefore they do not think; they are purely receptive beings."

Which is right? Neither. And the mistake arises from the fact that both these classes of people conceive of thinking only in its adult and complete form, that is, as reasoning; but while the former, who may be called the "positive teleiomorphists," assert that the child thinks, which is true, and deduct from that that he must reason, which is false—the latter, the "negative teleiomorphists," assert that the child does not reason, which is true, and infer that he does not think, which is inaccurate.

The error in interpretation arises solely from the fact that the adult process has been taken as the criterion of that of the child.

This example shows us clearly that interpretation as to complexity must always be subordinated to interpretation *as to function.* One must begin by discovering the meaning of a process and the part it plays *in the mental life of the child;* only after this will one discover what form the function assumes. Thus, to return to our illustration, one would consider whether thinking was going on in the form of reasoning, or in some other less elaborate form. One would also ask whether this process does not contribute in some way to the *development* of the individual, an idea which would have no meaning if applied to the adult, because in the adult the conditions for the functioning of the process no longer exist; exactly as one could not understand the gill slits in the frog if one did not remember that batracians are aquatic animals in their early life. I will not here elaborate this point, which has been sufficiently explained in connection with the genetico-functional problem.

This matter of interpretation being of great practical importance, it will be well again to quote one of Dewey's examples which illustrates clearly the method of genetico-functional interpretation.

Let us suppose that, as the result of inquiry, it is stated that 73 per cent. of eight-year-old children own to a predilection for so-called "criminal" literature, a kind of police-news romance, *Nick Carter,* and so on. Here is a fact. But how is it to be interpreted? What truth about child-nature can one get out of it? If we consider it only in the light of adult consciousness, the fact will not be of great interest; we make a note of it, catalogue it, give it a name, classify it—but we cannot explain it, nor get anything out of it. If, on the other hand, we interpret it by the genetic method it becomes a different matter, and this fact, so barren and dry, becomes fertile in results both theoretical and practical. We shall ask ourselves what it means; whether it marks a stage in mental development; and, above all, whether it supplies a need at a certain period in development. And then, since the fact cannot have its full meaning unless one considers it in relation to the circumstances in which it first appeared, we shall inquire into these circumstances and try to reconstruct the context. We shall get information especially about those other children, the remaining 27 per cent., who did not own to this criminal predilection. And one will perhaps discover, in following up this clue, that the predilection of certain children for stories about brigands is nothing else than a reaction against a too severe discipline which oppresses them; or it may perhaps be a phenomenon of compensation, destined to supply some deficiency in the environment, so that if the surroundings in which the child developed had been more favourable, the child's interest would have assumed an entirely different form.

One word more. I said just now that the child is *different* from ourselves. This is certainly the case. His psychological processes assume other forms than ours. Yet there is something in which the child is very nearly like and almost identical with the adult, viz. in the general function of activity. This function has as its aim the satisfaction of the needs of the individual—needs which are ultimately the maintenance of life, the extension and assertion of personality, the realisation of self. And certainly in the child as in the adult the law of activity is the same: desire and interest stimulate activity; and we cannot in any better way represent to ourselves what makes a child act, imagine, think, will, and make efforts, than by recalling what we do ourselves when we think, invent, or make efforts to attain some desired end.[1] The *means* which the child uses is different, but the psychological *end* is the same; just as in the tadpole, breathing has the same function as in the frog, although the function is accomplished by different means.

Likeness in the *raison d'être* of activity, difference in the *form* of activity, or, in other words, *community of aim, diversity of means*—such are the two relations between the adult and the child.

[1] This is doubtless what Barnes meant when he wrote that the study of personal reminiscences was the most useful method for schoolmasters and psychologists who wish to understand children. (Barnes, *Methods of Studying Children*, Studies in Education, 1896, p. 8.)

It is necessary that these relations should be kept well to the fore in the mind of the pedagogue.

Unfortunately it is not so. In the school the exact opposite of this formula has been adopted: the child is considered as identical with the adult as to the form of his mental functions, and it is in regard to the biological basis of this mental activity that he is considered as constituting a type *sui generis*. On the one hand, is it not a fact that from beginning to end of the eight or ten years of school-life the same teaching methods are used, as if the minds of the scholars from seven to eighteen years of age were alike! And these methods, these systems of exposition, are everywhere copies of the logic of the adult, and in no wise are they in accordance with the natural tendencies which characterise each successive age of the child. We teach (or think we teach) the mother-tongue by grammar and rules; drawing by rules and compass; arithmetic by syllogisms and abstractions!

And, moreover, it does not appear to dawn upon the mind of the pedagogue that the child is a living being whose motives are fundamentally the same as those of the adult—desire and interest. People neglect to provide favourable conditions, as if the scholar were some sort of a demi-god floating above the things of earth, capable of doing everything simply because he *must*, and without any of the conditions, empirical, psychological, or physiological, which engender action. Never would it occur to any one to demand from an adult work of any merit under the sterilising conditions of artificiality which the school imposes on its unfortunate scholars!

3. Apparatus

It would be out of place to attempt here to describe or even to enumerate the apparatus which the psycho-paidologist might need, and if I devote a paragraph to the subject, it will be chiefly with the intention of reassuring those who think that an elaborate laboratory is a *sine qua non* for paidological researches. I have at various times received letters from teachers who were anxious to undertake experiments on their pupils, asking me to furnish them with a list of the instruments which would be necessary. It is impossible to provide such a list, because the kind of apparatus and also its use vary according to the object of investigation; and I strongly advise beginners to procure instruments gradually according to their requirements, rather than to collect at the outset a large quantity of which the greater part might never be used. Still, if funds are available, one might purchase a few generally useful instruments, such as a *chronometer* and *registering cylinders* (kymographs). But let every one be fully convinced that many instruments are not in the least necessary in order to make useful observations. The teacher who is disposed to carry out some experiments may collect ample material in the way of records without having recourse to other apparatus than pencil and paper, *e.g.* experiment in association of ideas, mental images, memory, accuracy, intellectual types, aptitude for drawing, &c., inquiries into interests, play, fear, &c.

There is, however, one instrument which is very useful, the pocket-chronometer, marking one-fifth of a second, of which the hand is started and stopped by pressing a button, and which is well named a "stop-watch." It will prove useful in very many ways (measuring of association times, time taken in arithmetical calculations, or in other mental operations). It is moderate in price; it can now be purchased for less than a pound. There are some which cost from two to four pounds, but I do not find that they get out of order less frequently than those which cost less. In my opinion, if one can spend two pounds, it is better to buy two of the less expensive kinds (one to take the place of the other when it gets out of order) than one of the more costly sort. And for the consolation of those who cannot purchase a "stop-watch" of any kind we would add that in many cases an ordinary watch with a seconds hand can be used as a substitute for the chronometer; for the mental operations of children are generally slow, and measurement by seconds will in most cases be sufficiently accurate.

Other instruments, such as *exhibitors* (designed for displaying to the eyes of an observer a picture or word for a certain period of time), *weights* (for testing muscular sensibility or power to judge of differences), *æsthesiometers* with single or double points (for measuring sensations of touch), &c., may be easily constructed by the experimenter himself. Teachers who wish to record physical growth can for a small sum set up a six-feet measure by which to ascertain height.

BIBLIOGRAPHY

Methods of Research.—See psychological manuals, being careful to guard against the confusion indicated on p 76 For a general sketch of psychological method, see article by CLAPARÈDE, *Classification et plan des méthodes psychologiques,* Archives de Psychologie,

VII., 1908 (published separately by Kundig), and ALIOTTA, *La misura in psicologia*, Florence, 1905. LEHMANN'S little text-book, *Lehrbuch der psychologischen Methodik* (Leipsic, 1906), deals only with methods of measurement, errors in observation, and methods of ascertaining averages. The work of TOULOUSE, VASCHIDE, and PIÉRON, *Technique de psychologie expérimentale*, Paris, 1904, contains, especially in its second part, hints which will be useful to the psycho-pedagogue ; unfortunately the greater part of the methods and processes suggested have not been tested. In SOMMER'S *Lehrbuch der psychopatholog. Untersuchungsmethoden* (Berlin, 1899) will be found instructions concerning the registration of movements of expression. *Cf.* also BARNES, *Methods of Studying Children*, Studies in Education, 1896. STUMPF, *Zur Methodik der Kinder Psychologie*, Z. päd., Ps. II., 1900. RIBOT, *De la valeur des questionnaires en psychologie*, Journal de psychologie, 1904. IOTEYKO, *Méthodologie de la psychologie pédagogique*, Sixth International Congress on Psychology, Geneva, 1909, p. 423. CLAPARÈDE, *Die Metoden der tierpsychologischen Beobachtungen und Versuche*, Congress on Experimental Psychology, Frankfort, 1908 (reprinted by Barth, Leipsic, 1909). E. JONES, *Psycho-analysis and Education*, J. ed. Ps., Nov. 1910.

Methods of Interpretation.—*Cf.* the works of KING and MILLER quoted above. On the "Question of Mentality". CLAPARÈDE, *Les animaux sont-ils conscients ?* Rev. Philos., May 1901; *The Consciousness of Animals*, The International Quarterly, 1903; *La psychologie comparée est-elle légitime ?* Ar. de Ps., V., 1905; *Die Bedeutung der Tierpsychologie f. die Padagogik*, Z f. pad. Ps. und exp. Pädag., 1911. On "Objective Psychology": BECHTEREW, Rev. scientif., 1906, and International Congress on Psychiatry, Amsterdam, 1907, p. 20; NUEL, *La psychologie comparée est-elle légitime ?* Ar. de Ps., V., 1906, p 326. YERKES, *Comparative Psychology*, Journal of Comparative Psychology, 1906, p. 380; &c.

Apparatus and experimental methods.—SCHULZE, *Aus der Werkstatt der experimentellen Psychologie und Padagogik*, Leipsic, 1909 (an excellent introduction to experimental psychology, with numerous plates and descriptions of apparatus). For anthropometry: Giroud, *Observations sur le développement de l'enfant*, Paris, 1902 (a small practical guide to family and school anthropology). Advice as to methods of cephalometric measurements is given by MANOUVRIER and BINET, in An. ps. V., p. 558, and VIII., p 345.

CHAPTER IV

MENTAL DEVELOPMENT

It seems to us quite natural that there should be children, and that children should not come into the world "grown-up." But in reality there is no logical necessity for this. One can quite well imagine beings springing into the world fully armed, like Minerva, for the combat. Low down in the zoological scale we do indeed find animals which are born "grown-up"; they have no youth. But the higher we go in the scale of beings, the more we find the period of youth prolonging itself. Is not that something to be surprised at? A young human being, a child, is a creature very ill adapted to life; it is weak, it might easily become the prey of other animals; left to itself it cannot supply its own wants. Yet we know that the struggle for existence has constantly eliminated and pitilessly sacrificed, in the course of evolution, all those who were unfit and those who showed any trace of inferiority to their kind. Why, then, has nature, who generally shows herself so economical, not only protected this period of youth, but even developed and prolonged it? There is only one way out of the difficulty, which is to admit that if this period of youth has thus triumphed, it is because it has a certain utility either for the individual or the race.

This brings us to the point: "*Of what use is Childhood?*"

I do not think that pedagogues in the olden days, nor many pedagogues in the present day, ever asked themselves that question, which will perhaps be considered absurd. "Oh," they might say, "childhood is simply a period of intellectual immaturity which separates birth from adult life, an immaturity which depends on lack of experience of life." That is true to a certain degree. But the question is whether childhood is simply a contingent circumstance, secondary and accidental as it were, a necessary evil—as, for example, senility—or whether it has a particular function of its own. In other words, is the child a child *because* he has had no experience, or is he a child *in order that* he may gain this experience? Is the child little *because* he is not big, or is he little *in order that* he may grow big?

We shall see later on that this distinction is less subtle than it appears, and that the way in which it is decided is of considerable practical importance.

Before studying mental development, we must take a glance at physical development; firstly, because the destinies of mind are, as every one knows, closely connected with those of the body, and that to understand one is to understand the other. Next, because the phenomena of physical growth have a certain interest from the point of view of school work.

1. Physical Growth

We have said above that the child is not a miniature man, but that, on the contrary, he presents a special type. Nothing so clearly proves the truth of this assertion as the phenomena of physical development. It is already established that the growth of the child is not a simple increase in bulk, like the formation of a crystal; the adult that is to be is not already formed in the embryo, according to the theory of the "homoncule" of the physiologists of the

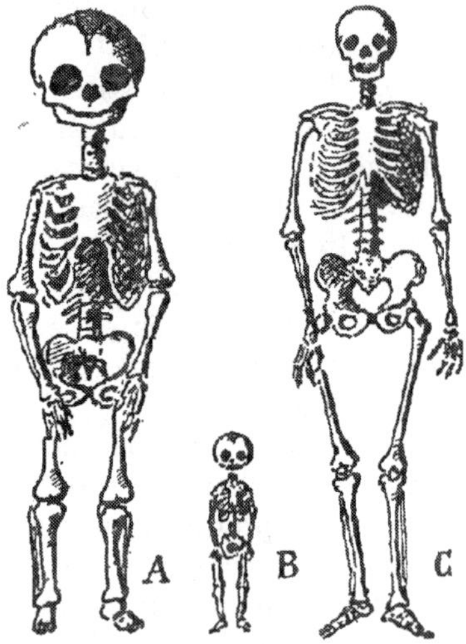

Fig. 1.—This plate is specially designed to show how much the type of the new-born child differs from that of the adult. To make this difference more striking, the skeleton of a new-born child (A) and that of an adult (C) are here represented drawn on different scales. (B) represents the new-born child drawn on the same scale as (C). (From a photograph by Prof. Sanford, published by S. Hall, *Adolescence*, I.)

seventeenth century. No; the development of the animal, and of that of man in particular, consists in a succession of creations, of new formations, appearing sometimes here, sometimes there, without apparent order—like a firework, from which rockets fall out into space, blazing up suddenly in the darkness without anything that could help us to foresee the place or time of their appearance.

Without entering into details about the individual development of the different organs, which would be of no direct interest to the educator—with the exception of that part which concerns the brain, about which a few words will be said later on—let us pass on to examine the general growth of the body by considering two chief aspects, *height* and *weight.*

If one measures and weighs a child regularly—say every three months—and records the results of growth by a curve on a chart, it will be observed that the curve of growth is not continuous and regular, but proceeds spasmodically, that is to say, there are times when growth is much more considerable than at others. The periods of this acceleration, of these *crises in growth,* vary according to different circumstances: of race (peoples of the south are more precocious); of social conditions; of state of health; and specially of sex. Moreover, the crises of increase in height do not correspond with the crises of increase in weight.

Let us take height first. There is a strong increase during the first year, then a slackening until about the age of six or seven, then a fresh up-shooting, but of short duration only, after which the annual increase in height becomes less and less till it reaches a minimum at about twelve years; then all of a sudden growth again becomes more rapid until about fifteen years of age. Then it steadies down, and though there may be increase until about twenty or thirty years of age, it will be barely perceptible.

The curve showing increase in weight has an analogous appearance; nevertheless, from the fifteenth year onward increase in weight is relatively greater than that of height, and it is a little slower. As may be seen by the accompanying chart, in the first years of

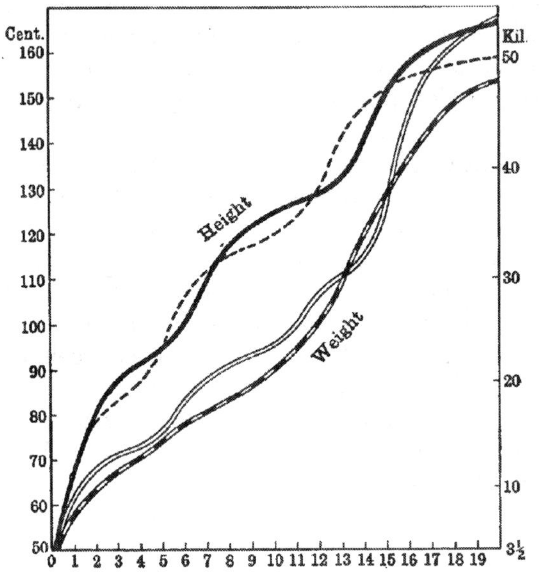

Fig. 2.—The continuous lines represent the curve of growth in boys, the dotted lines that of girls. On the lower horizontal line the figures represent years from 0 to 20.

life and up to the fifteenth year, the child increases in height more than in breadth; the chubby little child gives place to the tall and slender boy. After fifteen years of age the relation changes; height has attained its maximum, or nearly its maximum, while weight begins to increase considerably; the adolescent grows in breadth more than in height, he fills out, becomes stouter—his density increases, if we may so express it.

What is specially interesting from our point of view in the evolution of growth is the abruptness of these shootings-up, these crises or sudden increases often following upon a period of perfect calm. Each abrupt rise in the curve is preceded and followed by a flattening which seems to bear witness to the effort which the organism is going to make or has just made. Before the crisis there is a period of repose—as though the organism fell back and pulled itself together for making a better spring; then comes the upward leap, the outburst, as though some mysterious blast from a blow-pipe had suddenly kindled all the vital forces; then comes the stage of exhaustion: out of breath, and as if conscious of the effort it has made, the organism allows itself a well-earned rest.

The last of these crises is especially formidable; it is so formidable that it has been remarked upon by every one, in all times, and has received the name of *puberty*. It is true that this name is used in a more or less wide acceptation; while for some the period of *puberty* is that which corresponds to the nascent period of the sex functions (which is the true meaning of the term), for others it denotes the entire period of this crisis of growth of which we have just spoken. Hence confusion; the pre-pubescent period of the former corresponds with the pubescent period of the latter. It seems to me that, so far as possible, one should let words retain their own exact meaning; we shall, with Godin, let *puberty* denote the period when the reproductive organs mature, and to the period of rapid increase in height we shall give the name of *adolescence*, which is, by the way, the correct term (*adolescere*, to grow). And as it is convenient also to have a name for the period of calm, organic preparation which precedes adolescence, we will call it "the pre-adolescent period," or "pre-adolescence," for this will be less equivocal than the term "pre-pubescent."

What makes an exact nomenclature in this connection difficult is that the age when the crisis of growth takes place varies very much in individuals. In one case it takes place rather later than in another; in one case the change is very marked, while in another it might be represented by a very slight increase in the curve of growth.[1] That is the reason why curves constructed by means of averages based on large numbers of children are only slightly irregular. They do not show in a striking way the zigzags, the ups and downs, which would be recorded in the growth of *a single child*, for the individual zigzags cancel each other; the phase of active growth of one child superposes itself on the phase of quietude of another. In this way individual variation has been antagonistic to the establishment of a subdivision of the different periods of development, which might have had a somewhat general validity.

If individual differences are very great, the difference which exists between the sexes is still greater. The growth of girls, whether in height or weight, has, as a whole, the same appearance as that of boys, but it is less vigorous, less irregular, and consistently

[1] In what degree are these abrupt accessions of growth normal? Is comparatively continuous growth better than irregular growth? These questions are difficult to answer, for up to the present we lack data for comparison. In any case we may say that we have no authority for supposing that irregularity in growth is a sign of abnormality.

more precocious; the crisis of increase in stature belonging to second infancy, which with boys takes place when they are about seven years old, begins with girls when they are about six, or before; that of adolescence begins with the girl when she is about ten or eleven instead of twelve or thirteen, and it ends at thirteen or fourteen instead of at fifteen years of age, as with the boy. In other words, the comparative growth of boys and girls is like a running match; boys and girls start together, but the girls, outstripped for a moment by the boys, soon gain the advantage, then the boys catch them up and pass them, but the girls again take the lead until the boys definitely win the race.

Let us try now, in accordance with the foregoing data, to determine approximately the chief stages of physical growth, and to give them the names which correspond, or should [1] correspond, to them.

[1] The most complete confusion still prevails in these names: Lacassagne, for example, understands by *first infancy* only the first seven months; *second infancy*, from seven months to two years; *third infancy*, from two to seven years; *adolescence*, from seven to fifteen; *puberty*, from fifteen to twenty. Verrier makes use of entirely different terms: *earliest years*, from birth to seven years; *second infancy*, seven to fourteen years; *adolescence*, fourteen to twenty-one. Springer: *first infancy*, from birth to two years; *second infancy*, from two years to puberty (ten to twelve years); *youth*, from puberty to twenty or twenty-two years. Alvarez: *new-born infant*, from birth to sixteen days; *first infancy*, from sixteen days to three years; *second infancy*, from three to fifteen years (for this writer *adolescence* means all the period of growth from birth to twenty-four years). (Lacassagne, *Précis de médecine judiciaire*, Paris, 1886; Verrier, *Le premier âge et la seconde enfance*, Paris, 1893, Springer, *La Croissance*, Paris, 1890; Alvarez, *Anatomia y fisiologia especiales del nino*, Madrid, 1895; quoted from Chamberlain, *The Child*, 2nd ed., p. 70, London, 1906.)

It should be one of the tasks of a paidological conference in the near future to bring a little unity into this terminology, and it

	Boys.	Girls.
1. First Infancy .	From birth to 7 years.	From birth to 6 or 7 years.
2 Second Infancy .	From 7 to 12 years.	From 7 to 10 years.
3. Adolescence . .	From 12 to 15 years.	From 10 to 13 years.
4. Puberty . . .	From 15 to 16 years.	From 13 to 14 years.

The great oscillations of which we have just spoken appear to have an internal, inter-organic cause, and to depend on the rhythm of the processes of growth. There are others of less importance which seem, on the contrary, to depend on external causes; for example, on the seasons of the year. These secondary oscillations have the effect of causing the curve of growth to undulate slightly through all its course, independently of the great zigzags which it forms.

Research into *variations in growth as affected by the seasons* could well be carried on by a schoolmaster. It is true that the schoolmaster has not always a weighing machine at hand, but it is at least easy for him to measure the height of his pupils by placing them (without shoes) against a vertical wall, to which has been nailed a graduated rule, and by causing to slide longitudinally in this vertical rule a half-square, the horizontal arm of which would rest on the top of the head of the child who was being measured. By repeating this little operation every two or three months, he would get records of the changes that growth goes through during the school year.

The influence of the seasons on the process of growth

could be done all the more easily because these names are conventional and involve no doctrinal question; it would be sufficient to come to some understanding as to the physiological criteria (dentition, access of growth, sexual maturity) or psychological criteria (sensations, language, &c.) which are the most suitable for fixing the limits of these different periods.

is still the subject of discussion; observations do not agree. Some find that growth is accelerated during the summer months, while others have it that this occurs rather during the spring and autumn. Here again it is necessary to distinguish between height and weight. The very patient research of Malling-Hansen, Director of the Institute for Deaf-mutes in Copenhagen, who measured and weighed his 130 pupils every day for three years, show that there is alternation between increase in weight and increase in stature. Thus weight increases specially in the autumn, only slightly in winter and spring, and remains quite stationary in summer. The exact contrary takes place with regard to stature. Here the period of maximum increase is in the summer, the period of minimum growth in the autumn, and the intermediate period in the spring. But these measurements are of children in a northern country; it would be well to repeat the experiment by taking measurements of as many children as possible in other regions.

Variations in growth during the course of the year are not without interest for the educator. The question is, indeed, whether these variations are natural, or whether they are the more or less pernicious consequence of school régime. To solve the problem it would be necessary to compare either the variations, according to season, of children who do not go to school at all, with those who attend school regularly—or with the variations of children subject to a different school régime.

Ten years ago Binet hit on the ingenious plan of studying the way in which organic activity displays itself during the school year, by investigating another special phenomenon which accompanies this activity, namely, *appetite*—appetite being measured by the *consumption of bread.* Researches were carried on in the Normal Schools of France. The necessary information was gained from the school housekeeping book; this book shows the quantity (in pounds) of food bought each day for the school, and the quantity not consumed. Food-stuffs being very different in their value as nutriment, Binet took bread alone into consideration—bread, which is a complete food in itself, remains sufficiently invariable from one end of the year to the other, and the consumption of it is therefore a fairly exact measure of appetite; in schools, "when one is very hungry, one goes for the bread." Binet states that the consumption of bread diminishes during the course of the school year; and he draws the conclusion that intense intellectual work injures the appetite.[1] Schuyten, who has made a similar inquiry in Belgium, also states that there is decrease in the consumption of bread during the summer months. This decrease is very surprising, for child-development is along the lines of aggrandisement during the summer period, and this aggrandisement ought to be accompanied by a larger appetite in the summer; since this is not the case, there must be in the environment some disturbing factor. Schuyten incriminates the school; he says it is permissible to suspect the pernicious influence of the school whenever a phenomenon differs in its course of evolution from what one has a right to expect. The school, therefore, has a noxious influence on physiological activity. What is to be thought of this conclusion? It does not seem to me to be a certainty, for the

[1] Binet, *La Consommation du pain pendant une année scolaire,* Année psych. IV., 337; Schuyten, Paedolog. Jaarb., 1908.

phenomena with which one has to do are very complex,[1] but it might well be true. And this possibility alone shows us the vital importance of research of this kind, which school authorities ought to facilitate and even to encourage.

2. Repercussion of Physical Growth on Mental Functions

The chief interest for the teacher in the phenomena of physical growth lies in the fact that they have a repercussion on psychic functions and on the energy available for mental work. But what exactly the effect of this repercussion is has not yet been definitely determined.

Let us see, first of all, how far it has been possible to establish a relation of cause and effect between growth and mental energy.

Many writers have investigated how such or such a mental function evolved with age—*e.g.*, Bolton, Bourdon, Netschajeff, Lobsien, Pohlmann, Kirkpatrick, have studied the development of memory; Gilbert has studied the development of a series of functions (memory, reaction time, discrimination of colours, &c.); Stern, the evolution of the power of giving evidence; Guidi, of suggestibility, &c.[2] In schools researches of

[1] One might ask, among other things, whether the decreased desire for food during the summer does not arise in some degree from the fact that during that time the need for caloric is less. Schuyten has, however, observed that among labouring men there is an increase in the food they consume during the summer.

[2] Bolton, Amer. Journ. of Psychol., 1893; Netschajeff, Congress of Psych. at Paris, 1900; Bourdon, Rev. philos., 1894; Lobsien, Zeitsch. f. Psychol, 1902; Pohlmann, *Exp. Beitr. z. Lehre vom Gedachtniss*, 1906; Gilbert, Studies from the Yale Lab, 1894; Stern, Beitr. z. Psychol. der Aussage; Guidi, *Exp. sur la suggestibilité*, Ar. de Ps. VIII., 1908; Kirkpatrick, *Studies in Development*, New York, 1909, p. 6.

this kind can easily be undertaken. One might try to find out what is the average value of a certain

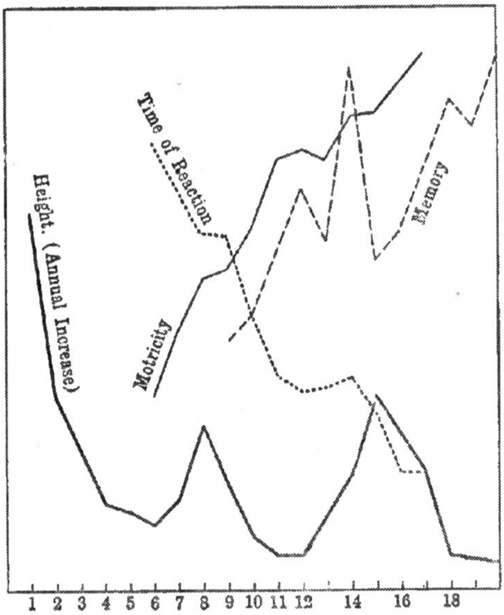

Fig. 3.—Curves of motor aptitude and of reactivity according to Gilbert; the curve of memory has been constructed according to results obtained by Pohlmann (*op. cit.*, p. 112). The lower curve represents the annual increments in height. It will be seen that the periods of depression in the curves of function correspond approximately to the periods of large annual increments. (The curve of reaction time descends from left to right; this does not signify that reactivity diminishes with age, but that reaction *time* diminishes more and more as reactivity increases with age. All these curves are constructed upon observation made on boys. The figures on the lower horizontal line indicate age.)

aptitude among children of one age; thus one would obtain a curve of its quantitative development.

Also it is observed that the curves thus obtained, showing the evolution of different mental functions, offer a striking analogy to those of physical growth; they, too, show during the time of adolescence a descent, followed by a more or less sudden ascent, and then a fresh descent. This zigzag is more accentuated among girls than boys.

Nevertheless, these curves of functional growth cannot be exactly superimposed upon those of physical growth; their minimum and maximum points do not precisely coincide—on the contrary, it is often found that a depression in the functional curve corresponds to a stage of accelerated growth in the physical curve, and one is confronted with the question whether the crises in physical growth, especially those in height, do not exercise a depressing influence on mental function. It is not, however, possible to say at what exact moment in adolescence this antagonistic influence is strongest. Is it at the outset, or, on the contrary, when adolescence is in full swing? The fact that the curves of functional development which we possess were not taken from the same children as the curves of physical growth, prevents any definite reply. The relations between the two groups of curves also vary according to the mental function considered. It always seems to me that one fact stands out constantly when examining these curves, especially those curves published by Gilbert, namely, that mental functions are unfavourably affected especially during the initial and final stages of adolescence. In order to elucidate this point it would be very helpful if more exact investigation of the *same* children could be carried on for several years.

However this may be, it is evident from the general

examination of the process of functional development that at a given moment this development is affected by physical growth ; it is therefore very probable that there is antagonism between the energy required for growth and mental energy. And there would be nothing surprising in such antagonism. The amount

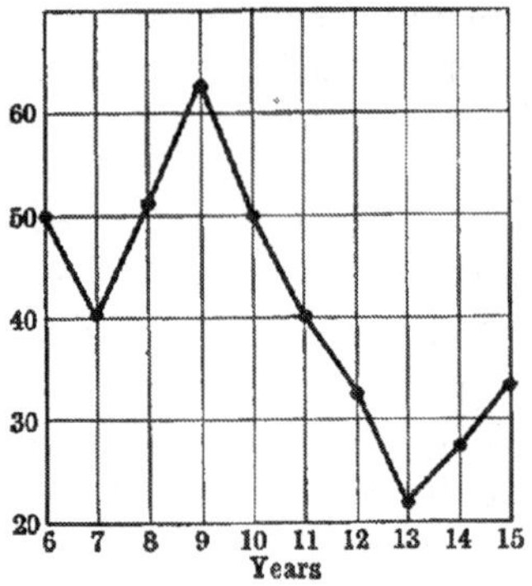

FIG. 4.—Evolution of suggestibility. It will be noticed that suggestibility has a general tendency to decline with age, but between seven and nine years of age and between thirteen and fifteen there occurs a heightening of the curve, which corresponds to the periods of vigorous growth. This diagram is taken from an article by Guidi (Ar. de Ps. VIII., p. 53), who measured the suggestibility of little schoolgirls in Rome by means of apparatus which suggested sensations of heat.

of energy which the organism has at its disposal is not unlimited, so there is nothing surprising in the fact that if it is employed in supplying the needs of organic growth it must be to the detriment of cerebral function. On the other hand, whenever growth is less vigorous, the energy set free is thus applied again to psychic work.

This equilibrium between the two regions of vegetative and functional processes respectively, which the living being is called upon alternately to flood with energy, is also met with in the alternations of sleep and waking: when the exhausted organism begins to monopolise for purposes of restoration the energy which previously was employed in the active life of waking hours, that activity ceases and sleep sets in. And sleep in its turn ceases when, the process of restoration being accomplished, this energy is once more set free.

The repercussion of physical growth on work and mental energy seems to be only a particular case of the general law of the alternation of vegetative and psychic activities, an alternation which arises from the limitation of energy furnished by the organism.

Whatever may be the explanation of this repercussion, it appears that the child is less apt for work during the periods of vigorous growth. This is a fact very useful for the educator to know If a teacher observes a certain slackness in his pupil, before punishing, let him reflect that this falling off is perhaps only the natural and inevitable result of the revolutions which are taking place in the very depths of the child's being.

It must be confessed that these two chief crises of growth both fall at a particularly unfortunate age—at six or seven, when the child's school life begins, and at fourteen or fifteen, when the preparation for important examinations begins.

The beginning of school life is an important time for a child, who, having been hitherto free in his movements, finds himself suddenly shut up in a room, often dark and ill ventilated, and forced into an immobility which is contrary to all his instincts—transported, in short, into surroundings to which, whether he will or not, he has to adapt himself. This compulsory immobility, above all, is probably very injurious to the development of physical power by the repression of one indispensable stimulus, that is, free movement. We must therefore try to make school discipline during this first school year as little coercive as possible.[1]

The mental tension and perpetual preoccupation which, about the fifteenth year, are made necessary by preparation for adult examinations, or even for the school examination at the end of the year—the apprehension which is thereby aroused—all this is very prejudicial to adolescence. It is just from this conflict between the mind (which would for its own needs direct organic energy into one channel) and the body (which will not give up that energy, for it requires it to carry on its own growth) that overpressure often proceeds, with the break-down which does not fail to follow. It is true that more often there is neither overwork nor break-down; that is because pupils, endowed with an instinct of self-preservation which triumphs over the desire to pass brilliant examinations, work with only half their

[1] According to Drs. Engelsperger and Ziegler, who have made minute inquiries in schools in Munich as to the influence on growth of the first two years of school life, school exercises a pernicious influence only on those children who are less than six years of age. But, as these writers admit, the investigation was undertaken in the autumn, which is a period of acceleration in growth; it is therefore possible that the effect of school life may have been obscured by the favourable influence of the season of the year. Other medical men, such as Schmidt-Monnard, are said to have proved the depressing effect on growth of entry upon school life. (*Cf* Engelsperger and Ziegler, *Beitr Zur Kenntnis der physischen und psychischen Natur des sechsjahrigen in die Schule eintretenden Kindes*, Z. exp. Pad. I., 1905)

powers, make memory supplement the real work of intelligence, and thus secure for themselves a régime of accommodation which enables them to double this dangerous cape with safety, fortunately for their health, but to the great detriment of their intellectual and moral education; for they have contracted the habit of doing things by halves, and they have derived from the work nothing that will be of benefit in the future.

The only method by which instruction can be harmonised with physiology appears to be the suppression of those absurd encyclopædic examinations which terminate the secondary school course. Adolescence does not preclude intellectual work, but what is hurtful is the undigested surcharge. Let us lighten the time-table, and have fewer subjects studied at one time; it would be an advantage both for health and for education itself. By hunting fewer hares at a time there would be less danger of returning home with an empty bag.

Growth is a process infinitely more delicate than is supposed: it puts the organism in a state of unstable equilibrium. Also, the organic disturbances coming on at the time of rapid growth may be very serious. The different organs are a collective whole; the evolution of one determines or regulates the evolution of another; it is therefore easy to understand that the arrested or retarded growth of one of these organs may have far-reaching consequences; the organ which does its work abnormally, or insufficiently, influences on abnormal lines the subsequent course of organic development which depends on it.

If, then, intellectual work is forced during one of the phases when mental energy ought to give way to vegetative energy, the growth of certain organs is checked and the remote effects of such accidents are only too real It is true it is no longer the teacher who is called upon to record them—it is the doctor.

The Health Note-book.—A knowledge of the course of the physical development and the state of health of his pupils is indispensable to an educator; so the institution of health note-books is called for on all sides, or "individual medical forms" for each of the children in a school, upon which should be recorded all the various incidents of a medical or biological nature which occur in the course of school life: illness, vaccination, crises in growth, accidents, &c.

If every one is agreed in the desire for these note-books (which would be of the greatest advantage not only to the doctor but also to the schoolmaster of the future, by stating the moral and physical characteristics of each scholar individually), people are by no means so agreed when it is a matter of determining what ought to be recorded in the booklets, and by whom it should be recorded. Complete information about a child ought certainly to include all that has to do with heredity: alcoholism and other diseases of the parents. But what would become of medical secrecy? One can foresee the difficulties in the way of carrying out the proposal. Some have laid it down that these note-books should be filled up by doctors only, and should be kept in such a way as not to violate professional secrecy. But there are many details of a moral or psychological nature which could only be entered by a teacher.

Among the facts to be noted in this book let us mention, in the first place, the records taken periodically from term to term of the height, weight, and, if possible, chest measurements; in the case of children with defective sight or hearing, the results of examinations, &c., upon the condition of these senses should be noted.

These health note-books, already adopted in many towns (including Geneva), will prove valuable documents for the sociologist and the demographer, who will be able to study with their assistance the influence of the hygienic conditions of such and such a school, or quarter of a town, or of the general social conditions, on the physical development of youth. For further details about these note-books and their uses, see articles by Drs. Letulle, Teissier, Roux, Dinet, in the *Reports of the First and Second Congresses on School Hygiene* in Paris (Paris, 1904 and 1906); Drs. Philippe and Boncour, Ed. mod., May, 1906; Binet and Simon, Revue Scient., January 26, 1907; Mathieu, L'Hygiène Scolaire, April 1907, p. 75.

3. Play and Imitation

Let us now begin to consider psychological development. The study of its mechanism will enable us to answer the question asked above: Of what use is childhood?

Psychological development is not accomplished entirely of itself; I mean, it is not simply the result of the unfolding of inner forces which the new-born infant received as an inheritance. No; the child must *himself* develop himself. The two means to which he instinctively has recourse to effect this development are play and imitation.

First, let us consider play, which comes first in point

of time, being made use of from the moment of birth: whilst imitation appears only after some months.

Play

What is play? And why does the child play? There are four theories which have been advanced for the solution of this, at first sight, embarrassing problem.

(1) *The Theory of Relaxation.*—This is the old-fashioned and popular theory: play is recreation, its purpose is to rest the tired mind and body. But this theory cannot be supported: why should fatigue incite to play rather than to rest? Moreover, as a fact, little children begin to play as soon as they awake in the morning, at the very time when they are not tired. And kittens and puppies, which play all day from morning till night—what work have they done that they should be so much in need of rest?

(2) *The Theory of Superfluous Energy.*—A child has an excess of vitality; his strength, not being used up by any serious occupation, accumulates. This excess of energy discharges itself as it can, flowing naturally along the channels that nature has already created in the nervous centres. The movements thus produced, having no immediate utility, constitute play. This theory, propounded first of all by the poet Schiller, and defended by Spencer, bears criticism very little better than the former. Doubtless superfluous energy favours play, but does it account for it? Not at all. This theory does not explain the *fixed forms* which play assumes in all animals of the same species. Indeed, it is incorrect to say that children rehearse in play their habitual actions; they rather perform

actions which are new to them. Also, children play till they are very tired and until they fall asleep over their toys. And convalescent children amuse themselves in their cots as soon as strength begins to return, without waiting for energy to be in excess.

(3) *The Theory of Atavism.*—Play is nothing but the rudimentary activities of foregone generations, which persist in the child, in accordance with the well-known "bio-genetic law" of Haeckelm: "The development of the child is a brief recapitulation of the evolution of the race." This theory, which was advanced later than one which we will examine presently, was propounded by Stanley Hall in 1902. Hall's idea is that play is an exercise which is essential to the disappearance of those rudimentary functions which have now become useless, "but must be exercised like the tadpole's tail, if they are to vanish." This idea is interesting, but it does not seem to fit in with the facts; it is not probable that an exercise so persistent as play can result in weakening rather than in strengthening the activities which it calls forth. Can it be that the little girls who play with dolls will afterwards be less good mothers than those who had a contempt for dolls? In a later work Hall appears to have slightly modified his opinion; the play of a rudimentary function has not as its object to make the function disappear by weakening it, but rather to make it possible for it to exercise a temporary influence on the development of other functions. Returning to the illustration of the tadpole, Hall modifies it thus: play exercises many atavistic functions which will disappear in adult life "like the tadpole's tail that must be both developed

and used as a *stimulus to the growth of legs*, which will otherwise never mature." [1]

This new point of view is much more fertile than the former; but I do not think that Hall, when modifying his illustration of the tadpole, wished to modify his original idea It is I, not he, who set up these two theories in opposition to each other. They seem to me to have a very different bearing: in one case play is nothing more than a means of elimination; in the other it becomes an instrument of production. This last-mentioned hypothesis seems to me to become confused practically with that which we are now going to examine, and which I have kept to the last because it is the crown of the whole edifice.

(4) *The Theory of Preparatory Exercise.*—This was formulated by Karl Groos in 1896.[2] This psychologist, at that time a professor at Basle, recognising the inadequacy of the theories of relaxation and of superfluous energy, was the first to recognise that, in order to solve the problem of play, it must be considered from a biological standpoint.

This biological standpoint, be it said in passing, is far too much neglected by psychologists, who would often gain thereby a deeper insight into mental activity and its disturbances; for the observer who takes up this standpoint is led to consider the various activities not only of human beings but of all animals —and to investigate not only the immediate end of

[1] S. Hall, *Adolescence*, London, 1904, p. 202. The passage in italics is not in italics in the original The first quotation is from the Ped. Sem. IX., 1902.

[2] Groos, *Die Spiele der Thiere*, Jena, 1896 (English trans., *The Play of Animals*); *Die Spiele der Menschen*, Jena, 1899 (Eng. trans., *The Play of Man*), *Der Lebenswert des Spieles*, Jena, 1910.

these activities but their functional meaning, the part they play in the maintenance of life.

And if from this exalted position a glance is cast at the ludic activity (*ludus*, play) in general, it is immediately recognised that play varies according to the kind of animal, and that the activity displayed in the play of a certain kind of animal resembles very closely the activity displayed by adult animals of the same species. There are, in short, nearly as many kinds of play as there are instincts; there is wrestling play, hunting play, fighting play, love play, &c. The kitten, for example, pounces on the piece of paper drawn in front of him, or on a withered leaf blown about by the wind, just in the same way as later he will pounce on mice or birds, his favourite prey. Kids amuse themselves by knocking their heads together, a prelude to future butting with the horns, &c. But one never finds in the play of one kind of animal an exercise of the instincts belonging to another kind: in vain would one rustle a piece of paper before a kid; he would never throw himself upon it; and, on the other hand, kittens do not play at butting each other with the forehead.

One is therefore led to think of play as preparatory exercise for the serious work of life. The greater part of inherited instincts are not sufficiently developed at birth (especially in the higher animals and in man) to fulfil their purpose at the outset; they have to be exercised or completed by new acquisitions. It is by play that they have to be completed. Just as it is necessary to have played scales in order to be a good pianist, so it is necessary to have been young in order to be a good adult.

Doubtless this preparatory process is reduced to a

minimum in the case of the lower animals; I do not think that a little oyster would have to play at oysters for a long time in order to become an accomplished oyster. But in proportion as the animal is high in rank the apprenticeship is long. A little rabbit must have played the rabbit for a certain time in order to become a perfect rabbit, a chick must have played the cock or the hen for some months in order to become a good one; the kid must have cut many capers before becoming a goat or a chamois worthy of the name. Also, our children must have played long years at being men and women in order to truly become men and women It may therefore be said with Groos that *it is not because the animal is young that he plays, but that he has youth because he needs to play.*

Many other writers before Groos anticipated more or less clearly this function of play, among others Souriau;[1] but it was the German psychologist who first perceived it in its entirety, and formulated its biological bearing. This new conception is, to my way of thinking, of capital importance to the paidologist and to pedagogy. I shall try to show this in the following paragraphs.

It must at the same time be recognised that the preparatory exercise of instinct is not the motive of all play; as Carr, an American author, has rightly shown, play has a more extended biological utility.[2] Among other things, it procures for the organism the stimulation which is necessary to the growth of its

[1] Souriau, *Le plaisir du mouvement,* Rev. scient., 3rd series, XVII., 1889.

[2] Carr, *The Survival Values of Play.* Investig. of the Department of Psychology of the University of Colorado, I., 1902.

organs. As has been said by experts occupied with the problem of variation of species in the course of evolution, the formative agents of the body of the animal do not all come from the mother-cell which produced it, but many are furnished by the outside world. The development of the individual is the result both of the natural tendencies (as yet but dimly understood) which have been transmitted by heredity and of the action of the surrounding world. It is for this reason that variation in environment can have a repercussion on the morphology of the animal: such as regression of organs which have become useless, and development of stimulated organs.

Play, then, acts as a stimulant to growth. It acts especially on the nervous system. At birth the nervous centres are far from having acquired their definite structure: the brain, above all, is not in a condition to function.[1] A great many of the nerve fibres of the brain have not yet acquired their medullary sheath, that is, the fatty covering which will isolate them from each other as an india-rubber covering isolates the wires of an electric installation. When they are without this sheath they cannot function. But the stimulation of these fibres is one of the factors which help them to acquire this medullary sheath, and therefore their functionary power. Play, by giving rise to and multiplying this stimulation, is therefore an important agent in the development of the nervous system. Observation verifies this view: if the eyelids of a new-born kitten are sewn together, a certain arrest in the development of the visual centres of the brain will be noticed, because

[1] Probst, *Gehirn und Seele des Kindes*, Berlin, 1904, p. 124.

they have not received the necessary stimulation.[1] The motor centres of the brain become atrophied in people who have had an arm or a leg amputated in childhood. In these cases we find a certain confirmation of the biological adage that it is function which makes the organ. The play of the limbs also favours muscular growth; the mere activity of a muscle is, as every one knows, a factor in its development (biceps of athletes).

Another use of play, to which Carr has also drawn attention, is to maintain *newly acquired* activities by constantly reviving them. This is specially true of the play of adults; in time of peace the soldier plays at war, shoots at a target, rides on horseback, just as the virtuoso between two concerts practises scales and trills in order not to grow rusty.

According to Carr, play has also a *social rôle* of first-class importance; parties, balls, matches, are useful in developing feelings of solidarity, &c. This appears to be very probable, but the sociological conception of play is not opposed to the biological conception of Groos, it is only a particular case of it.

Carr finally attributes to play a *cathartic*, that is a purgative, effect: we bring with us into the world a certain number of instincts, which still persist and which are generally injurious in the present state of civilisation; it is the rôle of play to purge us from time to time of these anti-social tendencies. When in tragedy men kill and fight, they give vent in a bloodless way to their sanguinary tendencies. In the same way, by boxing, or playing football, the child gets rid of his anti-social instincts while satisfying them

[1] Moles have atrophied eyes because they have not "played" enough with light.

at the same time. What is to be thought of this hypothesis? Might not the same objection be made to it as to Dr. Stanley Hall's? If in certain cases play develops instincts, why in other cases should it diminish them? It must be admitted that Carr hardly explains this point. But I think that this hypothesis is different from Hall's. Carr's idea is not that play *suppresses* these harmful tendencies, but that it directs them; as to the idea of a veritable purging, it might be maintained, it seems to me, if it were admitted that it is *emotions*, and not definite activities, which are thus expelled, and that they are only temporarily expelled. If one is angry, it is soothing and pacifying to break a plate, to slam a door, or to flog an arm-chair. By fighting with his companions, the child will not definitely eliminate his wrestling instinct, which it is necessary he should possess for legitimate defence, but he will temporarily give vent to the aggressive tendencies that this instinct gives birth to, and which will be socially inconvenient until a necessary struggle gives him the chance to express them in real earnest.[1]

Let us now consider some of the plays of children. We shall see that all of them exercise some physiological or psychological function, in accordance with the theory of Groos as completed by Carr. Some exercise the *general functions* of mental life, such as

[1] But one must not conclude from this cathartic hypothesis that a child can be purged of his warlike instincts by making him play at soldiers. Alas, no! Rigault in 1858 said in his charming article on Children's Playthings (*Conversations littéraires*), "Prussia is decidedly the leading power among lead soldiers!" The Prussians in 1870 do not appear to have lacked military aptitude because they played at soldiers as children, at the time when Rigault was writing his witty words.

perception, motricity, ideation, feeling; others exercise *special functions,* such as wrestling, hunting, love, sociability, imitation.

I. Games in the first category comprise sensory games, motor games, psychic games.

(1) SENSORY GAMES. — Children, especially quite young children, take pleasure in the simple fact of experiencing sensations. It amuses them to taste the most diverse substances in order "to see what that tastes like," to make sounds (with whistles, trumpets, castanets, rattles, musical boxes; vibrations of various kinds, such as that of string tightly stretched and played like a guitar, or of the nib of a pen placed on a table and made to vibrate by finger-taps, &c.); it amuses them to examine colours (tops, kaleidoscopes, coloured counters, painting in colours, &c.). Little children play at touching and feeling objects.

(2) MOTOR GAMES.—These games are innumerable; some develop co-ordination of movements (games of skill, cup and ball, jugglery, ball games, hoops); others develop strength or promptitude (gymnastics, running, jumping, stone-throwing). Language movements also have their part in this kind of play. We are all familiar with sentences that it is difficult to say quickly, such as "Peter Piper," or "Round the rugged rock the ragged rascal ran," &c.

(3) PSYCHIC GAMES.—These may be divided into intellectual and emotional games.

Intellectual games are those which call into requisition comparison or recognition (lotto, dominoes), association by sound (rhyming games), reasoning (chess), reflection or invention (enigmas and riddles), creative imagination (invention of stories, drawings). *Imagination* plays a very important part in a child's life; it enters into all a child's occupations. As imagination occupies a place of the highest importance in the mental life of a man, it is necessary that it should be exercised early. It is creative imagination which raises man above nature by enabling him to group elements in new combinations. Representation of this creative kind implies very considerable independence of the mind in reference to actual facts. Animals do not seem to possess it; and in acquiring it the human race has made an immense step forward. It is a comparatively new faculty, and it has to be "played" a great deal in order that the child may master it. It is not necessary to recall at length the inexhaustible power of fancy of which a child gives proof when, for example, it invests the most trifling object with all the qualities it is pleased that it should have; a piece of wood may represent to him a horse, a boat, a locomotive, a man. He makes inanimate things live, he personifies the letters of the alphabet, attributes to himself very diverse personalities, and transfigures reality till he really deceives himself.[1]

Sometimes this imaginative impulse oversteps the play boundary and a tendency to illusion in real life is observed: the child misrepresents truth and earns the name of liar; but he has nevertheless no intention of deceiving, he merely prolongs a comedy of which he is himself to some extent the dupe. This is a fact which should make us cautious in allowing children to be witnesses in courts of law.

[1] For the development of imagination, see Ribot, *Essai sur l'imagination créatrice;* and for instances of the part which imagination takes in the plays of children, see books by Compayré, Sully, Pérez, &c. On the tendency to personify, see Lemaitre, *Audition colorée et phénomènes connexes observés chez des écoliers*, Geneva, 1901, and Arch. de Psychol. I., 24.

Finally, there is another kind of intellectual play, that of *curiosity*, which with Groos we may define as intellectual experimenting, or as a play of attention.[1] Why is a child curious ? Why does he want to touch everything, to see what there is in the bellows that makes it blow, in the top which makes it spin ? Why does he want to know the why and wherefore of everything ? For the reason that he needs to do it in order to effect his development. Nature has not implanted in us an innate knowledge of the cause and effect of phenomena, but she has implanted in us the desire to procure it for oneself and the means of doing so, which is a thousand times more precious. This desire, which takes the form of a question, springs from the feeling of discomfort caused by the non-comprehension of things (maladaptation), and the means of satisfying it is observation, experiment, investigating the mechanism of things. Indeed, the curiosity of the child is nothing else than the preparatory exercise of this questioning and experimenting instinct which sets itself at work upon everything and nothing. This play-curiosity is distinct from the curiosity of the scientist, in that the pleasure of the former consists in the act itself, while that of the scientist depends on the desire for discovery : the child is curious because it is pleasant to be curious ; the scientist is curious because he wants to know. But that does not prevent the curiosity of the child from being very useful to his development, by drawing his attention to all things that are new to him, and consequently by exercising his attention and enriching his store of knowledge. It is also, as Groos so

[1] To be exact, curiosity is a need, an appetite, and it is rather the gratification of curiosity which constitutes a play of attention.

rightly points out, a salutary counterpoise to the fear of the new, an instinct which, however valuable it may be, would certainly interfere with intellectual development if it preponderated.

In *emotional games* pleasure is found in the arousing of the emotions, even of disagreeable ones. Grief is sometimes amusing if it is voluntarily accepted; immersion in an icy bath has in itself little charm, but there is a certain delight in braving the shivering that it produces. I remember that once upon a time my little companions and I used to amuse ourselves by striking each other on the calves with a stick "to see how much one could bear without crying out." The æsthetic sentiment is developed by a great many games (drawing, painting, modelling, music).

Fear also furnishes material for many games: stories of robbers which make one's hair stand on end; games of "wild beast," when a child hides in a corner and jumps out on his companions, who, though trembling with fear, try to find him; all sorts of practical jokes, such as ringing the front-door bell of some strange house and then running away as fast as one's legs can carry one for fear of being caught by the servant.

The exercise *of the will* gives rise to many childish plays, such as games of imitation, which will be mentioned later. We will here consider only *games of inhibition*, the essential of which is voluntary arrest or repression of movement. This is very important, for the more the adult human being is civilised the more he has to restrain his impulses; with animals, savages, imbeciles, and inebriates, impulse is immediately followed by action. But in order that an act may be intelligent it must be judged and its consequences weighed before being accomplished. "Thinking," said Bain, "means refraining from speech and action." Therefore, in order that a child may become a thinking being, he must first learn to restrain action. The exercise of this power of arrest gives occasion for many games: repression of laughter, of certain reflex movements (*e.g.* trying not to blink when a hand is brought near the eyes), repression of voluntary movements, exercises in immobility (the child plays at being a statue or at *tableaux vivants*); and, above all, by the "game of contraries."

II. We pass on to *games of special functions*. They are all well known, and it will be sufficient to mention a few by way of example.

(1) Wrestling Games.—Bodily wrestling; mental wrestling (in matches and discussions). Children fight and quarrel not only amongst themselves, but they often exercise their combative instinct against their master, whom they look upon as a dreadful tyrant. Carl Vogt relates in picturesque fashion what used to take place in this way at the Giessen *Gymnase* when he was a pupil there. "Learning and work were for the greater number incidental only; the greater part did nothing but tease their schoolfellows and annoy their masters. The study of the peculiarities of character of these scholastic tyrants soon showed us the weak side of each, and after some experiences, of which some were truly smarting experiences, we knew how to get at the weak point without running the risk of punishment. All the time spent at school was nothing but a continual war against the teaching body, sometimes single combats or skirmishes at the outposts, sometimes combined movement directed by 'scientific' tactics—a

war, interspersed sometimes with momentary truces, but never followed by a lasting peace." [1]

That took place in 1830, but things have not improved since then. There is still between masters and boys a hostility of which, in a very fascinating article, M. Cousinet explains the cause.[2] There is between them great divergence of interests; their aims, motives, and ideals are different. This is true; but there is also, no doubt, the pleasure of fighting for fighting's sake. It is not necessarily out of hatred that a schoolboy plays pranks on his master; it may be simply for the pleasure of playing a trick which satisfies some want in his nature.

(2) Hunting Games.—These are first of all games of pursuit, hide and seek, &c. Then those which are more closely allied to real hunting: birds-nesting, hunting flies or butterflies, gathering fruit or flowers. In this class may be placed the collecting instinct which is so strongly developed in animals who have to hibernate. This instinct in the child gives rise to collecting plays: collections of stamps, insects, &c. There need not necessarily be any dominant idea in the work undertaken. The mere fact of filling an empty space in a stamp-album constitutes pleasure. The child collects for the pleasure of amassing The

[1] Carl Vogt, *Aus meinem Leben*, Stuttgart, 1896, p. 70.

[2] R. Cousinet, *La solidarité enfantine*, Rev. phil., Sept. 1908. In some later articles (Bull. S. ps. E., Jan. 1910, and Ed. Mod., July 1910) Cousinet considers the "ragging" of the boys to be an instinctive expression of their contempt for those masters who have no authority, "whom they feel to be inferior to themselves." The "ragging" is said to be a kind of punishment that the pupils inflict on a master quite unfitted for his work (as is *being laughed at* in the theory advanced by Bergson). This view is doubtless very near the truth; it is no less true that the "ragging," whatever may be its final cause, covers, in the scholar, a purely playful character.

quantity is to him more than the quality. He takes everything. Have you ever seen the contents of a child's pocket? It is a genuine museum of curiosities: little white stones, postage stamps, tram-tickets, shells, old nails, dried flowers, silver paper, corks, unnameable fragments, pieces of lead, wood, and putty, all that has attracted the attention of the boy and has been carefully preserved by him. With what an enchanting imagination has he surrounded all these little objects? What intimate signification has he given them? In order to understand it we must go back for a moment to our own childhood; but, alas, on the road of time there is no such thing as retracing one's footsteps!

(3) Social Games.—Under this heading come "chums," excursions, the formation of camps, of clans, and of little childish societies in imitation of the societies of grown-up people, with a president, secretary, &c. Most games concur indirectly in furthering the development of social instincts.

(4) Family Games.—One may thus designate those games which are based on the maternal or on the family instinct. The place of honour here is accorded to the doll, the most widely spread and perhaps the most ancient of plays, which calls out the instinct of maternity, of domination, authority, and imitation, all at the same time. Little girls and boys sometimes join together to play at being "Father and Mother"; they make their home in the window bay, adorn it with imaginary furniture, and do not fail to correct little Miss Dolly, their daughter, if she should object to swallow the bowl of diluted chalk which does duty for a cup of milk.

(5) Games of Imitation.—Imitation is a very

valuable auxiliary of play. Let us here make two delicate distinctions: *the game of imitation*, in which the child imitates for the mere pleasure of imitation (*e.g.* the monkey game: a child makes faces or gestures more or less absurdly funny; other children have to imitate them as closely as possible); and the *imitative game*, in which the purpose of imitation is to provide elements for the carrying out of the game. Thus, in their wrestling, children imitate Redskins if a troupe of Red Indians should happen to be performing just then at the fair; or they will be Japanese or Boers if a war in the extreme East or in the Transvaal should be engrossing public attention at the time, &c.

This rapid sketch is sufficient to show that, according to the biological theory, every kind of play is indeed the preparatory exercise for some useful activity or function. It is hardly necessary to say that many plays exercise many different functions at once: movement, imagination, reflection, &c.

We will now mention an objection which is often brought against this theory of preparatory exercise: it is not the purpose of play, it is said, to prepare for future activity, and play is not characteristic of the young only, for adults play. But, we answer, all activities and all faculties are not wholly developed nor entirely acquired in the adult, and if the adult experiences an instinctive want to exercise or keep up certain activities, it is because those very activities, the exercise of which is play to him, are just those which are not yet entirely developed nor definitely acquired. In regard to those imperfectly developed activities which he feels inclined to exercise, is not the adult still young? There is no play, indeed, that is not the exercise of some activity *more or less im-*

perfect. The performance of an action which can already be perfectly accomplished is not a game. Thus it is play even to an adult to throw stones or shoot with a rifle at a target situated at a certain distance from him; it would certainly be no longer a game if the target were placed sufficiently near for him to be certain of hitting the bull's-eye at every shot.

Further, every adult is young in relation to subsequent generations of adults, and his games prepare for acquisitions which will be useful to them. The history of humanity shows the influence that play has had on scientific and industrial progress: the game of chess has given rise to various mathematical problems; the amusements of "Popular Science" have been the cause of many important discoveries; it was in play that the properties of electricity were discovered; also it was play that led to the invention of the bicycle, that useful means of transport, the child of the velocipede of former times, a simple instrument of amusement. Aeroplane races and competitions, which are at the present moment games and sports without immediate utility, are preparing for the period of practical usefulness upon which aviation will soon enter, as balloons have already done, for balloons too were at one time mere toys. And, in a general way, was it not by playing with natural phenomena that great scientific geniuses discovered the great laws of nature, which they would never have perceived if their experiments had had nothing in view but material benefit?

The question remains: What is the psychological nature of play? Why does play please the child so much? In what category of methods can it be entered?

The answer to the first question is easy. Play is pleasant because it satisfies a need. It is a general law that everything that has to do with development of life and of the personality is accompanied by pleasure (eating when one is hungry, sleeping when one is tired, &c.). There is therefore nothing mysterious here.[1]

Is play an instinct? This is chiefly a question of terms. If it is held that an instinct is a definite act, it is certain that play is not an instinct, since it brings into working the most diverse activities. This is Groos' opinion, to which no objection can be taken. Play is related to instinct, apparently, in the sense that, like it, it consists in the spontaneous performance, in response to some internal or external stimulus, of a complicated act, the mechanism for which is registered in the nervous centres, and of the purpose of which the individual is not conscious. We will say, then, that play is an *instinctive impulse*. Physiologically it is based on the excessive excitability of the nervous mechanism, which excitability itself depends perhaps on the fact that the neurons in process of growth are in a state of instability which facilitates their disturbance.

It is now time to pass to a second factor in mental development, that of imitation.

[1] The special attractiveness of play has led writers on the subject to introduce into the discussion, in order to explain it, *the joy of causation* and the *feeling of liberty* which fill the soul of the child who plays. But this joy and feeling do not seem to me to be the *causes* of the attraction of play, but themselves to proceed from the objective conditions of liberty, which are necessary to play in order that it shall be play.

IMITATION

Imitation is a very important function with which earlier psychologists did not much concern themselves, and which gives a great deal of trouble to those of modern times. Its limits are undefined: on one side imitation is confused with simple motor adaptation, on another with habit, which in a way is imitation of oneself, and again with a voluntary act which may be regarded as the imitation of an idea. And then comes the question, as with play, whether imitation is a separate instinct, or whether it is only the name given to the starting of certain sensory-motor co-ordinations which already form part of definite instinctive tendencies. Finally, what is the relation between imitation, suggestion, and mental contagion?

I hope to be excused from discussing all these points, which indeed matter little to the present study, the aim of which is simply to determine the place which imitation occupies as an agent in mental development.

There are three ways in which a child can be put in possession of the functions necessary to his existence as a man: (1) heredity, (2) personal experience, (3) imitation.[1]

Heredity, as we have seen, is insufficient in itself, and play has to come to its assistance, not only in order to reinforce the lines imprinted by heredity on the nervous centres, but to make new ones. And

[1] Instruction by others, didactic teaching, may be included under the heading of imitation. To profit by a lesson is to imitate the experience of others of which the lesson has given an account, or to prepare to imitate it as soon as occasion offers.

even this is not enough. If there were only these two factors childhood would have to be excessively long, for every one would have to rediscover for himself the greater part of the experiences of preceding generations. Fortunately imitation spares us this continual beginning again, by inviting us to profit by the experience of others.

Imitation is, then, an instrument of capital importance for development. But this instrument is not given to us all ready for use: we have to acquire it, as other functions have been acquired, in play.

In order to clearly understand the rôle of imitation, let us see what psycho-physiological process the act is based upon. To imitate is to reproduce oneself what one has seen done or what one has heard. In order to imitate, it is necessary that a visual or auditory percept should evoke precisely those movements of the limbs (or of the larynx if it is a question of sounds) suitable for reproducing it. This evoking implies the existence of an association between this percept and the motor images which control the movement. In physiological terms one might say that this evocation presupposes the existence of a connection between the neurons of a sensory centre corresponding to this perception, and the group of motor neurons which control the movement.

But the greater part of these motor-sensory associations are not furnished by heredity, and this is not astonishing, for those which man needs to have at his disposal are indefinite. He must then create them for himself. This is the use of imitation-play. The little child who tries to reproduce the movements which he sees made, or the noises which he hears, appears to concentrate all his interest in the mere reproduction of these movements or sounds.

Up to this point things go on by themselves. But this is where the situation becomes complicated—not for the child, but for the psychologist · (1st) Why has the baby a tendency to reproduce what he sees? (2nd) Why does he repeat these reproductions until he has succeeded in copying his model?

The simplest answer would be to attribute these tendencies to instinct: the instinct of imitation. This is what is generally done. But there is a difficulty in such a supposition. An instinct is, by definition, a very definite act, such as the construction of a nest, the seizing of prey, &c. But the acts which one imitates, or which one might be called on to imitate, are undefined. ·Must we therefore conclude that imitation is not an instinct? This is the opinion of Groos, for whom imitation is nothing more than a particular case showing the motor power of images.[1] It is a fact that all our images have a tendency to translate themselves into movement: you probably know the little parlour game which consists in asking every one what a rattle is; nine out of ten times the person questioned will illustrate his answer by a rotatory gesture descriptive of a rattle. This tendency of an image to pass over into the action which expresses it, which is incontestable, solves, I quite admit, the first question; but it throws no light at all on the second. The motor tendency of images certainly explains that a percept starts a movement, and that this movement may be imitative when the sensory-motor co-ordination already exists, but it in no wise explains the tendency of the child (who as yet possesses no co-

[1] Groos, *The Play of Man*, p. 289 (Eng. trans.).

ordinations) to *repeat a movement till it is like* the model.

It is in this phenomenon of the search for conformity —entirely neglected by psychologists—that lies, to my thinking, the instinctive element in the process of imitation. This search after conformity is the same in all imitated acts, whatever they may be. It is, then, a well-determined tendency and always uniform; we are perfectly justified, therefore, in considering it an instinct: the *instinct to conform.* I am not now speaking of voluntary imitation, in which this search after conformity is clearly perceived and becomes the aim of the subject; while with the child the end is pursued without conscious purpose, which is what characterises an instinctive act. This instinct reveals itself in consciousness as a "desire for conformity," just as the alimentary instinct is revealed through hunger.

We now know why the child imitates, and how he imitates. There is yet another obscure point to be cleared up: What does he imitate?

The child, as a matter of fact, does not imitate everything.

To begin with, the power of imitation is limited by the anatomical structure, which predisposes the individual to reproduce certain phenomena rather than others: if linnets were placed with larks when young they would adopt the song of the latter; but they would not adopt the barking of a dog if they were brought up with dogs.

Yet among the models which are suitable to serve as copies the child makes a selection, a choice. What prompts this choice? The necessities of develop ment; a great many potentialities which we bring with us into the world when we are born are not susceptible of development without the impetus given by imitation.[1] That is to say, the choice will vary with age, and according to the needs of the moment. The child will imitate what it is important he should imitate in the interest of perfect development.

But the child reproduces many acts only recently acquired by the human race—such as reading a newspaper, smoking, or turning the steering-wheel of an automobile—acts of which the physiological element was certainly not transmitted by heredity. If he is induced to imitate them, it is in consequence of the ascendancy that is exercised over him by persons who are older than he is, or whom he feels to be in some way superior to himself. It is surely to the advantage of his development that he should constantly try to conform to that which appears to him to be above his level, and it is this interest in copying adults in general, or such and such a person in particular, which determines his individual choice in the acts he reproduces. The child imitates an act much less because the act itself interests him than because he is interested in the person who is accustomed to perform that action.

A fact that introduces a certain amount of confusion into the question of imitation is that, in the case of the young child, imitation is hunting two hares at one time. On the one hand, the little child imitates in order that he may learn to imitate—this is just the

[1] An American psychologist, Berry, has stated that in the case of certain kittens the instinct to devour mice is aroused by the stimulus of imitation only · if they are brought up apart from their kind, so that they never see cats devour mice, they play with these animals without hurting them. (Berry, *An Experimental Study of Imitation in Cats*, Journ. of Comp. Neurol , XVIII., 1908.)

play which accompanies "the instinct to conform";[1] on the other hand, he imitates in order to acquire other knowledge by means of imitation. The imitative function is both the end and the means. And it is both at the same time. It is educative while it is still being educated. The student in the training college has to give lessons in the schools in order to learn his work as a teacher; he is at the same time master and pupil. This is precisely the condition of imitation, which educates itself by educating, and which educates while educating itself.

It would be useless to return now to the spontaneous exercise of imitation, which is only a particular manifestation of the ludic function; let us rather ask ourselves what it is that is educated by means of imitation.

We may subdivide into two groups the acquisitions which are due to it: (1) Acquisition of general functions; (2) acquisition of special functions.

(1) *Acquisition of General Functions.*—These functions are motor adaptation in general, voluntary movement, and the comprehension of our environment.

Motor adaptation:—we have stated that imitation is confused in one direction with simple motor adaptation. When a young child follows with his eyes the light that passes in front of him, or tries to reach with his hand the ribbon on his cradle, he is in a sense trying to imitate with his eyes the movement made by the candle, or to imitate with his arm the space which separates him from the ribbon. The idea of

[1] Groos, for whom imitation implies no instinct, is rather perplexed how to account for the play of imitation, since all play is the preparatory exercise of some instinct (*Play of Man*, p. 289, footnote); this difficulty disappears if one recognises in the act of imitation the instinct to seek for conformity.

imitation becomes confused here with the idea of play-adaptation.

Voluntary movement :—in order that volition may be efficient in a movement, it is necessary that there shall be, not only a representation of the whole act, but that this representation shall stimulate the motor images or the motor neurons which control its execution. Imitation, which, as we have said, creates and multiplies sensory-motor and ideo-motor associations, is therefore an important agent in the acquisition of the power of voluntary motricity.

Comprehension :—*i.e.* comprehension of things, for to comprehend or understand an object is to know how to use it, and it is imitation which makes it possible for us to acquire a knowledge of the handling of things. Further, there is the understanding of the emotions, the understanding of others : by instinct we are inclined to reproduce the facial expression of those who surround us ; serious faces make us wrinkle our foreheads, smiling faces smooth out these wrinkles, enthusiastic faces stimulate our being and incite us to action. Having reproduced, having imitated expressions of grief, joy, transport, or admiration, we have also by the same act ourselves experienced and understood the different emotions. Imitation of this kind is at the root of that sympathy which we, members of one society, ought to feel for each other. As an English writer has rightly said, "Being children, we imitate everything without understanding it, and by virtue of this imitation, we have learnt to understand it."[1]

(2) *Acquisition of Special Functions.*—These acquisitions are innumerable, and it is superfluous to name

[1] Hirn, *Origins of Arts*, London, 1900, p. 79.

them: by imitating the dancing-master one learns to dance, by imitating the carpenter one learns to plane, &c. Among the more important of the acquisitions gained by the help of imitation, language should be mentioned. In the domain of morals imitation plays a very important part: every one knows the power of example.

4. Of what Use is Childhood?

We are now able to reply to the question with which this chapter opened: "Of what use is childhood?" Childhood is for play and imitation. A child is not a child because he has no experience, but because he has a natural necessity to gain this experience. It is not because he is not full grown that a child is young, but it is because a secret instinct urges him to do all that is necessary in order to become full grown. And (we have just seen) this instinctive tendency to develop shows itself by play and imitation.

Juvenile activity, the childish mind, it should be carefully remarked, is in no way a necessary consequence of simple lack of experience or development, as popularly supposed. Insufficiency of function is by no means sufficient to create the child type. A cow, for example, is certainly very deficient as far as reflection and social virtues are concerned; but it is not a child. It is not the fact of a child's ignorance that makes him a child; it is the fact that he wants to know, that he tends to become something more than he is. The little calf is a cow-child, because it tends to become a cow; but the cow is not a child-man (in spite of her insufficiency with regard to human mentality) because she shows no tendency to become a man. I, who am no musician, am not a child in the art of piano or harp playing, because I have no tendency whatever to become a pianist or harpist (I am in this matter nothing at all, not even a child); on the other hand, a pupil at the Conservatory who has not finished his course will be a child, a young thing, in relation to music, because he has the wish to develop himself musically still more.

The essential quality in the child, then, is not that he is insufficient, but that he is a candidate.

We understand now why animal species which have a long childhood have survived in the course of evolution: it is because those animal species were the kinds which by this fact attained a higher degree of development. Indeed, the longer childhood is, the longer is that plastic period during which the animal plays, imitates, experiments, that is, multiplies its possibilities of action, and augments by the fruit of its individual experience the too small capital which was transmitted to it by heredity.

Adult age is crystallisation, petrification; the aim of infancy is to defer as long as possible that moment when "being," losing its aptitude for "becoming," congeals, takes its definite form, like a piece of iron which the blacksmith has allowed to grow cold.

Thus girls, who, as we have seen, arrive more quickly at maturity than boys, pay for this precocity by attaining a less degree of intellectual development. This relation between the inferior evolution of feminine mentality and the shorter extension of their period of childhood is of the highest biological interest. It shows how, in spite of strong individual variations and economic and social conditions which seem to have turned upside down the mechanism of selection and evolution, one finds the hard-and-fast law of nature which regulates the destinies of species always vigilant. It is necessary in the interest of the race that woman should be more passive, more conservative, that she should have in a less degree the taste for research and for those enterprises which would carry her far from the domestic hearth, and from those children with whose fate her own should be associated. It seems as if this comparative abbreviation of the period of childhood were the means that nature has used to put restraint upon the intellectual evolution of the woman. On the other hand, the woman has a more developed emotional life than her male companion, and in this she may find ample consolation for her inferiority in the region of abstract thought and in the power to make new acquisitions.

5. Attractive Education

I affirmed that the manner in which this question of the significance of childhood should be solved had considerable practical importance. The time has come for demonstrating this.

If childhood were nothing more than a *pis-aller*, an accident, a secondary consequence of development, all those phenomena without any immediate utility that childhood brings in its train (play) ought to be repressed, dammed up, swept away as rubbish—just as one sweeps away the cinders caused by combustion in a furnace; in no case would it be well to stimulate and to make capital out of them from an educational point of view. Pedagogy would then have to be in a great measure repressive, disciplinary, and rigid.

Such a conception of education has prevailed for a long time, and, alas, still prevails. But this was not always the case; the ancients, who had in many respects a much juster conception than we have of normal life, gave to games, in education, the place of honour which is now being restored to them and which such thinkers as Plato and Aristotle accorded to them. But later in the Middle Ages, under the dominion of perverted religious creeds, began a crusade against everything which could bring any joy into life: the arts, including music, were proscribed; also good living, and even bathing and walks. Children's games were included in this pernicious ostracism, for it was believed that virtue and suffering were necessarily allied, and that a lesson in order to be useful must necessarily be tiresome. This fatal conception still weighs down modern pedagogy; schools and colleges are still synonymous with prisons of youth. The present school system is dominated by authority, intimidation, coercion, the repression of natural inclination, and consequently by *ennui*.

And this would be more or less justified if childhood were nothing but an accident, the reverse of growth, without more significance in itself than the wrong side of a piece of tapestry. But all that has gone before has abundantly shown—at least I hope it has—that childhood is not an accident, a wrong side, but that it is the *actual form* that development of the being assumes. The most trifling manifestations of the characteristics of this childish state should be followed with the greatest care by the educator, who, far from thwarting nature, could not do better than follow it, for fear of ending in failure. Nature does well what she does; she is a better biologist than all the pedagogues in the world, and the way in which she sets about turning a child into an adult should be our sole guide.

And what do we see? We see that nature has implanted in children certain wants, certain desires, corresponding to developmental necessities, and that everything which is capable of satisfying these wants, or of realising these desires, has a particular attractiveness. The actual accomplishment of these educative activities is play; even when imitation intervenes, it is always in the form of play, or in connection with play.

We have here the fundamental elements of a pedagogy which is, I believe, the true one. It consists in exercising a child's activity only when he feels the natural need for doing so, or after having skilfully *created the need*, if it is not instinctive—in such a way that the object of this activity may captivate the child, may excite in him the desire to acquire it, provided always that the activity itself shall have the characteristics of play. An education which has due respect for the laws of natural development of the child—the only effective education—ought to be attractive: the subject-matter taught should interest the scholar; and the activity which he will display in order to acquire it, the work that he will accomplish in order to assimilate it and to master it, will then quite naturally take the form of play.

I know very well that by saying this (which, by the way, is no new thing) I am bringing a hornet's nest about my ears. Moralists, dogmatisers, and pedants of every shade of colour, who from the depths of their arm-chairs prescribe what the child ought to be without ever having asked themselves what he is, will rush upon me, or, if not upon me, who am unworthy of the honour, at any rate upon psychology, as capable in their eyes of overthrowing all the old sacrosanct principles. Just think! Make school attractive! But all school-work would be nothing but amusement! Nothing would be taken seriously any more! It is necessary that the child should be trained to make effort!

It is necessary that the child shall be trained to make effort! This, out of all the protestations, is the only one worth taking up. Yes, no doubt the child should be enabled to make effort. Yet we must not, under pretext of training him, disgust him with effort or make him incapable of it for ever.

A distinction should be made here: do not let us confuse the teaching *of* effort with teaching *by* effort. It is not by any means clear that the latter will realise the former. It is not by compelling a child to make unseasonable efforts that his power of making effort later in life will be developed, any more than by compelling a babe to eat beef-steak will he be trained to have a good appetite and robust digestion when he is grown up. Aptitude for effort is not an autonomous faculty which can be developed by exercise as one develops a biceps muscle. Do you seriously think that *because* you have made a schoolboy grow pale with doing Latin prose, that this same boy, when he is grown up, will be the better able to resist the temptations of life, will conduct himself better, will show more civic courage . . . ? No, certainly not; school ineptitudes have not these virtues. If we look around, we find quite the contrary: we find men suffering from nervous break-down in consequence of having made too great efforts; and we see others capable at any given moment of surmounting enormous difficulties, because they must, although nothing whatever in their manner of life has previously habituated them to such a display of energy.[1]

If apprenticeship in effort-making is not the uniform result of the discipline imposed by the school, it is nevertheless certain that, for the greater part of the scholars, study means effort: children are taught *by means of* effort. The idea of work also implies the idea of difficulties to be overcome. But it does not follow from this circumstance that play should not be the root-principle in education and instruction. On the contrary, it is only when effort is solicited under cover of play that it will be executed in an efficient manner, and that the effort-maker will derive the

[1] This is not the place to expatiate on what the teaching of effort should be. We will only remark that if the moral gain were proportionate to the painful effort demanded in the course of study, a much more highly developed morality ought to be found among the unintelligent than among the intelligent, since the unintelligent have had much more trouble than others in following the school curriculum. And further one would arrive at the amazing conclusion that it is advantageous in the education of character and of will to be a simpleton! All this has not convinced my excellent friend Professor P. Bovet; in the *Journal de Genève* of 17th July 1909 he regrets that I have not "based on facts" this affirmation that aptitude for effort does not develop, like the biceps, by exercise. That is, I know, a point of capital importance, which deserves to be thoroughly threshed out, and which the limits of this book will not permit; I hope to return to it elsewhere. I should, however, like to draw the attention of Prof. Bovet, and of many others who doubtless agree with him, to the following questions: If the exercise of effort suffices *in itself* (inasmuch as it is exercise) to develop the aptitude for effort, how can it be accounted for that so many young men, who, having been subject all through their youth to strict and severe paternal discipline, to which they submitted without resistance, sow their wild oats as soon as they reach their majority, and suddenly show an absolute incapacity for applying themselves to continuous work? Another question: Why, if the method of

satisfaction to which he is entitled. It follows that, far from being decreased, the effort which a difficult piece of work requires will be all the more vigorously and victoriously carried out if the work assumes the psychological characteristics of play.[1] This is quite easy to understand.

Let us ask ourselves under what circumstances we make efforts. We make an effort when work is difficult or painful, and when it is necessary to rivet our attention upon it, because our attention has an inclination to wander. It is precisely this compulsion of a volatile attention when it tends to wander which constitutes effort. Why does our attention want to wander? Is it not possible for attention to remain fixed on an object? Certainly; when we are at the

drudgery has had such good results, is there such an outcry on all sides at the failures of the schools, which certainly have not failed to make abundant use of this method? Third question. Is there not a kind of opposition between the idea of exercise and that of effort? When you try to do something which, to begin with, gave you a great deal of trouble, the thing becomes more and more easy, thanks to habit; that is, by exercise one develops habit, not effort. Even if the exercise has to do with different kinds of work, certain general habits may be developed (sitting at one's table, shutting oneself up, using tools, &c.) which diminish the effort required. Is not the mistake of attributing to the development of an effort-making power that which proceeds simply from a diminution in the resistance to be overcome, the source of the belief in development of effort by exercise? A fourth question: If the fact of development by exercise of an aptitude for effort-making can be demonstrated, would it not be incumbent on those who arrogate to themselves the right to apply to the child, of set purpose, the method of coercion and *ennui*, to furnish this demonstration themselves?

[1] Think for a moment of the really considerable work and persevering effort accomplished by the little child when it is learning to talk; the fact that this work and this effort constantly assume a playful character does not in any way injuriously affect the success of the result. (See p. 178.)

circus, for example, we can watch for a long time consecutively the acrobat or circus-rider. If, when engaged upon difficult work, attention refuses its services, it is because attention is induced to behave thus by the general wants of the organism, which is so made that it protects itself against fatigue. Our organism is a good fat animal which has never been able to understand how it is that the mind should exhaust itself in trying to solve difficult abstract questions, or by undertaking other tasks of which it does not itself feel the immediate need. Its only care is to preserve itself in perfect health. Thus, as soon as the Mind sets to work upon a task after its kind, that is, some work without apparent utility, the Animal does all it can to put a stop to it, for this prolonged intellectual work is going to use up its cerebral cellules. Its way of putting a stop to it is by bringing into action its defensive reflexes, of which it pulls the wires. These reflexes are at first momentary inhibition, or the turning aside of attention, weariness, disgust, then fatigue, and finally sleep. It is against such reflexes that the working mind has to fight. And the feeling of conflict between the interests of mind and those of the animal is precisely this feeling of effort.

What must be done so that mind may be victorious, so that effort may be efficient ? It must do what always has to be done in order to be victorious : be stronger than the enemy. The superior interest of mind must be stronger than the limited interest of the organism. If my interest is strong enough to enable me to take my attention by the collar and put its nose to the grindstone of my work, for me to despise fatigue and even sleep, then I shall get to the end of my task, and I shall be rewarded for my effort.

Let us return to the child. You wish him to make an effort. For this, as we have just seen, three conditions are necessary: a difficult piece of work, defensive reflexes which will divert him from this work, and a superior interest which will make him capable of definitely triumphing over them. How are these conditions, or at least how is the third, to be realised—for, as to painful work, you, schoolmasters, will undertake without any help to supply him with that, and with defensive reflexes he is already armed to the teeth? But what must be done in order that the mind may not be immediately floored or put to flight by these defensive weapons, in order that it may be able to maintain the struggle for one instant (of effort-making) and, if possible, gain the victory? You will succeed if you can arouse in the soul of the child an interest sufficiently powerful to hold in check the antagonistic reflexes of which we have just spoken.

Interest! One always returns to that in whatever way one may be treating the problem of education. But what sort of interest can be aroused in the soul of the child? One alone: the play interest, for one might define a child as a being who is interested in nothing but play, who is captivated by nothing but that which will bring about his development in conformity with natural evolution. It will only be by enlisting for work the joyousness and attractiveness of play that we shall succeed in retaining the attention of the child and of giving him the psychological strength necessary for the accomplishment of his task.

But here the adversaries of attractive education will return to the attack, crying out that they too stimulate the interest of scholars in that they punish them if they do not do their duty. Is not the interest in not being molested one of the most powerful to which recourse can be had ?

This objection is specious. Observation shows, as a fact, that the value and fertility of work are in direct proportion to its intrinsic interest. By substituting for this intrinsic interest an extrinsic interest (like that of avoiding punishment) one cuts off the spontaneous assistance of the mind; for, not having created in mind any desire for knowledge that the accomplishment of work might satisfy, one has not set in motion any of the mental processes specially adapted for securing its accomplishment. This inferior form of work is what is called *drudgery*. Drudgery, since it does not respond to any need in our nature, repels us, as a meal repels us when we are not hungry; also it sets in motion a crowd of defensive reflexes (disgust, inattention, &c.) which, to begin with, have to be kept in check, and this entails expenditure of energy without any effective work to show for it. Drudgery is therefore particularly exhausting and discouraging, since for a minimum of work it exacts a maximum of energy.

The more interesting a difficult piece of work is in itself, the less it arouses defensive reflexes which would have to be subdued. If the interest be complete no defensive reflexes at all will be aroused: the only opposition to be overcome will be the purely passive resistance inherent in all "work," the resistance of nervous matter against that modification to which even the pursuit of a desired end tends to give rise. The fact is that when interest is complete the pursuit of the object of interest responds to an immediate want. And the Animal of which we spoke just now, whose incentive is always the gratification of an immediate want, ceases to act as policeman and becomes an ally of Mind by giving up to it the energy it requires.

But it is precisely in play that this superior form of work is realised, and in which interest depends quite as much on the means used as on the end pursued.[1]

Let us suppose, however, that by some sufficiently imposing disciplinary artifice, one has succeeded in making a pupil "swallow" a lesson which is for him entirely devoid of interest. Still one would not be at the end of the trouble, for the wearisome lesson is not only distinguished from attractive study by difficulty in absorption, but also by impossibility of assimilation; for the mind, like the body, refuses to assimilate and to make part of itself what is repugnant to it.

One could not form a better idea of what drudgery is in relation to normal work than by comparing a meal which one forces oneself to swallow to please one's host—a drudgery-meal—with a meal eaten with appetite. If you do not like oysters, and you were to find yourself obliged to eat them, you know what trouble you would have to cause the viscous mass to make its way through the isthmus of the throat. All the defensive reflexes are set up and do all they

[1] Let it be clearly understood that the word "play" is here used in its widest sense, and that it is not synonymous with "amusement." The dictionaries, it is true, do not make any great difference between play and amusement, which they define the one by the other, or which are both made synonymous with diversion; but it is necessary to make a distinction between the two ideas: "amusement" implies ease and passivity, while "play" is essentially active

can to make the repugnant food take the contrary route to that which indirect interest wishes to make it continue to take. At last you find yourself the conqueror in this first struggle . . . but in appearance only, for as the mollusc does not stimulate the interest of the stomach (that is, its contractions, or the processes of gastric secretion adapted to its digestion), it will "lie on the stomach" and will very soon be returned intact to the light of day.

This drudgery-repast, whatever the virtue of the effort that it called forth, has profited nothing.

The intellectual meals that the school prepares for its young guests are subject to the same laws as other meals. They must be consumed with relish if they are to do good to those who eat them.

If it be once admitted that play and attractiveness *ought* to be the pivot of all education, we shall still have to find out exactly up to what point the realisation of this desideratum is *possible*. We agree that it is often difficult to give an attractive form to certain teaching. The difficulty arises from the fact that, with the human race, social evolution has proceeded much more quickly than the evolution of the individual; to such a degree is this true that the latter still possesses no instinctive desire to know and to do a number of things that the social necessities of a world (a so-called civilised world) oblige him to know and to do. If the kitten is consumed with the desire to leap upon everything which resembles a mouse, the little boy, on the contrary, does not feel the least desire to know the affluents of the Yangtse-kiang or the ports of Chili. It may well be, it is true, that the dose of these subjects, which do not respond to any natural interest, might be considerably diminished. But I will not here enter upon a discussion of this kind. It is a fact that many things ought to be learnt although they are devoid of immediate interest, because later on one will want to know them (the multiplication table, for example, spelling, or reading). Can the study of these things be a game? Not directly, perhaps, but indirectly. These different studies can be associated with the natural interests of a child, and thus an attractiveness they do not possess may be transmitted to them. In some cases this might be difficult; that is just where the educator's skill would come in. I cannot here touch on a question of pure application.

This necessity for making education and instruction attractive has been emphasised by all pedagogues worthy of the name; [1] but it is still entirely misunder-

[1] It suffices to mention the names of Fénelon, Rousseau, Pestalozzi, Herbart, Spencer. "Notice a great defect in ordinary systems of education," said Fénelon; "all the pleasure is put on one side and all the trouble on the other; all the trouble into study, all the pleasure into amusement . . . Let us try to change this order: let us make school pleasant; let us hide it under an appearance of liberty and pleasure" (*De l'éducation des filles*). "What must we think of a barbarous method of education which sacrifices the present to an uncertain future, which loads a child with chains of all kinds, and makes him miserable to begin with in order to prepare him later for I do not know what pretended happiness? . . . Love childhood, encourage its games, its pleasures, its lovableness," cried Jean-Jacques (*Emile*, Bk. II.). Herbart has made interest the centre of pedagogy. Quite recently W. James (*Talks to Teachers*) has reminded us how much it would be to the advantage of the teacher to ally himself with the interests of the child. K. Groos declares that work which assumes certain playful characteristics, that is, work with which is associated the joy of creating and the pleasure of overcoming difficulty, is "the highest and the most noble form of work" (*Play of Man*, p. 400). And a mathematician, Laisant, in his little work *L'initiation mathématique*

stood in the everyday practice of schools. The present school system ought, in this respect, to be revolutionised from top to bottom, in accordance, by the way, with the desire of many parents, who tacitly support the above-mentioned idea by their unconsidered demands about what it is "worth while" their children should know, if "knowledge" must be acquired under conditions which absolutely nullify assimilation.[1]

(Geneva and Paris, 1906), has given excellent examples of the way in which pupils can be interested in arithmetical problems, simply by formulating them in a picturesque fashion. "Above all," says this author, "set yourself to interest and amuse the child, do not oblige him to learn anything by heart. . . . Let the play periods—they should not be called lessons—never be prolonged beyond the time when attention flags, or curiosity ceases. . . . We will make a pedagogical use of amusing questions, to arouse the curiosity of the child, and thus succeed in getting into his mind, without effort imposed from without, the most essential elementary ideas." "Our schools," adds another mathematician, "might be a place of pleasure. Let people say this to themselves: When the school ceases to be attractive to the child, *it is always the school that is in the wrong*" (Camescasse, *L'initiateur mathématique*, Paris, 1910).

It is interesting to oppose to these smiling declarations the following mournful recommendation which Brunetière made to a College Principal: "You must not give your scholars to understand that the hours of study and rest will be arranged in such a way that work may seem to be amusement. Instruction is not amusement!" (letter published by the *Débats*, 20th July 1903). Villeneuve, from whom I borrow the following quotation, comments thus upon it: "Though the effort which brain development demands, occasionally but rather rarely affects the rhythm of hilarity, it (brain development) might become a joy if wisely conducted. . . . It is amid shouts of laughter that a baby learns from its mother to name familiar objects, and, in spite of M. Brunetière's sermons, we see no danger in mixing a few chocolate letters with the infant's first alphabet" (*L'ennui scolaire*, L'Hygiène scolaire, Jan. 1904).

[1] "If your schools really achieved their purpose," wrote a Geneva pedagogue, who died prematurely—A. Tschumi—"pupils would leave school with a desire to learn. Their memory would be less loaded with useless things, their knowledge would be less frag-

The chief mistake which people make when insisting that the child should make efforts from the pure love of duty, or from genuine respect to abstract discipline, is to forget that the child is not a man, and that in place of the scale of values which prevails amongst adults he has a corresponding scale of other values of his own The manifold values which have to do with the necessities of social and industrial life, with the moral or æsthetic side of activity, with the ideal of truth or of science, with moral, social, or economic obligation—these do not exist for him, and ought not to exist for him. One simple and only function replaces them all : this is play. With the child play is work, is good, is duty, is the ideal of life. Play is the only atmosphere in which his psychological being can breathe and, consequently, act

It is true that by coercion one can obtain from certain very docile scholars some school successes. But see what comes of it later ! Tired out, disgusted, without initiative, incapable of energetic action, the unhappy beings never succeed in being men because they have never been children

By exacting from the child work-efforts founded on anything else than play, one is behaving like the imbecile who shook an apple-tree in spring to make it give him apples ; far from getting apples, he wholly deprived himself of them by shaking down the very blossoms which should have produced the autumn fruit.

mentary, and they would not carry away with them into life that feeling of satiety and of disgust which they get from most schools. . . . Pedagogy ought to become entirely experimental and to be based on numerous observations." (*Revue de Genève*, Dec. 1886)

6. Psycho-Biological Conception of Interest

We have spoken again and again of *interest* as an important factor in directing mental tendency to one end or another, and we shall still often have to allude to it. Before going further it would not be unprofitable, therefore, to understand clearly the meaning of the term, of which the use is somewhat elastic.

We say that something is interesting if it is important to us at the moment when we are considering it, if it responds to a physical or intellectual *want:* food is interesting to a starving man because it is important to him to possess it; a rare flower interests the botanist because it is important to him to know it, &c.

The word "interest" expresses an adequate correspondence, a relation of reciprocal convenience between the subject and the object. An object is never in itself interesting; it always derives its interest from the psycho-physiological disposition of the subject who considers it: indeed, an object never interests unless the subject is disposed to be interested by the object; and further, the subject never feels any interest in the presence of an object unless this object means something to him. It follows from this duality of the factors implied by the phenomenon of interest that this term can be applied equally to the object which interests and to the psychic state aroused in the subject by the object which is important to him. One may either say, "Botany has great interest for Paul," or "Paul takes great interest in botany." The latter is *psychological interest*, and its corresponding objective should be called the *interest-object.*

But usage admits of other and different extensions of the word "interest." There is, to begin with, an objective extension of it: interest is made an abstract quality, an attribute in things which are interesting, *e.g.* "Botany is full of interest." This might be called the *interest-attribute.*

Also there are two subjective extensions: Sometimes one applies interest to the subjective *cause* of interest, that is, the want to be supplied (a want which may exist in the absence of the object fitted for its satisfaction); "Paul does not find anything to satisfy his interest." Sometimes the name "interest" is applied to the subjective *effect*, attention, activity, *e.g.* "This flower monopolises Paul's interest (attention)," "Botany is his sole interest (occupation)." These are special ways of looking at the psychological interest.

Finally, the word "interest" is also used in the utilitarian sense of profit or gain, as when one says, for example, "It is to the interest of Paul to study botany." That is the vital and practical sense of the word "interest." In this case one might speak of *biological interest.* Biological interest is that which is useful to the being from the point of view of his preservation, or the development of his personality.

A *viable* being (a creature capable of living) is by definition a being who reacts every moment in such a way that this reaction is useful to the maintenance of his existence (since if it were not so he would die). That is the same as saying that *to live is, for a being, to act at every moment along the line of his greatest interest.* Interest here is to be understood in its utilitarian or in its teleological sense, that is, biological interest. Biological interest is therefore implied in the idea of life.[1]

Interest-object, psychological interest, interest-attribute, practical or biological interest—these are many interests! That is true, but this plurality is not inconvenient, for all these words relate in reality to one psycho-biological phenomenon. These expressions differ according to whether, in thought, the interest centres in the object or in the subject, but they are in reality absolutely equivalent; to say, "This flower is an interest for me," or "This flower has an interest for me"; or, again, "I take an interest in this flower," "It is to my interest to consider this flower," is to state *one and the same fact*.

A few words must, however, be said to explain a little difficulty about this statement as to the equivalence of these different interests.

Does the psychological interest always correspond to the biological interest? In other words, is that which really interests us, which holds us enthralled, always that which *ought* to interest us from the point of view of our preservation, from the biological point of view?

Among animals the psychological interest always coincides with the biological interest, that is, animals are always interested in that which it is to their advantage to be interested in, and they are not attracted by that which might harm them. But we must recognise that, for man, this is not always the

[1] It is interest thus understood which is the spring of all our actions, of all our thoughts, which gives them an orientation adapted to the necessities of the moment. Every instant it is interest which determines the kind of reaction; I have proposed calling this fundamental biological fact "*the law of momentary interest*" (Arch. de Psychol. IV., 1905, p. 280).

case: he is often interested in that which is not advantageous to him; often, too, he is not interested in that which would be profitable to him. To quote one example only, the drunkard has a love for alcohol, the absorption of which is nevertheless directly contrary to his personal biological interest and to that of his race.

This abnormal divorce of the psychological and the biological interests arises from the partial deterioration of instinct in man, a deterioration for which reason and acquired experience are called upon to atone. As the result of this circumstance, little by little a divergence has been created between the psychological and the biological interests. But it is evident that this divergence cannot increase very much, for those who act against their interest, that is, who are (psychologically) interested in that which is not to their interest (biologically), are very quickly eliminated. The families of drunkards, for instance, soon become extinct. This auto-elimination of those who show an aberration from the psychological interest, or an inversion of it, ensures and maintains a nearly perfect agreement between the biological and psychological interests. So in the following pages we shall consider these two aspects of interest as equivalent; this equivalence is the rule in the case of the normal individual, if one considers as normal the individual whose acts tend to the preservation of his species.[1]

[1] With man, in consequence of the development of his intellectual and social life, the system of interests is very complicated. There are many degrees of interests which are not always in harmony with each other. Also, an act which may satisfy an interest of one kind may be contrary to an interest of another kind, *e g.* the tortures to which a woman submits in order to be in the fashion. The European woman by squeezing herself in corsets, and the Chinese

Once it is recognised that, with mankind as with animals, it is interest which decides what act shall be accomplished at a given moment, there still remains the question by what mechanism this wonderful adjustment can be carried out. As a matter of fact, at every moment an organism is exposed to a considerable number of excitations, and its reactionary possibilities are multiple. How is the organism going to make its choice, its selection of the most suitable reaction?

Old-fashioned psychology settled the difficulty by placing in the individual an entity (Soul, Ego, Will, Apperception) which had just this "faculty" of choice, of decision. But that does not solve the problem; it simply avoids it by substituting a word for an explanation.[1]

In order to explain this process of choice, we must not attribute the power to one special faculty, but we must show how choice results from the given circumstances at the moment when the decision occurs. These circumstances are in the main the following: there is a need to be satisfied, and an object (per-

woman by crushing her foot, act according to their immediate biological interest, which is to conform to custom, to harmonise with what the taste of the time considers beautiful. But they are acting at the same time against their more remote biological interest, which is not to injure their health by compressing or mutilating necessary organs. It need scarcely be stated that in a community absolutely normal, and conscious of what is good and what is bad for itself, all these individual interests, social and racial, would harmonise, so that, by satisfying one, others would be satisfied at the same time.

[1] In contemporary psychology, the "Centre O" of M. Grasset is an entity of this kind. But if this Centre O is useful in indicating the place, so to speak, of the reflective and volitional activity, yet it gives no account of it, in spite of the anatomo-physiological aspect of its name.

ceived or represented) capable of satisfying it. These circumstances concur in giving rise to the reaction adapted to this object. The choice as to which reaction shall take place among the thousand reactions possible at any given moment is the resultant of the above-mentioned need and of the perception (or representation) of an object adapted to its satisfaction.

Suitable choice ("choix adapté," *i e.* a decision that harmonises with the well-being of the organism) is a process of the reflex-action type. It is not some mysterious power that chooses, but it is the want and the object combined which together effect the selection of the reaction most appropriate to the organism. One can conceive how this process of choice is carried out in a purely mechanical fashion; we all know "the penny in the slot" automatic distributers of chocolate, which are so constructed that they bring out a tablet of chocolate when they contain one, and return the coin when they are empty. Our organism is similar to this apparatus, with this difference, that instead of having been made all at once, its interior works have been fashioned little by little by the experience of preceding generations, by heredity and by selection.

Let us now try to picture to ourselves how this physiological mechanism can be worked, by virtue of which only those stimuli which correspond to the interest of the moment are permitted to set up a reaction, while those stimuli which awaken no interest remain a dead letter for the organism.

Let us suppose that there is in the organism a large reservoir of energy, the function of which is to irrigate with energy and to bring into play useful reactions. This reservoir is furnished with a number of taps, each of which controls the irrigating pipe of a special reaction, so that when one of these taps is open the energising force carried through the pipe will start the reaction which depends on the opening of this particular tap. Each tap is provided with a lock, and the key is the stimulus or exciting cause. In a viable organism it is evident that the tap would not be capable of being opened unless the reaction it controlled were of use to the organism. To ensure this, the opening of each tap would depend not only on the stimulus but also on the need of the moment. These double dependences would be realised if the lock of each tap were provided with a keyhole which varied in its shape according to the wants of the organism, so that each tap could only be turned by a key which fitted the keyhole (that is, by the stimulus corresponding to the need of the moment). By this arrangement a key (a stimulus) would only be able to turn on the tap of a certain reaction if the turning on of the tap by this key were for the good of the organism—and consequently the dynamogenisation of useful reactions would take place only in conformity with the well-being of the organism.[1]

This is a very rough outline! It appears to date from the time of Descartes, who, in order to explain reactions, introduced little pipes running all over the body. But the physiology of to-day hardly permits of any more exact metaphor. And it may be said that things do go on *as if* this reservoir, these taps,

[1] In some previous works I gave the name of "reaction of interest" to this process of opening the tap of energy, of dynamogenisation by that particular stimulus which has a right to excite reaction because it is in touch with present interest.

and these locks, with their variable, changeable key-holes, really existed. The exact way in which these arrangements are made in the nervous system matters little to us psychologists. What is most important here is to convince ourselves that the selection of a reaction can be carried out mechanically by the stimulus, under the influence of interest.

7. Evolution of Interests

Interest is a symptom of want; in children it is a symptom of some want connected with the growth of mind or body. In fact, the objects or actions which arouse sympathy in a child vary with his development. How does this progressive variation of interest proceed? or, in other words, what is the evolution of interests? This is evidently the question which the educator should put to himself, if he desires to work in accordance with nature, and to adapt the course of his teaching to the natural course of psychological evolution.

This problem admits of two kinds of solution: one may try to fix the *date* when each category of interests appears; or one may try to determine the *order* in which interests appear. The second question is the more important. By reason of the individual diversities in children, it would not be very profitable to fix the exact age when such and such interests appear; while, on the contrary, the order in which interests succeed each other exhibits remarkable constancy: it corresponds to the successive stages that the development of the being goes through in its inflexible course.

How is one to discover this order of the evolution of interests?

Two ways present themselves to us: the former,

the extrospective method, will consist in observing the *conduct* of the child, his activities and games, and in noting the variations which they undergo with age. From the nature of the activities one will be able to infer the interests which excited them, and from the interests one will infer the wants of each stage in development, since an object is only interesting to a child in so far as it responds to some want.[1]

A child's *works* may also be considered: his drawings, short stories, &c. Drawing is one of the most appropriate of all the means by which the child-soul reveals its preoccupations to us:[2] one child affects men, another engines or motor-cars, &c. One prefers to draw what he sees, another draws what he imagines. Apart from these individual preferences, the observation of a large number of drawings by children of all ages teaches us that children draw first of all human beings, then animals, and only later, plants and inanimate objects. Drawing shows us further what it is in any special object that strikes or does not strike a child, and how a certain detail in the external world attracts his attention more and more as he grows up. To take one example only: the neck is generally forgotten in the drawings of men made by the youngest children; under eight years of age the child rarely draws this part of the body (at six years of age, only 20 per cent.).[3] And this can easily be understood: what interest could this neutral and

[1] I am, of course, alluding now only to those interests which have a certain permanence, a certain duration, not to those interests which are essentially temporary, which respond to fleeting wants, such as eating when one is hungry, or sleeping when one is tired.

[2] *Cf.* Katzaroff, *Qu'est-ce que les enfants dessinent?* Ar. de Ps. IX., 1910, p. 125.

[3] Partridge, *Children's Drawings,* Stud in Educ., II., p. 167.

comparatively motionless part of the body have for a child, especially as in close proximity to it are parts which concentrate attention on themselves—the head, the arms, and the chest with its row of buttons?

Language, the reflection of inner life, furnishes information as to the evolution of a certain category of interest; every advance in language arises from the fact that a new group of qualities, feelings, or ideas has aroused interest in the child: it may be interest in objects (substantives), in qualities (adjectives), in the tenses of verbs, in abstract words, in methods of expression.[1]

The other way open to us of discovering the interests of the child—and which is not practicable in the case of younger children—is **the introspective method**: children are questioned about their interests, their preferences, their wishes, their ideals. This procedure can give no tangible results unless it is applied to a number of children. For example, the pupils in a class might be asked to answer in writing the following question: "*What person whom you know or have ever heard or read of would you most like to resemble?*" That was the question put by Miss Darrah, the first author who undertook a study of this kind (in 1898).[2]

[1] Conradi, *Children's Interest in Words*, Ped. Sem. X., p. 359; Stern, *Die Kindersprache*, Leipsic, 1907.

[2] Darrah, *A Study of Children's Ideals*, Pop. Science Monthly 1898. See also Vostrovsky, *A Study of Children's Reading Tastes*, Ped. Sem., 1899; Taylor, Wissler, ibid., 1898; Earl Barnes, ibid., 1900, and Studies in Ed., vol. ii; Goddard, Ped. Sem., 1906; Varendonck, *Les idéals d'enfants*, Ar. de Ps VII, 1908; Friedrich, *Die Ideale der Kinder*, Z. pad. Ps., 1901; Lobsien, *Kinderideale*, Z. pad. Ps., 1903; Stern, ibid, 1905, Wiederkehr, *Statist. Untersuch. uber die Art und den Grad des Interesses bei Kindern der Volkschule*, Neue Bahnen, 1908 (*cf.* Keller's review of same, Z. ang. Ps. III., 97).

The question might also be stated thus: "*Who would you like to be? And why?*" as was done by Friedrich in 1901. Or again: *What lesson or branch of study do you prefer? Which is your favourite book? the game you like best?* &c. One must not forget to ask children to give reasons for their choice or preference; that is a very important point.

This kind of inquiry, very easy to initiate, brings to the educator a quantity of useful and often unexpected information, and is capable of suggesting ideas very fertile in results for his practical work.

We cannot here give the detailed results obtained by procedure of this kind. We will only add just a few words about the chief stages in the evolution of interests.

Every one who has taken up the subject of childhood has been led to subdivide it into a certain number of periods. It seems at first sight as if it might be chimerical, or at least very arbitrary, to wish to cut up into distinct periods anything so continuous and insensibly progressive as an unfolding life. But let us not forget that development proceeds by leaps and bounds, as we have already seen. The main stages into which authors divide psychological evolution correspond on the whole with the various stages in physical growth, such as are shown in the chart on p. 105.

Here, for example, is Stumpf's [1] subdivision:

1st period, from birth to the appearance of language;

2nd period, from the appearance of language to the school age;

3rd period, from the school age to adolescence;

4th period, adolescence itself.

[1] Stumpf, Z. päd. P. II., p. 2.

However justifiable this division into periods may be, periods which, as Stumpf says, present each "its own particular problems and difficulties," it still remains to be determined what it is that characterises each from the point of view of psychology, that is, what is the great interest that culminates during the course of each, and what is the fundamental motive of the corresponding activities?

The physiologist Sigismund has described the first stages in mental development by means of the principal activities which they exhibit, and he has given them some charming names: stages of the *Saugling* (suckling), *Sehling* (seer), *Greifling* (grasper), *Laufling* (trotter), and lastly of the *Sprechling* (chatterer). Sucking, looking at things, taking hold of them and handling them, walking, then trying to speak—those are in reality the great leaders in the way of interest which successively direct the baby's activity during the first two or three years of existence. But afterwards?

Afterwards interests diverge and multiply. Different functions develop along parallel lines, and I think we should be unduly forcing things if we tried to arrange one after the other, in order of time, the periods during which each of these functions monopolises the activity of the child. But always, in spite of this parallelism in development, there is a culminating point in the reign of each interest during which that interest often predominates over, if it does not eclipse, all other contemporary interests. The following is *a rough sketch* of the order of succession of the main classes of interests, based solely on their periods of predominance.[1]

[1] The ages indicated in this table are obviously approximate only, on account of the great individual diversities; ages are men-

I. Stage of Acquisition and Experimentation

1. Period of perceptive interest, during the first year.
2. Period of glossic interest (Gr. *glossa*, tongue), during the second and third years.
3. Period of general interests; intellectual awaking (questioning age); from three to seven years.
4. Period of special and objective interests, from seven to twelve years.

II. Stage of Organisation and Valuation

5. Period of sentiment; ethical and social interests; specialised interests; sexual interests; from twelve to eighteen years and after.

III. Stage of Production

6. Period of work. The various interests are themselves subordinated to a superior interest; it may be an ideal, or simply the interest of personal preservation, and in reference to this they are simply a means to an end. Adult age.

If we try to deduce the general law which governs the succession of interests, the guiding lines of their evolution, we shall observe that this progression is :—

from the simple to the complex ;
from the concrete to the abstract ;

tioned only for the sake of making more definite the idea we wish to convey.

A Hungarian author classifies the different stages in the evolution of interests as follows: (1) *Sensorial* interest, from 0 to 2 years. (2) *Subjective* interest, from 2 to 7 years. (3) *Objective* interest, from 7 to 10 years. (4) *Specialised* interest (permanent, "beständig"), from 10 to 15 years (5) *Logical* interest, after 15 years. (*Die Entwicklung des Interesses*, Z. exp. Päd. V., 1907.)

from passive receptivity to spontaneity ;

from indetermination to specialisation (this means that, to begin with, various objects are interesting only inasmuch as they give rise to the play of general functions—feeling, adapting a movement, seeking for the cause or the "wherefore"—while later, interest specialises in certain objects, certain occupations, certain problems) ;

from subjectivity to objectivity (understanding by these terms that at first objects are interesting only in so far as they are a pretext for bringing functional activities into play, and that later only are they considered for their own sake) ;

from the immediate to the mediate in space and in time (at first there is interest only in the immediate environment, and in the present ; later on the distant, the past, and above all the future, in turn insist on their share in interest).

To enter into the details that the examination of these different evolutionary periods would admit of would exceed the limits of this paragraph. Nevertheless a few words may be said about each :—

1. **The Period of Perceptive Interest.**—In early days we see the child interested in everything which strikes his senses : he watches attentively the curtain of his cradle, the shadow which flickers on the ceiling, &c. He also takes interest in his own movements in so far as they help him to reach the objects around him. In short, this first period is characterised by interest in what is at hand, in the immediate surroundings, of which the child's body and limbs are a part, for he treats these as strange objects which he must learn to handle.

The interest of the baby is not concerned with

objects considered in themselves for their intrinsic interest, but with objects in that they are things upon which he can exercise motor adaptation. An object is for him simply something "suckable," "seeable," "followable with the eyes," "takeable," "touchable," "feelable," "tearable"—not a body made up of different component parts. Only much later will he distinguish these parts. At first the object is perceived *in toto* only. Perception, in fact, like all our mental activity, is controlled by interest; we perceive things in the way in which it matters most to us that we should perceive them at that particular moment. If we look at a tree, we shall see it differently according to whether we look at it from the point of view of one who is only taking a walk, or from the point of view of a botanist; in one case our vision will be spherical or integral, in the other it will be analytical. Perception is not analytic, unless we have some interest in analysing. And the child evidently has to begin with interest only in the object as a whole, considered as a coloured mass, more or less extended, more or less irregular in form, and which requires, in order to be seized or looked at, such or such movements of the head or arms. He must be indifferent to the details, as we are indifferent to the details of an engine or of a motor-car which we have to get out of the way of in order not to be run over.

This fact of "vision of the whole," of the perception of the general appearance of things, is so marked in children that it is worthy of a special name. I proposed elsewhere[1] to give it the name of *syn-*

[1] In my note *Exemple de perception syncrétique chez un enfant*, Ar. de Ps. VII, p. 195. See also the remarks on integral perception (*perception globale*) by Jonckheere, ibid. II., p. 296, and VII., p. 84.

cretism, by which term Renan designates that "first general, comprehensive, but obscure, inexact view," in which "all is heaped together without distinction," which is the first view of primitive man.[1] Let us remark in passing that this syncretic and *confused* perception is a fusion of the whole and has nothing in common with perception of the *complex*. We have said that the mind proceeds from the simple to the complex; the fact that the child sees the whole before perceiving its parts does not contradict this statement. For the child, the whole not being a collection of parts, but, on the contrary, a block, a unity, to go from the simple to the complex is to proceed from the whole to its part. This remark is important from the educational point of view: what is simple for us is not *ipso facto* simple for the child; let us beware of judging the perception of the child by our own adult standard, and let us not require him to proceed from the complex to the simple by treating subjects in an order which *for us* (who have gone through the work of analysis) proceeds from the simple to the complex.

This is the irrational mistake made in teaching reading. For the person who has grasped the mechanism of written language, the letter is undoubtedly more simple than the syllable, the syllable more simple than the word. But this is not at all the case with the child who sees the written text for the first time. For him the word, or even the sentence, makes a drawing the general appearance of which engages his attention much more than the drawing of isolated letters, which he does not distinguish from the whole word; so it is often an advantage to teach children

[1] Renan, *L'avenir de la science*, p 301.

to read by beginning with words in place of isolated letters.[1]

It is above all during the first year of life that this interest in the perceptible characteristics of objects, and in their external configuration, is predominant. Doubtless long after this the child will open wondering eyes at the things around him, but this perceptive interest will not be long in allying itself to other interests—the glossic interest, such as knowing the names of things; or the intellectual interest, such as knowing the why and wherefore of phenomena.

2. **Glossic Interests.**—With the second year springs up a new interest, which monopolises the mind of the child for a long time: interest in language and in words. Long before this the baby has given vent to a charming gurgling of syllables, but it is only towards the end of the tenth or twelfth month that he begins to attach some meaning to a few of them.

We shall not now speak of the beginnings of language and of the psychogenetic problems raised by them. We will only call attention to the pleasure that the child takes in carrying through the colossal task which confronts his feeble powers: learning to speak. There could be no better example of the

[1] This is the well-known method of Dr. Decroly. For details, see his articles published in collaboration with Mademoiselle Degand in the Rev. scient., March 10, 1906, and in the Ar. de Ps. VI., 1907. With intelligent children learning to read by the current method is so easy that it does not seem that there would be any advantage in introducing Decroly's system into ordinary teaching, especially if reading is not begun too early. But for backward children, or the mentally deficient, this system produces remarkable results, and makes children *take to* reading who otherwise dislike it. I have had opportunities myself for noticing with what facility an abnormal child succeeds in writing correctly from dictation whole words, such as "nest," "tree," &c., *of which, however, he may not know a single isolated letter.*

persevering effort a creature can make to accomplish a piece of work in which his interest is enlisted.

The brain is so made that, at a given moment in its development, it needs to fabricate or assimilate words, just as it needs to assimilate phosphates and to fabricate neurons. So we see the child bent on storing up words and expressions even if he does not understand their meaning. The word itself is for him sufficient explanation and justification. If, seeing on the table an unknown tool, he asks what it is, and is told "pincers," he is satisfied. His curiosity does not go beyond the name of the thing.

He loves the word for its own sake. To have learnt a new word is a delight to him. For a while this amounts to a veritable mania: he hunts for words; he makes a collection of them; when he finds a rare one he brings it home in triumph. He fills "his mouth"[1] with words, as later he will fill his pocket with everything he has picked up on the road. His instinct to collect displays itself first of all in collecting words.

Master Baby occasionally takes stock of what his "shop of words" contains. One can hear him in the morning, in his bed, unpacking his store. He repeats the words, puts them together, one after the other, making most delicious nonsense; he turns them this way and that, plays with them, and seems to find pleasure in the simple fact of possessing them and of jingling them—as the miser, shut up in his room, enjoys the tinkling of the crowns tumbling between his fingers.

[1] At four years of age, my little boy, who had been reproved for not having used the right word to designate some object, replied quite shamefacedly: "And I had chosen it so carefully from *the shop in my mouth.*"

The purpose of this sort of glossic[1] passion may easily be imagined. Just think of the great quantity of words and expressions which the child has to learn at an age when his voluntary attention is relatively weak, even if it exists, and when no system of logical classification could as yet help him with his stupendous task. The pleasure alone of the sound of hearing words stimulates him to remember those that he has heard pronounced, and to pronounce those that he has remembered, until they are definitely engraved on his memory.

The evolution of language comprises in itself quite a series of successive interests: at the outset the child makes use of substantives only, designating concrete objects; then verbs appear in his vocabulary, then conjunctions, then adjectives, then numerals, and then pronouns. This order (into the details of which I need not enter) is very constant. We wish to call attention to this constancy because it is of great theoretical importance; it is one of the most patent proofs of the strict connection between the different phases of mental development.

This order of succession is, moreover, independent of the age at which language may appear and of its mode of acquisition. Thus, in the case of Helen Keller, that celebrated and brave American blind-deaf-mute, the development of language took place in

[1] The word "glossic" seems to me preferable to "linguistic" for designating that which has to do with the psychological process involved in language. "Linguistic" really means "that which has to do with the *science* of language," and not with its acquisition. It is therefore incorrect to speak of "pre-linguistic babbling," as in Sully's *Studies of Childhood*; a chapter in this same book is entitled "The Little Linguist." But linguist is a name applied to one who studies language, not to some one who is learning to speak.

identically the same order as in that of a normal child, although she did not learn to speak till she was seven years old, and by means of touch.[1]

Pedagogy should make better use than it does of this natural aptitude for the acquisition of language which the child possesses. It is especially in the first years of school life that foreign languages ought to be taught (I am speaking of modern languages only). But they should be taught in the same fashion as the mother-tongue—by conversation.[2]

[1] But her progress was more rapid: she spent only seven months in going through the different stages, while the normal baby spends two years over it. See, on this evolutionary parallelism, Stern, *Helen Keller*, Berlin, 1905.

[2] A Belgian schoolmaster who conceals his name under the pseudonym of Eddy objects, in his *Causeries pédagogiques* (Ostend, p. 212), that "the mother-tongue should first be well known to children before they begin to study a second language, otherwise the whole of education may suffer." I confess I do not understand very clearly why this should be so. The acquisition of a language (I understand acquisition to mean the power to speak a language, not the knowledge of its linguistic curiosities) is a matter of habit, and not of reflection or reasoning; let us, then, take advantage of those years when the mind is not ready for logical work. Thus we should be in harmony with nature; and it would be so much to the good later on. There is ample illustration of the astonishing facility with which children who have had the chance of learning two or more languages in childhood have assimilated them, while those who have only learnt them by the ordinary school methods are incapable, in a foreign country, of asking merely for a railway-ticket without having recourse to a dictionary, and even then they cannot be understood because they do not know how to pronounce the words. Lacombe, in his *Esquisse d'un enseignement* (p. 117), demands that the study of language shall be relegated to the two latter years of school life, from 16 to 18 years. This author starts with the idea that a language can only be well learnt by passing six months in the country where it is spoken, it would therefore be useless to encumber the school with instruction which could be acquired without trouble in an out-of-school fashion. Doubtless this method would have its advantages; but we should be leaving the sphere of psychology if we were to discuss it here. All that

3. **General Intellectual Interests.**—Long before the time has passed away when the child cultivates the word for its own sake, a crowd of new interests invade his life. These interests are connected with all those things that set ideation and imaginative fancy at work. We spoke above of imagination in play, and shall not return to it.

Then appear in their turn interests which are essentially intellectual, and they soon predominate. The child is preoccupied with the relations of things, with their origin, their constitution. It is "the questioning age" of Sully, which begins with the third or fourth year. Every one knows how endless and how odd are the questions of children, which the mothers—and often also the fathers—find very hard to answer: "Why is the moon round? Why has the cat hairs on its nose?" &c.

It is true that, if this desire to know is imperious, it is also very easy to satisfy. A child, having asked his nurse, "Why are pavements hard?" and she having replied, "Because all pavements are hard," considers the thing explained. To explain is for the child, as for ourselves, to bring a particular case under a general rule, a law.

Most grown-ups are accustomed to consider these incessant questions as a sign of foolishness, of inquisitive curiosity, and to answer them frequently with a dry "Be quiet," or again with an ironical "Because." This is quite wrong; far from repressing this desire to know, it should be encouraged, for it is the fulcrum

psychology can say is that *if* one wishes to teach a language to a child at school, it is advantageous to place this teaching as early as possible, on condition, I repeat, that it shall take the form of free conversation.

upon which the lever of instruction should be placed. And without it no cultivation of mind is possible, as is seen in the case of idiots.

Childish curiosity should disappear from the list of vices, in order that it may be inscribed on the list of virtues.[1] In schools, the various subjects of instruction are often entered upon without the pupil having been shown to which of his "whys and wherefores" they will furnish an answer. This is a grave fault, which nevertheless can easily be remedied. *A lesson should be nothing else than an answer*, an answer which a child will welcome with enthusiasm if he has himself been led to formulate the questions to which it is a reply.

Among the questions asked by a young child, those which concern the uses of things preponderate. One can turn to account this utilitarian attitude of mind by getting a child to define objects. One will receive a number of answers of this kind: A knife "is to cut with," a horse "is for drawing carriages," &c. A pupil in a primary class said to me one day: A mother "is for getting dinner ready and washing up the plates." And a little girl questioned by Binet said: A snail "is for crushing."[2]

Parents or teacher might often exploit these utilitarian inclinations with a view to education. By showing a child the practical reason of an order, or prohibition, or lesson, given to him, one would over-

[1] Ribot (*Psychol. des sentiments*, 1896, p 360) describes three stages in the development of curiosity: (1) *surprise*, which is a shock, and which one notices from the fifth month; (2) *astonishment*, a more stable state than surprise; (3) lastly, *interrogation*. Stanley Hall and Smith have made a study of the first signs of curiosity in a child. Out of 465 questions asked by children, 75 per cent. had to do with the *cause* of things (*Curiosity and Interest*, Ped. Sem. X., 1903)

[2] Binet, *Perceptions d'enfants*, Rev. philos., 1890, II.

come without any trouble the instinctive resistance that he offers to the accomplishment of what, in his eyes, responds to no want.[1]

4. **Special Interests.**—When once the general psychic functions have developed, such as perception, adaptation of movement, expression of desire by language, measurement of space, seeking cause and purpose, then interest specialises, concentrates itself on certain objects, on certain occupations, on certain more definite problems. And so special instincts become one after the other the source of a child's play. In what order do these different interests appear ?

Many psychologists agree that the order is the same as that in which they appeared in the course of the development of the human race. According to this view, the life of each child would be only an accelerated and abridged recapitulation of the different phases through which its human ancestors have passed.

This idea of parallelism between the psychological development of the individual and that of the race is not new ; one meets with it in a more or less explicit form in the eighteenth century and at the beginning of the nineteenth, in the works of such writers as

[1] That pupils do really suffer from the ignorance in which they are kept with regard to the purpose and the utility of their studies is shown by the following words quoted from a pamphlet which I published on leaving College, and in which were expressed the impressions, at that time quite fresh in my mind, of my years of secondary studies: "Would it not be reasonable for a professor, in the first lessons, to give a logical analysis of the course, as well as some idea of the usefulness of the subject-matter he proposes to teach, either from a practical point of view, or from the point of view of intellectual development; to show what are the special points to be insisted on, either because they are of importance in themselves, or because they would be helpful in making other points intelligible ?" (*Quelques mots sur le Collége de Genève*, Geneva, 1892, p. 9).

Lessing and Herder, of poets such as Goethe, of philosophers such as Rousseau, Hegel, Aug. Comte, Spencer, and of the pedagogue Ziller, who have shown the important bearing of this parallelism on education. "Education must reproduce in miniature the history of civilisation," said Spencer; and Ziller expressed himself in the same fashion. This conception has been named the "Theory of civilisation epochs" (*kulturgeschichtliche Stufentheorie; Culture-epoch theory*). At the same time an analogous hypothesis was developing itself in the region of morphology and embryology: naturalists were also discovering striking resemblances between the successive forms through which the human embryo has passed and the forms which compose the animal series; this "recapitulation" of racial development by the individual, dimly perceived by the physiologist Harvey in 1628, then rediscovered in turn by G. St. Hilaire, Meckel, von Baer, Agassiz, Serres, was supported by the solid arguments of Fritz Müller in 1864, and raised by Haeckel to the dignity of a law, the **Fundamental biogenetic law**, expressed by the following celebrated formula: *ontogenesis = phylogenesis* (development of the individual = evolution of the race).

We cannot here examine in detail the strong and weak points of this theory, which in these latter days has been attacked by the embryologists themselves: it is a fact that this biogenetic law has a great many exceptions, and that the parallelism which it enunciates is only approximate. Thus, to take one example, there is exaggeration in affirming that the mammifer passes, when it is very young, through a fish stage, because even if it does possess for a while gill slits and a spinal cord like a fish, it has not at any time in its life the heart or the eye of a fish; on the other hand, one finds it in possession at this same epoch of a quantity of organs quite unknown among fish. Also, the child *is* not, at any age, psychically a "primitive man," or a "savage." The characteristic features (cruelty, nature worship, &c.) which these ancestors have bequeathed to us may be more evident in the child than in ourselves, but the mentality of the child never ceases to be *childish* mentality; while, if one interpreted the biogenetic law literally, the child would be successively a *man* of the stone age, then a *man* of the bronze age, &c., which is obviously not the case, since he has none of the adult characteristics which primitive man possessed, such as sexual instinct, courage, &c.

However, there are many phenomena which bear out the recapitulatory hypothesis, and which can hardly be explained without it. As, for example: Why have the embryo of certain fish teeth, when the perfected animal has none? Why is a tail of vertebræ formed in the horse, which retrogrades afterwards, and in the grown-up animal is nothing more than a tuft of hair? Finally, what is the meaning of those branchial arches which are so clearly traced in the human embryo? And in the realm of psychology, in what other way than by innate instinct can the liking for playing at Indians, for pursuit, for ruses

[1] Further, if the mentality of a young child recalls in certain respects that of an animal, the parallel must not be carried far; very quickly do the lines of interest followed by the child on the one hand and by the animal on the other diverge, as has been demonstrated in a striking fashion by the experiments of Katz and Révész on the memory of fowls compared with that of a baby (*Z. f Ps.*, vol. 50, 1908, p. 107; *cf.* also Shinn, *Notes on the Development of a Child*, p. 229).

and surprises, so general among children, be explained? Whence can come to them that passion for living in the open air, for climbing trees, for building houses, for digging caves and establishing themselves therein in improvised colonies, of paddling in streams, of making primitive weapons, and of parading on hobby-horses made of a simple stick? And is not the uniformity in these manifestations of child-life in all climates and latitudes most astonishing? There is more in this than imitation: imitation alone would not cause the child this joy which is the invariable symptom of the satisfaction of a vital instinct.[1] These facts, and many others, show that an incontestable parallelism exists between the evolution of the race and that of the individual.[2]

But what is the fundamental reason for this parallelism? Two theories offer themselves: some there are who think that this likeness arises from a genuine *repetition* by new generations of the phases that former generations passed through—this repetition being an effect of heredity; others hold that this likeness is nothing more than simple *conformity*: if the development of the individual recalls the de-

[1] Ferrièro, *La loi biogénétique et l'éducation*, Ar. de Ps. IX., pp. 168, 173. In a work entitled *Spontaneous Constructions and Primitive Activities of Children analogous to those of Primitive Man* (Amer. J. Ps., Jan. 1910), Acher describes the buildings children love to make out of sand, soil, snow, blocks of wood or stone; he also describes other activities, emphasising their analogy to those of primitive peoples. The author shows that imitation is not sufficient to account for the greater part of the activities. (The data for this study were provided by an inquiry made by Stanley Hall.)

[2] From the biogenetic law has been derived a method of investigation called the *comparative genetic method*, of which mention was made above, p. 85; the evolution of the race and of the individual, when compared, mutually elucidate each other.

velopment of the race, it is because living beings are all formed in accordance with regular laws, and nature employs identical means for effecting the evolution both of the individual and of the race.[1]

These two conceptions, far from being contradictory, ought not, it seems to me, to be separated; each mutually implies the other, for the development of an organism is assuredly under the influence of heredity. Nevertheless, it would be possible to adopt the first without the second, and to see in the onto-phylogenetic repetition nothing more than the simple echo of past forms, atavistic rudiments, which no longer play any part in the *actual* development of the individual, and only reappear from force of habit, as one might say. But this point of view would be untenable: for it is very evident that all these transitory organs, which last for a certain time in the embryo of vertebrates and are replaced by definite organs, have something to do with these latter, which they either engender or help to form. Their temporary presence is, indeed, to the building up of the organism what provisional scaffoldings are to the construction of a building.

In the same way, in the region of psychology, we have to look at these transitory stages in relation to their genetic-functional utility (see above, pp. 70 and 94). And if the child goes through certain stages which recall the animal, the savage, or barbarian, we should consider these stages as necessary to his ulterior evolution. As Tyler says, the barbaric period of childhood is a stimulus to the development of the

[1] In pædology, the former of these theories is represented by the school of Stanley Hall (see above, p. 122), the latter by the school of Dewey.

capacities of the adult, just as the dorsal cord of the embryo is a stimulus to the ulterior formation of the vertebral column.[1] In conclusion: One is justified in calling to one's aid the history of the primitive ages of humanity in order to understand the successive stages of progress in the child-mind, and in order to adapt to them the different steps in teaching.[2]

Certain authors,[3] however, hold that education has nothing to gain from the analogy between the child and his primitive ancestors, for the child, finding himself in quite different circumstances from the savage or the barbarian, ought to be immediately adapted to his actual circumstances, without its being necessary for him to trace again all the deviations and errors of the evolution of humanity. That is right to a certain extent; it is obvious that it is only *cum grano salis* that the biogenetic theory can be applied to practical education. When it is said that certain "savage" or "barbaric" impulses of the child should be allowed free expression, because it is useful to development, no one means that he must be taught to handle the boomerang, to hunt the bear, or worship idols. We must be careful, however, for it is quite possible that what seems to us and to our pedantic reasoning "deviations and errors" may be in reality the shortest way to the goal, because it is the way that nature herself has made—and it may possibly be the only practicable way. It may be a *détour* for the frog to pass through the tadpole stage; might it not

[1] Tyler, *Growth and Education*, Boston, 1907, p. 55.

[2] It is especially for the teaching of mathematics that people have been anxious to retrace the route that the human race has traversed; *cf.* notably Branford, *A Study of Mathematical Education*, Oxford, 1908, chap. v.

[3] Such as Lange, *Ueber Apperzeption*, 10 Aufl., Leipsic, 1909.

be simpler that the frog should be born with feet, and, above all, without that tail which is only "a *détour* and a mistake"! But this *détour* is no doubt necessary; you do not imagine that the formation of grown-up frogs would be much hastened by cutting off the tail of the tadpoles . . . which would probably be done if the frogs had schools!

But let us return to the evolution of special interests. W. Hutchinson describes four distinct periods in the evolution of the child, which recall the phases of the evolution of civilisation, and which are each marked by some characteristic interests: 1st, interests of the chase, of capture, and of war; 2nd, pastoral interests, by following which the child attempts to tame and train animals, and amuses himself by digging holes and by building huts; 3rd, agricultural interests, which show themselves in playing at gardening; 4th, and last, commercial interests, which lead to barter, the selling of objects of small value to realise profit.[1]

The truth is, we still stand in need of facts for establishing ever so uncertainly the scale of special interests. As we have said, each of them reigns for a rather long period, but only culminates during a relatively limited period. For a knowledge of this period of culmination the comparative method does not help us, and it is necessary to have recourse to the psycho-statistical method: we find out how many amongst a hundred children of each age have a given interest. We may thus describe the curve of the interest: the point of culmination of the curve will correspond to the age at which we most frequently come across the interest in question.

[1] Hutchinson, quoted from Varendonck, Ar. de Psy. VII., p. 381.

Let us take as an example the collecting interest, which has been dealt with before apropos of plays (p. 134). An author named Burk has shown that this interest increases up to the age of 10, and then decreases very gradually.[1] Or, again, doll play: the famous inquiry by Stanley Hall (of which we spoke in our Introduction, p. 6) has furnished, among other things, wha tis not lacking in interest, the curve of the evolution of doll play (among girls); it is from 7 to 10 years of age that the passion for dolls is greatest among the little Americans, and the apogee of the passion is found at 8½ years of age (see fig. 5).[2]

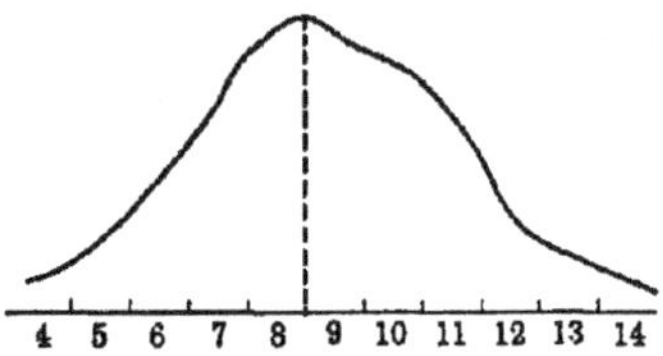

FIG. 5.—Curves of frequency, according to age, of playing with the doll. (After Ellis and Hall.)

Each interest, we have said, progresses on its own lines, in certain definite directions. Collecting, for example, which deals at first with objects indiscriminately, specialises gradually. The direction of the interest which it excites also changes; at first the child collects for the immediate pleasure of amassing and of possessing. Later it is in consequence of a more objective interest, and for a more remote end; it attaches a certain value to the things themselves.

If we observe play in general, this progressive

[1] Burk, Ped. Sem. VII.

[2] The diagram is unfortunately based upon only 98 observations. To secure the necessary information, the authors asked some women students in a normal school to indicate, according to what they remembered, the age at which their passion for the doll had been strongest (Ellis and Hall, *A Study of Dolls*, Ped. Sem. IV., 1896, p. 156). In the article by Croswell, *Amusements of Worcester School*, Ped. Sem IV., 1899, diagrams of the evolution of various plays are to be found.

specialisation is also found, and the constant movement from the concrete to the abstract, from the immediate to the mediate. At first all that comes into the hands of the child serves to amuse him; afterwards the plays are specialised, then concrete amusements, involving a toy, make room for amusements of an abstract nature.

This centrifugal progression of the mind continues

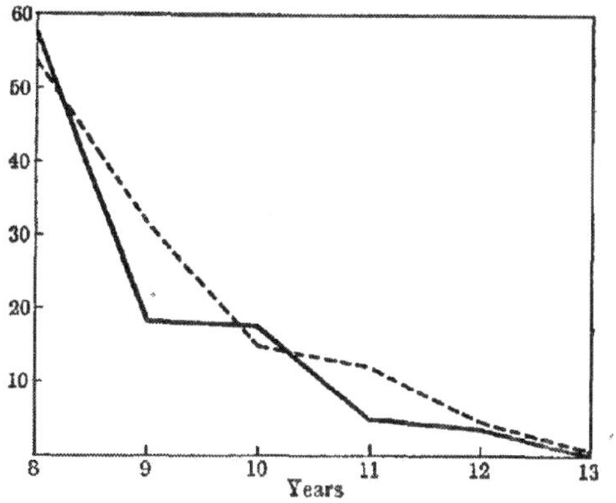

FIG. 6.—Diagram representing the variations in the choice of father and mother. Dotted line for boys, continuous line for girls. (After Varendonck, quoted above.)

to be met with, again in a very clear manner, in the answers which children give to questionnaires on their ideals. At the very first, it is the immediate intimates, parents, big brothers and sisters, who are chosen as "ideals" by the children who are asked, "What person would you wish to be like?" But parents quickly lose ground, as is seen by one of the diagrams, drawn up by Varendonck (fig. 6), and the ideal is found in a less immediate sphere: in contemporary celebrities, the heroes of history, or those in books (fig. 7).

If we make inquiries into the *reasons for the choice* of such or such an ideal, we find that young people are preoccupied above all with material possessions or pleasure; for example: "I should like to be like M. Paul, who is a veterinary for dogs; because I like that" (boy of 8). "I should like to be like Martha V., because she has lovely ear-rings" (little girl of 9). "I

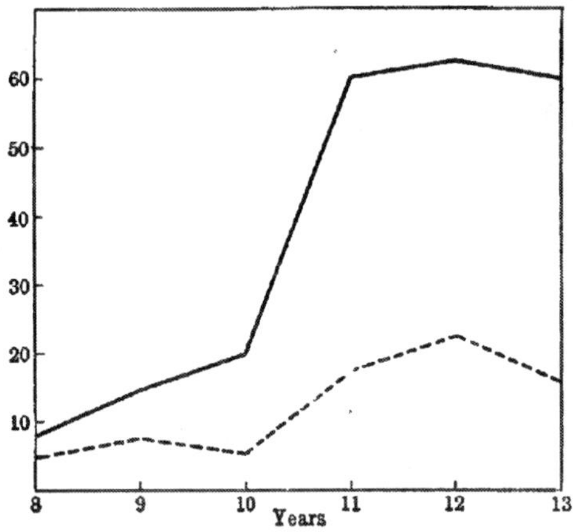

Fig. 7.—Diagram representing variations in the choice of historical or contemporary personages, and of authors.

should like to be like M. Rothschild, because he is a millionaire" (boy of 11).[1]

But very soon material considerations influence the

[1] These examples are taken from the work of Varendonck, already quoted. We may add this one, more interesting, however, from an economical and social point of view than from the purely psychological: "I should like to be like Marie V.," writes a little girl of 10, "because she has two woollen petticoats and I have only one. She works at a dressmaker's, and I have not had any work for five weeks." "Is not this a proof," justly remarks Varendonck, "that no high ideal can be attained when one is not provided with the necessities of life?"

N

choice of ideals less, above all among boys (girls, according to Varendonck, remain longer attached to them), and then it is the intellectual, æsthetic, or moral qualities which dictate the choice (fig. 8); and declarations of this kind are obtained: "What I should like to be, is to know how to write well like the great authors" (boy of 12). "I know a girl whom I admire very much. She has a heart of gold and helps poor people who are in want. . . . She is very kind to everybody. If she sees any one ill-treating an animal she weeps bitterly at the man's brutality" (girl of 12). "I should like to be like one of the good, charitable souls who help the unfortunate, rescuing them from misery" (boy of 15).

The way in which the interest for the different branches of study evolves has very great pedagogic importance. One cause of error to be avoided in this kind of inquiry is the fact that the pupils may detest a certain branch in spite of its intrinsic interest, simply because it is badly taught, or because a child has a personal dislike to the master in charge of it. It is necessary, therefore, to work upon a great number of scholars, belonging to different schools, or even in different towns, so as to be sure that the interest, or the lack of interest, for such and such a branch does not arise from accidental circumstances.

Researches of this kind—which every director of a school ought to repeat for himself—show that the branches preferred or disliked vary from one year to another. It is evident that if a study generally preferred at the age of 8 falls to the rank of those generally disliked at the age of 12, this proves either that the mind of the child is more apt in assimilating this branch at 8, or that the method employed later is bad, or that we have not followed, in teaching this branch, an order conforming to the natural development of the mind.

And, *vice versâ*, if a branch preferred later is disliked by the younger pupils, this indicates that its teaching is commenced too soon, or that it is badly presented. To give a single example, taken from the work of Stern: the religious lesson—which never appears anywhere among the branches preferred!—is found to be less detested by the older than by the younger pupils. Such a statement makes us suspect

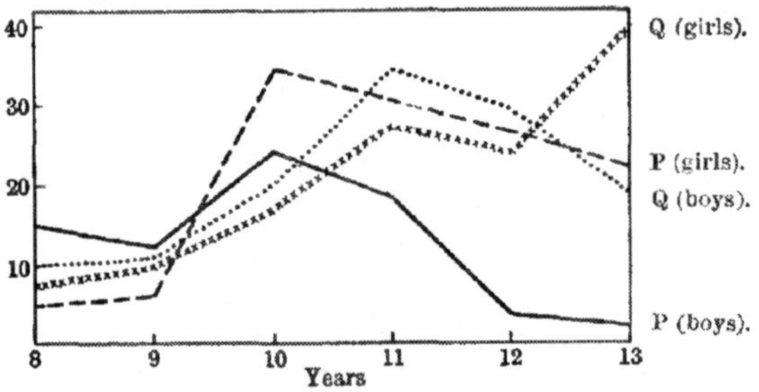

FIG. 8.—Variation in children's reasons for their choice. Q = intellectual qualities, P = material possessions.

that the way in which this lesson is given to classes of little ones in Germany is not in accordance with the degree of development which the pupils have then attained.

It is during this period, from about seven years, that interest commences to be objective. The child no longer acts for the pleasure of acting, but is interested in the concrete aim of its action, the *success* of its effort; that is to say, it consciously apprehends the relation between the means employed and the end to be attained. It is easy to understand all the advantage that pedagogy may derive from this propensity of the mind.

Lastly, interests vary according to *sex:* common with the little ones, they differentiate more and more with age. The running games and physical exercises, which persist among boys until the end of adolescence, rapidly decline amongst girls from about the eighth to the ninth years. On the other hand, they more and more prefer manual occupations.[1]

Psycho-statistical researches of the kind indicated above (inquiries concerning ideals, favourite readings, &c.) clearly bring to light the difference of interests of boys and girls, differences which stand out more prominently in proportion as the children advance in years. Thus, whilst boys prefer to read accounts of adventure, inventions, history, and science, the library of young girls is composed, above all, of purely imaginative narratives (myths, legends, novels), and especially of narrations concerning children.[2] Here is an example, simply by way of illustration, to show the great difference existing between the sexes: in his inquiry upon the reading matter preferred, Vostrovsky found that 76 per cent. of the boys, and 24 per cent. only of the girls, showed a taste for narratives of adventures; on the contrary, books in which children are the heroes are only liked by 12 per cent. of the boys, while they are liked by 52 per cent. of the girls In a word, as is said by Brittain, the interests of boys have pre-eminently a *dynamic* character, while those of girls have rather a *static* character.

Free drawing is a test which also reveals very marked differences in each sex. In looking through the

[1] Always excepting drawing, which is preferred by boys (see Ivanoff, *Le dessin des écoliers de la Suisse romande*, Ar. de Psy. VIII., p. 21).

[2] Vostrovsky: article quoted, Ped. Sem., 1899; Brittain, Smith, and Guillet, various articles in Ped. Sem., 1907.

drawings of more than 2500 children—drawings furnished by the collective experiment previously mentioned (p. 34), Katzaroff found that the boys, as compared with the girls, drew by preference animals, scenes of life, boats, railways, men on horseback, and bicycles; while the girls preferred to draw flowers, geometrical patterns, and various objects (furniture, utensils, &c.).[1]

Girls have a more lively and precocious sentimentality than boys; they show their feelings of friendship and affection in effusions which are often exaggerated. Boubier, having collected a certain number of "notes" which the pupils of a primary school had written to each other during lessons, remarks how clearly they show the profound psychological difference of the two sexes.[2] "As compared with the little girl, the little boy is not very fond of writing. As a rule he restricts himself to writing a few words under a caricature, so that its meaning may be better understood by the recipient. His notes, properly so-called, convey little more than a more or less trivial insult, some naughtiness more or less heinous, or a simple joke more or less witty. For example: 'Chaffinch, chaffinch, how are you? Tell me if you always sleep in your bed, or in the moon, or in the stars, or in the sun.' Another specimen, relating to a fat boy of the name of Grombal: 'The sea-mammal Grombal gives 150 kilogs. of sindon and 220 of cod-liver oil. A grombal weighs 370 kilogs. This animal was discovered in 1901 by the celebrated physician Dupen.' Dupen is another comrade

"As for the young girl, on the contrary," Boubier shows, "the note is her great preoccupation, her fixed

[1] Katzaroff, article quoted, Ar. de Psy. IX

[2] Boubier, *Les jeux de l'enfant pendant la classe*, Ar. de Psy. I, p. 56 and following

idea, in which she delights, because she is able to put into it all her mind, all her soul. As a rule there is not the least need of drawing to embellish what she writes, the words are everything. . . . She is more preoccupied with chatter and gossip, while war or politics already powerfully interest the boy to a high degree." Her epistles are often full of tender words, such as these. "I love you, I love you, I love you more than myself, more than myself; I love you more than myself." Or again: "Adieu, Helen, I am come to bring some eggs and I am come to say good-morning to you; adieu, my well-beloved."

We might notice other differences in interests according to age and sex, but these examples suffice to show in what way we can bring them to light, and to inspire teachers with the desire to enrich our knowledge of the subject.

5. **Social or Ethical Interests.**—The age of 12 is an important date in the history of the development of the child: it marks a turning, a changing of direction, of orientation. Unsuspected regions suddenly disclose themselves to his eyes; social consciousness awakes, and the axis of interests is changed.

At this age, the child, who until then has hardly concerned himself at all about the rôle which he was able to play in society, becomes conscious of his character as a member of a collective whole. He seeks to gain the esteem of certain persons, and becomes more sensitive to their influence. As, at this moment, his sensitiveness to the influence of others is still not tempered or governed by the critical spirit or any definite ethical ideal, the boy of 12 is particularly sensitive to evil suggestions.[1] It is therefore at this

[1] Marro, *La puberté*, p 67; King, *The Psychology of Child Development*, 1903, p. 193.

moment that it is necessary to supervise the acquaintances that he makes, and the comrades with whom he associates.

The child, at the same time that he becomes conscious of others, also becomes conscious of his own personality. To become conscious of oneself and to become conscious of others are, in effect, only two aspects of the same act of differentiation, of classification. The individual defines himself only in relation to the collective whole. The essence of self is made up of the feeling of responsibility, of duty, of the rôle that we are called to play: sentiments which are evidently of social origin and significance.

The period of adolescence is also characterised by concentration of interest upon a small number of objects. Often we find a single dominant interest, which is the centre around which gravitates all the occupations, all the thoughts, of the young man or the young woman: painting, music, a certain kind of charitable work, of collection, or of society. The value (moral and æsthetic) of these occupations begins also to dominate their purely intellectual interests.

Then follows the crisis of puberty, a crisis which is both physiological and psychological. The importance of this phase is so great that a whole volume ought to be devoted to it. The culminating interest is the interest, more or less conscious, and more or less avowed, for all that relates to the other sex, for all that is able to attract it: coquetry, dress, physical beauty, the reading of forbidden novels. . . .

This is the period of forbidden fruit. A new life bubbles up in the depths of the soul; yet we cloister the adolescent in the four walls of a college, or in the workshop of a boarding-school!

But the nascent instincts are no more able to

remain long confined than the sap of spring-time: if an obstacle prevents their normal ascent, they break out by some lateral way.

It has often been remarked how much puberty predisposes to religious exaltation. In his statistics upon the age of conversion, Starbuck has shown that this phenomenon has its maximum of frequency at 16 among boys and at 13 among girls.[1] It seems undeniable that the religious emotion and the sexual instinct may have some common psychological roots. Religion, like love, proceeds from a sense of imperfection, of personal insufficiency, of isolation or distress, of want; like love it supplies the individual with an opportunity for self-sacrifice, for intercourse with others, which are felt as needs by the adolescent, because they are in the interest of the race. By brutally repressing, in the name of some "positive" dogma, these religious tendencies, we may produce amongst young men, and above all amongst young women, grave troubles, notably among those who are of a nervous temperament or predisposed to hysteria. Even supposing that religion does not correspond to any objective "verity," it may be, for the moment, of great utility by serving as a support and a means of expression to those sentiments which in themselves are very real, and the expansion of which undoubtedly permits the personality to pass through a difficult stage of development.[2] To ask if such an interest is

[1] Starbuck, *The Psychology of Religion*, London, 1899.

[2] By suddenly destroying the religious beliefs of an adolescent, we risk producing a gap in his mental system. Given the instability which characterises this period, it may be followed by a complete disorganisation. If this mishap takes place just at the moment when the young man has taken these religious beliefs as the support of all his ideas, as the fulcrum of his conduct, this sudden demolition is likely to bring on a catastrophe: a crisis of melancholy, pes-

a "verity" or an "error" has no meaning for the paidologist; the only thing he has to take into account is whether it has biological utility. When the little baby sees a ship in a piece of straw which floats with the current of the water, we may ask ourselves if this belief is useful or useless to him, but it is no use whatever to raise the question whether it is true or false.

To hinder an adolescent, who feels the natural need for it, from normally accomplishing his religious evolution, under the pretext that religion is not "true," is to act as a dogmatic who *decrees* what is true and what is false, and what ought to be believed—not like an impartial psychologist who *finds out* what responds *in fact* to a need of growth, nor as a pedagogue who ought to promote the natural evolution of the mind, by guiding where this is necessary, but without thwarting it. One might as well hinder a baby from walking on all-fours when he does not know how to stand up on his feet, under the pretext that to walk on all-fours is an "error."

Repressed by circumstances, the sexual instinct is still able to express itself, apart from the religious inclination, under various forms of substitutions for love: uncontrolled friendship for comrades of the same sex,[1]

simism, or suicide. Proal has noted in his *L'éducation et le suicide des enfants*, 1907, p. 127, the complement furnished to suicide by adolescents through precocious scepticism. Suicide is the natural and logical termination of a being in whom has been destroyed the interest which was the motive-power of life.

[1] Marro (*La puberté*, p. 64) publishes some curious specimens of letters by young girls in a boarding-school, written to one another: "Why, mademoiselle, are you ashamed to write to me? You do not know, then, that a word from you makes me happy . . . If you knew what a void I indeed feel in my heart, you would hasten to fill it. . . . I look forward so much to the end of your holidays that I might come to meet you, to see you again and repeat to you

passion for animals, the cultivation of art, of philosophy, &c.

But we must stop. . . .

The question of the evolution of interests requires new and conscientious researches. From this moment, however, we can affirm that this evolution follows a definite and constant progress. The suggestions which spring from this fact are clear: 1st, education ought not to thwart this natural evolution; 2nd, it ought as far as possible to assist it. Varendonck rightly says in his study: "If education precipitates or retards these stages of development, it may result in a void in the character, perhaps a serious disorganisation." As we have already remarked apropos of physical development, the various stages of growth are bound up together. To pass over one stage is to do a wrong not only to the processes the development of which corresponds at this stage, but also to all the succeeding stages which they condition. To wish to begin a piece of education before being assured that the development has attained the point when it is able to support the burden, is to build in the air, as we should build in the air if we wished to commence the construction of a story of a house before the lower story upon which it must rest had been built.

By making the interests of each step in education correspond to the natural interests which characterise the various stages of infantile evolution, teachers would bring to an end that "radical unintelligibility"

by word of mouth that I love you! Do you remember the day of your arrival? If we had been alone I do not know what I should have done to you, without exaggeration, I should have smothered you with kisses . . ." &c. Another ends her letter thus: "If you wish to see me somewhat comforted, mademoiselle, continue to turn on me, from time to time, a kind and loving look." See also Smith, *Types of Adolescent Affection*, Ped. Sem., 1904, p. 178.

which M. Cousinet, in the article to which allusion has been previously made, shows to exist between the pupils of a class and their master. "There is no common measure," says M. Cousinet, "between children and grown-up people. The children live in a world constituted by means of an insufficient experience and a confused imagination, an unreal world for us, but very real for them. That which interests us is to them unintelligible; that which interests and enthrals them, their plays, and all the details of that world which is for them *the* world, appears to us insignificant and puerile. . . . This divergence of interest is one of the principal causes of the little confidence which children show in the grown-up people. . . . Not only does the master consider the ordinary occupations of the pupils contemptible, and not only do his thoughts remain unintelligible to the pupils, but he is also opposed to satisfying their childish desires; he destroys, as though it were a house of cards, the romantic world which so delights the child, and he forces him to accept as motives those interests which he (the master) judges to be superior. . . ."

That this unintelligibility exists is quite certain, and M. Cousinet very rightly shows on what it depends; that it must necessarily exist is, on the contrary, very doubtful, and I am unable to share the pessimism of our author when he writes . "Whatever progress may be made by pedagogy and child psychology, and whatever effort may be made by one to adjust itself to the other, even with schools 'made to measure' (like clothes) as advocated by M. Claparède (which, by the way, is, in my opinion, unrealisable), there will remain between the child, and above all between a group of children, and the master a radical unintelligibility."

But why should the teacher not be able to espouse

the interests of the child as the doctor espouses, for example, the interests of his patients? Doubtless, in order to do this, he must know these interests. And this is exactly the aim of child psychology, to draw the attention of the educator to them, and to invite him to determine them. Now, if a master is incapable of bringing down his mind and heart to the level of the heart and mind of the child, it shows that he has chosen a profession for which he unfortunately has no vocation.

Let us conclude this too long chapter. The child develops naturally by passing through a certain number of stages which succeed each other in a constant order. Each stage corresponds to the development of a certain function or aptitude, and the play connected with each of these gives pleasure to the child. All objects susceptible of bringing into play this new-born function or aptitude naturally interest the child, captivate him, and attract him, while those which do not correspond to the play of any existing aptitude leave him indifferent or are instinctively repugnant to him.

The secret of pedagogy consists in making use of these natural aptitudes of the child, instead of reprimanding him because of those which he lacks—those with which he may not be endowed, or which he does not yet possess.

BIBLIOGRAPHY

Physical Growth.—QUETELET, *Anthropométrie*, Brussels, 1870. MALLING-HANSEN, *Perioden im Gewicht der Kinder*, Copenhagen, 1886. SCHMID-MONNARD, *Ueber den Einfluss der Jahreszeit und der Schule auf das Wachstum der Kinder*. Jahrb. f. Kinderheilkunde, 1895. COMBE, *Korperlange und Wachstum der Volksschulkinder in Lausanne*, Z. f. Schulgesundheitspflege, 1896. WIENER, *Das Wachstum des menschlichen Korpers*, Karlsruhe, 1890. VIERORDT, *Daten und Tabellen*, Jena, 1888. WARNER, *The Study of Children*,

London, 1897. BURK, *Growth of Children*, Am. J. Psy. IX., 1898 (containing a good bibliography). GODIN, *Recherches anthropométriques sur la croissance*, Paris, 1903 (chiefly anatomical, and without immediate interest to pedagogues). Masterly résumés of all the preceding have been made by VARIGNY in the article *Croissance* in Richet's Dictionnaire. HOESCH-ERNST, *Anthropolog.-psycholog. Untersuch. an Zuricher Schulkindern*, Thèse de phil. de Zurich, 1906 CHAUMET, *Croissance des enfants des écoles de Paris*, Thèse de Méd. de Paris, 1906. BIANCO, *Enfants de Madrid*, Rev. de l'Hypnot., Feb. 1910. KING, *Measurements of the Physical Growth of two Children*, J. ed. Psy., May 1910 On the *Growth of the Brain*, see MANOUVRIER, art. *Cerveau*, Richet's Dictionnaire. DONALDSON, *The Growth of the Brain*, London, 1905. HEUBNER, Z. pad. Psy. II., 1900, p. 73. PROBST (quoted, p. 126). For *Anthropometry*, see GIROUD, MANOUVRIER, SCHULZE (quoted, p. 100), MELZI, *Antropologia pedagogica*, Arona, 1899.

Repercussion of Physical Growth on Mental Functions—GILBERT, *Researches on the Mental and Physical Development of School-children*, Stud. from the Yale psych. Lab. II, 1894. DAWID, *Schwankungen in der geist. Entwickel*, III int. Congress f. Psychol. Munchen, 1896, p. 449. LOBSIEN, *Schwankungen der psychischen Kapazitat*, Berlin, 1902 (Conclusion: Physical and psychical development do not progress on parallel lines during the course of the school year).

Play.—Besides the works of GROOS and CARR, that of COLOZZA, *Psychologie und Pädagogik des Kinderspiels*, Altenburg, 1900 (much historical information upon play in pedagogy; the original Italian edition of this work was unfortunately published before the works of Groos appeared). QUEYRAT, *Les jeux de l'enfant*, Paris, 1905 (a very good résumé, inspired by the theory of Groos). WINCH, *Psychology and Philosophy of Play*, Mind, XV, 1906 GROOS, *Das Seelenleben des Kindes*, 2nd edition, Berlin, 1908 (the title of this book is a little misleading, it is not so much a treatise on infantile psychology as a treatise on general psychology, with, it is true, many examples taken from recent researches on the child. In chapter vii., devoted to play, Groos replies to the criticisms of Carr). RACINE, *Les jeux à l'école*, Ed. mod., 1907. HUGUET, *Jeu des enfants dans le Nord-Afrique*, Ed. mod., 1906. SMITH, *Play of Japanese Boys*, Ped. Sem., June 1909 ROUMA, *Jeux educatifs*, Ed. mod., 1908, p. 171. GULICK, *Psychol., Pedag, and Religious Aspects of Group Games*, Ped. Sem., March 1899. For playthings, consult FOURNIER, *Histoire des jouets et des jeux d'enfants*, Paris, 1889 (in anecdotical and literary form). HILDEBRANDT, *Das Spielzeug im Leben des Kindes*, Berlin, 1904 (a brief survey of the innumerable toys and playthings sold everywhere in shops). H. D'ALLEMAGNE, *Les jouets à la World's fair en 1904 à St. Louis*, *histoire des jouets*, with plates, Paris, 1908. ENDERLIN, *Das Spielzeug in seiner Bedeutung fur die Entwicklung des Kindes*, Kf, 1907.

Attractive Education—BRIDOU, *Le rôle de la gaieté dans l'éducation*, Arch int hyg scol, I, 1905. ASSAGIOLI, *Gli effetti del riso e le loro applicazioni pedagogiche*, Riv. di Psy., 1905. LUCIE BÉRILLON, *L'éducation attrayante*, Rev. de l'hypnotisme, March–May 1909 (an excellent article, showing clearly that "attractive education, far from suppressing effort, provokes, on the contrary, spontaneous and joyous impulse, which leads to voluntary effort, and maintains attention." It contains numerous quotations from authors, from which I select the following. From Montaigne: "One should give nothing but that which tempts the appetite, or the result is donkeys loaded with books." From Rollin "What we want to get is will, and it is gained by sweetness, persuasion, and especially by the attraction of pleasure." From Georges Sand "The child who studies has already all the needs of the artist who creates. By closing him up in a bare and dull room, you stifle his heart and his mind as well as his body." From Michelet: "One only works well when happy." From Anatole France: "The art of teaching is nothing but the art of awakening curiosity in young souls in order to satisfy it afterwards. And curiosity is only lively and healthy in happy minds"). J. GIRARD (woman inspector), *L'éducation de la petit enfance*, Paris, 1908. ROUMA, *La vie heureuse au jardin d'enfants*, broch., Brussels, 1908. CHANTAVOINE, *L'éducation joyeuse*, Paris, 1910. An interesting attempt to apply attractive instruction to the study of solfeggio and music has been made with great success by JAQUES-DALCROZE (professor at the Conservatoire of Geneva), *Gymnastique rythmique*, Neuchâtel, 1906

Interest—HERBART, *Pédagogie générale*, 1806. OSTERMANN, *Das Interesse*, Leipzig, 1895 J. DEWEY, *Interest as related to Will*, second suppl. to the Herbart Yearbook, Chicago, 1895; *The School and Society*, New York, 1899. DE GARMO, *Interest and Education*, New York, 1902. W. JAMES, *Talks to Teachers* The fundamental rôle which interest plays as a factor of our mental activity has not been noticed by German psychologists Wundt, for example, never speaks of interest; in the fourth edition of his Psychology, this term is not even indicated in the alphabetical index of subjects; in the fifth edition, it is only indicated accessorily (æsthetic interest). English psychologists, on the contrary, have clearly perceived the importance of this ultimate factor in the determination of our acts and thoughts: see, for example, the *Principles of Psychology* of W. James, 1891. In my work on *L'Association des idées* (Paris, 1903) I have several times insisted on this selective rôle of interest, on the dynamogenisation of the useful reactions which it causes (see pp. 136, 172, 230, 378, &c). See also my communication to the Congress of Psychology at Rome (1905), *L'intérêt principe fondamental de l'activité mentale.* The primordial rôle of interest has also been clearly attested by ENGLE, *Analytic Interest Psychology*, Baltimore, 1904, and by LUQUET, *Idées générales de psychologie*, Paris, 1906. See also MÜNCH, *Unterricht und Interesse*, Z. päd. Psy., 1910 (the author is of the opinion that, in order that the pupils may not lose the habit of effort, the master should not make his instruction more interesting than is necessary to make the pupil feel that it is worth while to make an effort). For curiosity: INGEGNIEROS, *Psicofisiologia de la curiosidad*, Arch. di Psiquiatria, June 1910.

Imitation.—BALDWIN, *Mental Development*. HASKELL, *Imitation in Children*, Ped. Sem., 1894. FREAR, ibid., 1897. PISTOLESI, *L'imitazione*, Torino, 1910.

Biogenetic Law.—F. MÜLLER, *Für Darwin*, 1864. HAECKEL, *Morphologie générale*, 1866. For a general exposition, see CHAMBERLAIN, *The Child*, pp. 51–64. FERRIÈRE, article quoted above. VIALLETON, *Un problème de l'évolution*, Montpellier and Paris, 1908 (history and criticism). BALDWIN, *Mental Development*, chap. i. LUKENS, SEELEY, DEWEY, &c., *The Culture Epochs*, Second Yearbook of the Herbart Soc., 1896. Criticism of the biogenetic law, from the morphological point of view: HERTWIG, *Eléments d'anatomie et de physiol. générale*, 1898. From the psychopedagogic point of view: BOLTON, *Unsoundness of the Culture Epochs Theory of Education*, Journ. of Pedagogy, 1903, p. 136. Compare also CHAMBERLAIN, *Note on some Differences between "Savages" and Children*, Psy. Bulletin, 1909, p. 212.

Evolution of Interests.—See the good bibliography given at the end of the work by I. KING, and consult the collection of the Ped. Sem. *Cf.* TRETTIEN, *Psychol. of the Language Interest of Children*, Ped. Sem., 1904.

General Development.—Besides the works of Tiedemann, Lobisch, Sigismund, Sully, &c., quoted in Chapter I., see Mme. NECKER DE SAUSSURE, *L'éducation progressive*, 1828–1838. PÉREZ, *Les trois premières années de l'enfant* (1st edition, 1878); *L'enfant de trois à sept ans* (1st ed. 1886). COMPAYRÉ, *L'évolution intellectuelle et morale de l'enfant*, Paris, 1893. BALDWIN, *Mental Development*, London, 1895 (this work, although containing paidological observations, has especially a philosophical interest; the author tries to show that imitation is the foundation of the adaptation and progress of the mind). VINAY, *La psychologie du nouveau-né*, Sem. Med., 1897, p. 33. AMENT, *Die Entwicklung von Sprechen und Denken beim Kinde*, Leipsic, 1899. SIKORSKY, *Die Seele des Kindes*, broch., Leipsic, 1902. TRACY, *The Psychology of Childhood*, Boston, 1903 (very concise compendium; succinct résumé of the observations made on the development of the different faculties). IRVING KING,

The Psychology of Child Development, Chicago, 1903. STERN, *Tatsachen und Ursachen der seelischen Entwicklung*, Z. ang. Psy., Bd. I., 1907. PHILIPPE, *La psychol. des écoliers*, Ed. mod., 1906. BUCHNER, *Die Entwicklung der Gemuthsbew. im 1. Lebensjahre*, Kf. 1908, p. 166. VECCHIA, *Nei primi anni di vita di due bambini*, Riv ped., 1909.

Monobiographies (journals) relating to the development of a child. —During these last years a great number have appeared, some of which we quote: TAINE, *L'acquisition du langage*, Rev. philos I., 1876. DARWIN, *A Biographical Sketch of an Infant*, Mind, 1877. POLLOCK, *An Infant's Progress in Language*, Mind, 1878. EGGER, *Observations sur le développement de l'intelligence et du langage*, Ac. des X. Morales, 1879. PREYER, *Die Seele des Kindes*, 1882, tr f. *L'âme de l'enfant*, Paris, 1887. ESPINAS, *Obs. sur un nouveau-né*, Ann. de la Fac des Lettres de Bordeaux, 1883 SHINN, *Notes on the Development of a Child*, Berkeley, 1893–1907. MOORE, *The Mental Development of a Child*, Ps. Rev. Mon. Suppl. 1896. ST.-YBARS, *De un jour à dix ans.*, Ed. mod., 1909–10 (notes by a mother). GHEORGOV, *Die ersten Anfange des sprachlichen Ausdrucks fur das Selbstbewusstsein bei Kindern*, C R 2nd Congress of Philosophy, Genève, 1905, p. 520. . *Zur grammatischen Entwicklung der Kindersprache*, Leipsic, 1908 ; *Le vocabulaire dans le langage des enfants* (in Bulgarian), Sofia, 1910. WHIPPLE, *The Vocabulary of a Three-year-old Boy*, Ped. Sem., 1909. STERN, *Monographieen uber die seelische Entwicklung des Kindes*, Leipsic, 1907, 1909. CRAMAUSSEL, *Le premier éveil intellectuel de l'enfant*, Paris, 1908 (2nd ed. 1910).

Autobiographies.—LOTI, *Le roman d'un enfant.* H. KELLER, *Histoire de ma vie . sourde, muette, aveugle*, 1904.

Adolescence.—MARRO, *La puberté*, Paris, 1901. STANLEY-HALL, *Adolescence*, 2 vols., London, 1904 (an important work, a rich mine of documents and ideas. M. COMPAYRÉ has made a résumé, unfortunately too concise, of some of its chapters in a little book, *L'adolescence*, Paris, 1909). SCHMIDKUNZ, *Die oberen Stufen des Jugendalters*, Kongress Kinderforsch, Berlin, 1906, p. 245. MENDOUSSE, *L'âme de l'adolescent*, Paris, 1909. LEMAITRE, *La vie mentale de l'adolescent*, St. Blaise, 1910 (a collection of observations on mental anomalies of scholars). MOLL, *Sexuelle Erziehung*, Z. päd. Psy., 1908. WILLE, *Die Psychosen des Pubertätsalters*, Leipsic, 1898. AXEL KEY, *Die Pubertatsentwicklung und das Verhaltnis derselben zu den Krankheitserscheinungen der Schuljugend*, 10th International Medical Congress, 1890 Mme FRANCILLON, *Essai sur la puberté chez la femme*, Paris, 1906 (a thesis by a doctor of medicine, a physiological and medical study). SIREDEY, *La puberté et l'éducation des jeunes filles*, Arch. int. d'hyg. scol., IV., 1907.

Consult also the paidological periodicals, which contain numerous articles on all these questions.

CHAPTER V

INTELLECTUAL FATIGUE

THE question of fatigue is undoubtedly one of the most important of those which concern pedagogy, since it involves the study of the resistance of the organism to work. This study has been completely neglected by the old school of pedagogy, which concerned itself with decreeing what the pupil *ought* to do, without ever concerning itself with what he *was able* to do. But—according to a figure borrowed from Professor Kraepelin, the eminent psycho-pathologist of Munich—to subject a child to a programme of studies without having previously considered whether that programme can be followed without inconvenience to his brain, is to act like a mariner who ventures his ship upon the high seas before having tried it in port.

How is school work borne by the child? How much ought we to impose upon him? What relation is there between the manner of presenting or apportioning the various lessons and the fatigue which they create among those who study them? What are the different factors conditioning intellectual work, and capable of counteracting, retarding, or, on the contrary, augmenting fatigue? Such are some of the innumerable questions which present themselves to the educator who cares about his responsibilities.

The solution of them is by no means obvious: far from it. It is, in most cases, very difficult for a master to realise, with any approach to exactness, the degree of exhaustion of his pupils, or the progress of their fatigue. Here is a very striking example of this: Mr. Winch, a London psychologist, who carried out an investigation with a view to find out if evening classes were in any special way fatiguing, found that exhaustion was produced much more rapidly during such evening lessons than during the day lessons. Nevertheless, the teachers of the evening courses, "men having a long experience of day schools and evening schools," all declared—with only one exception—that the mental capacity of their pupils increased in the evening.[1]

Vague appreciations and "impressions" ought to be replaced, here as elsewhere, by precise facts. The first thing to do, to arrive at these, is to obtain a means of measuring fatigue. It is indeed indispensable to be able to express by *figures* the amount of fatigue, if we wish to appreciate the manner in which it varies under the influence of circumstances. We proceed, therefore, at once to review briefly the principal processes for measuring fatigue.

1. Measurement of Fatigue

This is a problem which has for a long time preoccupied psycho-physiologists. It is far from being solved, and it is very necessary that the various processes so far proposed should still be closely studied.

These processes divide themselves into two groups: one consisting of those for estimating the lowering of the capacity for work, which accompanies a state of fatigue—these processes are called *direct*, because they measure intellectual fatigue by intellectual work; the others, the *indirect* processes, determine the modifica-

[1] Winch, *Some Measurements of Mental Fatigue in Adolescent Pupils in Evening Schools*, J. of Ed. Psy., Jan. 1910, p. 17.

tions which follow fatigue due to mental work in various other functions, such as sensibility, muscular energy, pulsations of the heart, &c.

A. Direct Methods

1. **Dictations.**—We give the pupils a dictation at the beginning of a lesson, and another at the end of the lesson, both being similar in length and difficulty. Afterwards we count the mistakes in each of the dictations, leaving out of account those due to ignorance, so that we have only those due to inattention. The amount by which the number of mistakes is increased in the second dictation enables us to estimate the fatigue produced by the lesson which interposed between the two tests. We are able also to take into account the corrections and erasures, which increase with fatigue.

As an example we give the results obtained by a German teacher, Friedrich, drawn from a very great number of experiments of this kind : [1]—

40 mistakes in the morning before lessons.
70 mistakes after 1 hour of lessons.
160 mistakes after 2 hours of lessons.
190 mistakes after 3 hours of lessons, without any break for recreation.

We see that the differences are very clear and considerable.

This process, contrived by Sikorsky in 1879, is simple and good, and best adapts itself to school experiments. If we wish to compare the results from the different classes, it is indispensable that we should express in percentages the amount of increase in the number of mistakes made in the test carried out during a condition of fatigue.

[1] Friedrich, Z. f. Ps., vol. 13, 1897.

2. **Counting Letters.**—This test, which has to be done before and after a lesson, consists in striking out or counting, as quickly as possible, certain letters (for example the *e*'s) in a printed text. The more letters there are struck out (or counted) in a given time, the less is the fatigue. This method was first made use of by Oehrn (counting) and by Ritter [1] (striking out), but it possesses few advantages. The difficulty of finding texts exactly alike, of counting the letters omitted, and the very marked influence of practice, are some of its disadvantages.

3. **Calculations.**—In these the counting is replaced by simple arithmetical calculations: additions or multiplications. For example, sheets of paper are distributed to the children, and upon these are printed the additions or multiplications to be done, and the children have nothing to do but carry out the calculations. The value of the work done may be estimated in two different ways: either by counting *the number of figures* that have been added (or multiplied, &c.) in a given time, three minutes, for example; or else by counting *how much time* was necessary in each case to carry out a certain number of given operations. The second method is evidently not practicable if a collective experiment is to be done, except by asking each pupil himself to take note of the time that he takes to do his work.

But, besides the quantity of the work, there is also the question of its quality; and the *number of mistakes* made ought also to be taken into account, especially if the experiment is made with children. The fatigue will then be determined by means of the quantity of

[1] Oehrn, *Stud. z. Individualpsychologie*, Diss. Dorpat., 1889, and Ps. Arb. 1.; Ritter, *Ermudungsmessungen*, Z f. Ps., vol. 24, 1900, p. 424.

work done—the less the additions done in a given time, or the greater the amount of time taken for a given calculation, the greater the fatigue; and by means of the mistakes made—the greater the number of mistakes, the greater the fatigue.

The determination of the number of mistakes is often more important than that of the amount of work, for it may happen that, in consequence of the decline (due to fatigue) of the quality of the work, its rapidity is increased. But, on the other hand, we cannot neglect the amount of work done, for it is evident that if the work is done very slowly mistakes will not be made.

It is necessary, therefore, to take account of both of these two factors: speed and mistakes. As this duality is rather inconvenient in practice, we shall try to bring the two variables to only one, by determining the percentage of mistakes made in the work done. This will give us figures which will express both the quantity and the quality. This figure, however, will have only a rather doubtful value. If, in one minute, Peter does 100 additions and has 10 mistakes, while, in the same time, John does 10 with 1 mistake, their coefficient of error will be identical, viz. 10 per cent. But it is quite obvious that Peter's work is worth more than that of John, since he has done 10 times more work in the same time, with relatively the same number of mistakes—for John will, in fact, require 10 minutes to make 100 additions and 10 mistakes. I give this example to show what care we ought to take in the interpretation of experiments of this kind.

Another method which may be used with the collective method, to eliminate the *mistakes* factor, will be only to take account of tests which are wholly correct. We shall thus base our estimate exclusively upon speed: the number of operations executed. A certain number of scholars having engaged in adding for three minutes, we retain only those tests having no mistake, and we take the average of the number of additions done. By repeating this experiment under varying conditions, we shall see whether this average increases or decreases. But here, again, it may happen that a cause of error may slip in arising from the fact that the number of pupils calculating correctly does not remain the same for another test. It is evident that if the number diminishes much with fatigue, in such a way that the average depends on the strongest pupils in arithmetic, the result of the experiment will be wholly false. In order that a comparison may be made between various experiments, it is necessary that the conditions shall remain approximately the same.

We can also, and this method is certainly the simplest, allow the pupils enough time for all of them to do all the operations: no longer taking account of the speed of the work, but only of the number of mistakes made. But we are able to employ this method only with pupils who calculate so badly as to be certain to make some mistakes—it is true that if we count the mistakes of the collective effort considered *en bloc*, we shall be sure nearly always to find some!

The method of calculation was employed for the first time by Burgerstein in 1891,[1] and has been much used since; for, in spite of the inconveniences which have just been pointed out, it is very serviceable. It is more particularly made use of when we wish to determine the curve of fatigue. (See section 2 of this chapter.)

Instead of easy calculations we can give more diffi-

[1] Burgerstein, *Die Arbeitskurve einer Schulstunde*, Z. f. Schulgesundheitsflege, 1891.

cult problems as a test. This was done by Mr. Winch in the researches mentioned above. We assign a value to the work done by a numerical mark, or a quality mark (G., F., &c.), in the same way as for work done in an examination. By giving tests of equal difficulty before and after a lesson, we shall see how the marks vary. This method requires that the marking of the worked problems shall be done by men accustomed to marking, and marking exactly.

4. **Copying Letters.**—Schuyten [1] has made use of this method, which is easily adaptable to a collective experiment. The teacher writes upon the blackboard a certain number of combinations of the letters *a, e, i, o, u, v, r, n;* and the pupils are given five minutes for copying them. Exercises of the same kind take place at various times during the day, morning and evening. Fatigue is estimated according to the number of mistakes or omissions made

5. **Filling in Blanks.**—This tests ability in associative activity and in judgment.

In 1895 the town council of Breslau, wishing to know if the system of teaching, which consisted in having five consecutive lessons in a morning, did not produce overpressure, appointed a commission composed of teachers, doctors, and the psychologist Ebbinghaus, to study the matter experimentally. It was then that Ebbinghaus conceived the *method of blank filling*, which consists in putting before the pupils a printed test in which certain words or syllables are omitted and are replaced by lines.[2] The pupil is required to reconstitute the text by filling up the blanks as quickly as possible. The more fatigued the pupil is, the fewer blanks he fills in, and the more mistakes he

[1] Schuyten, Ar de Ps IV., 1904, p. 116

[2] Ebbinghaus, Z. f. Ps., vol. 13.

makes. The method is complicated, and the counting of the mistakes made is difficult, for the point is not only to estimate the quantity of mistakes but their quality.

6. **Memorising.**—We can conceive a number of yet other tests of the measure of fatigue based upon the variation of work done. We will mention only one more. This is also due to Ebbinghaus, and consists in reading to the subjects of the experiment a series of figures, asking them to write them down immediately after. Errors or omissions made in the reproduction of the series are counted, and these are found to be more numerous according as the attention is more fatigued at the moment when the series is presented to the subject. This method is little to be recommended, as the numbering of the mistakes is very difficult—for example, when two figures have been correctly reproduced, but are interchanged as to the given order; and besides, the retention of the series depends too much upon variable factors, *e.g.* mnemonic means, for it to be able to constitute a reliable measure of fatigue.

Criticism of Direct Methods

The direct methods which measure fatigue according to the decrease of work have some advantages and some drawbacks. It is expedient to give some account of each of these.

Advantages.—The methods of this kind have, firstly, the advantage that they explore intellectual fatigue in a direct manner. In order to understand the fatigue of the mind, tests are employed which appeal to the mind. It would seem, therefore, theoretically at any rate, that they come closer to the thing to be measured than the indirect methods of which we shall speak presently.

Another advantage, especially for school researches, is that they lend themselves very well to collective experiments, which can be done in class, and that they serve so much the better because many of them have all the appearance of being ordinary work (dictations, for example, and calculations).

DRAWBACKS.—There are very many of these. The most serious is this: fatigue is not the only factor which intervenes in a task; there is also the question of willingness and the effort made by the worker, which are able to make up for the depressing effects of fatigue.

Another drawback is found in the fact that the test itself is a cause of fatigue. This fatigue adds itself to that which it is desired to measure, and it is not known according to what laws this addition is made: whether the increase of fatigue produced by the work of the test is proportional to the amount of fatigue existing before the test. We notice that the carrying out of the tests is done mostly by writing. The writing movements also help to fatigue the subject, and that in a proportion unknown.

The tests submitted in the different experiments in a series are not exactly of the same difficulty. It is difficult to find two dictations of exactly similar difficulty, or two problems equally intricate. But this drawback disappears if the experiments are repeated sufficiently often to eliminate this cause of inequality.

In the direct methods the errors are difficult to compare as to their value. Do all the errors denote fatigue? Are there not some which come from unskilfulness, from confusions or omissions, from inattention connected with a cause other than fatigue? And the errors supposed to come from fatigue, do they all express the same quantity of fatigue?

Yet other drawbacks : the tests take time, and they are to a large extent affected by practice or habit.

Let us add that most of these drawbacks might be avoided by a suitable arrangement of the experiments. Besides, if our aim is less to study fatigue in itself than simply the effective capacity for work (whatever may be the factors on which this capacity depends), the direct methods alone are applicable, and they are capable of rendering very great services from the point of view of the school.

B. Indirect Methods

1. **Æsthesiometry.**—We pass now to the methods of the second group, namely, those which measure the fatigue resulting from a certain functional activity, by the correlative variations of other functions, such as tactile sensibility.

Everybody knows—since the psychologist Weber made the discovery in 1829—that if the two points of a compass are placed upon the back of the hand, it is necessary to separate the points by several millimetres in order that they may be perceived as double : less than a certain distance, which we call the *threshold* of touch discrimination (or "Weber threshold"), the two points are fused in a single contact. Now, a doctor of Mulhausen, Griesbach, has noticed that, in the case of a fatigued person, the separation necessary for distinguishing the two points is considerably more than that for the same person when fresh.[1] He thought he had in this way a means to express fatigue in millimetres. the lowering of the tactile sensibility being proportional to the fatigue.

[1] Griesbach, *Ueber Beziehungen zwischen geistiger Ermudung und Empfindungsvermogen der Haut*, Arch. f. Hygiene, vol. 24, 1895. See also his more recent work, in which he replies to the criticisms which have been addressed to him, Ar. int. hyg. Scol. I., 1905.

Here, by way of example, are the figures of a number of experiments made by Vannod in the schools of Berne.[1] In the morning, at 8 o'clock, the threshold of sensibility (measured on the forehead) of a boy 16 years of age was equal to 3 millimetres. At 10 o'clock, after two hours of lessons, the threshold rose to 3.5 mm.; at noon it attained 4.5 mm.; at 2 o'clock it had fallen to 2.5 mm. (this fall is due to the midday rest till 2 o'clock); finally, at 5 o'clock in the evening, the threshold had again risen to 3 mm.

The instrument by which we set the points for determining the threshold of tactile determination bears the name of "Weber's compasses" or "double-point æsthesiometer." Various models of this instrument are made, of which some are reproduced on p. 221. The working of them is easy to understand: little by little the two points of the instrument are separated until the subject perceives two distinct contacts, and we immediately note, by reading off from the graduated scale on the instrument, the distance in millimetres which separates the two points. It is impossible to enter here into the rather complicated details of the construction and of the manipulation of the apparatus, which ought to be familiar to those who propose to work with it.

Instead of the compass, of which one of the points is separated more or less from the other, we can also use (as Binet has done) a series of little cardboard plates, each having two needles fixed in their thick part (see fig. 9). The distance between these needles varies in a series, in such a manner as to form a scale including, at least, the following distances: 0 mill. (this absence of distance is represented by a cardboard

[1] Vannod, *La fatigue intellectuelle et son influence sur la sensibilité cutanée*, Rev. méd. Suisse rom., 1896.

having only one needle); 5 mm., 10 mm., 15 mm., 20 mm., 25 mm., 30 mm. The skin of the subject is touched successively, and for a certain number of times, with the needles of the various cardboards, and we note the responses—"one point," or "two points" —which are given *for each distance*. When the experiment is finished, a statistical summary is made of the responses, and we thus see from what distance the responses "two points" began to be more frequent than the responses "one point." The threshold is represented by the distance which has furnished an equal number of responses of each kind.

Here are the results of an experiment made by Binet, which illustrate better than a long description the nature of the method.[1] The table is made up of the measurements taken in a school before and after lessons. The first column shows the various distances of the needles, and the following columns show the number of responses for "one point" and "two points" which were given for each of the distances:—

Distances (in millimetres).	Before fatigue. "One point."	Before fatigue. "Two points."		After fatigue. "One point."	After fatigue. "Two points."	
0	124	12		126	10	
5	113	23	163 (5–15)	126	10	108 (5–15)
10	89	47		112	24	
15	43	93		62	74	
20	9	127		20	116	
25	9	127		2	134	
30	1	135		2	134	

[1] Binet, *Sur la fatigue intellectuelle scolaire*, An. ps. XI., 1905. Æsthesiometric cardboards of this convenient type, and so made that any one can easily make them for himself, have been devised by Buzenet (Bull. S. ps. E., 1905, p. 633). The needles used by Binet are number 8; they are fixed in the piece of cardboard by the point.

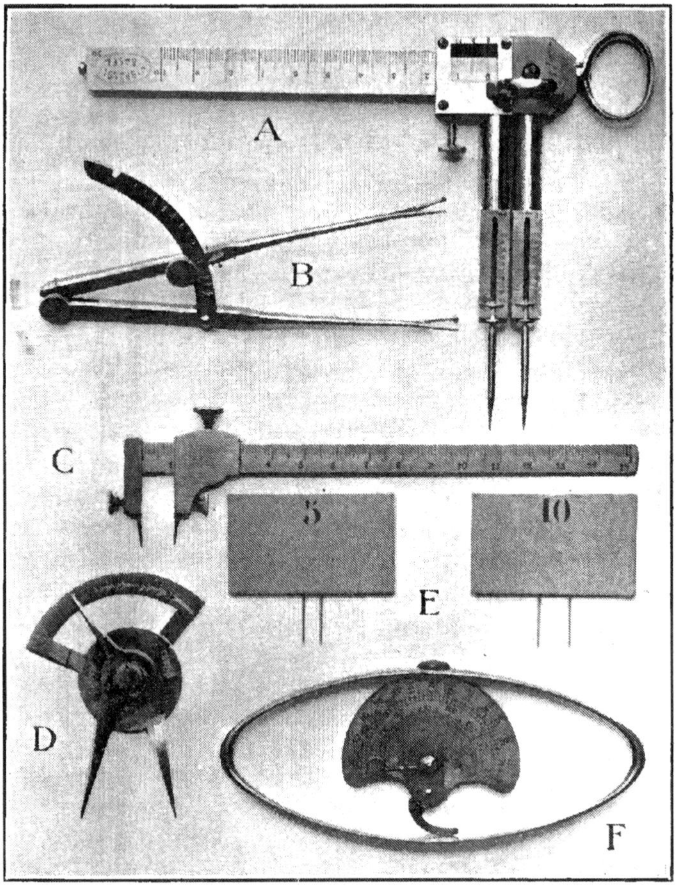

FIG. 9.—A. Griesbach's æsthesiometer (with an arrangement which permits of the measurement of the force of pressure of the points). B. Compasses with each leg bifurcated at its extremity, with one point blunt and one sharp. C. Sliding compasses. D. Simpler compasses. E. Two æsthesiometric cardboards, with needle distances of 5 and 10 mm. F. Collin's dynamometer.

As we see, the number of responses "one point" increases after fatigue, for the small distances, whilst the responses "two points" diminish. Thus, for the distances of 5, 10, and 15 mm., we have *before* fatigue a total of 163 responses "two points"; whilst *after* fatigue this number falls to 108. That is to say, the points are less well distinguished—and more often confused—after fatigue than before.

This method of determination (by the cardboards) has received, from Binet, the name *Method of irregular variations;* and it constitutes a special form of the psychometric method well known under the name "Method of true and false cases," or "Method of constancy" (*Konstanz-methode* of Müller). The method of determination by compasses works, on the contrary, by means of continued variations, and belongs to the "Method of barely perceptible differences," or "Method of limits" (*Method der Minimalanderungen*, or *Grenzmethode*, of the Germans). I give these particulars as a guide to those of my readers who may wish to seek, in general treatises on psychology, more ample information, theoretical and practical, about these methods.

The question of the value of the æsthesiometric method has given occasion for lively discussions—notably at the International Congress on School Hygiene at Nuremberg in 1904. Whilst some, with Leuba, Germann, Ritter, Bolton, Kraepelin, completely reject it, others, on the contrary, with Vannod, Wagner, Blazek, Ley, Schuyten, Sakaki, Bonoff, Noikow, and Abelson, affirm that they have proved a fixed relation between fatigue and the raising of the threshold of Weber. This relation appears to be incontestable. Binet, after having denied the possibility of measuring the threshold of the double sensation,[1]

[1] Binet, An. ps. IX., 1903, p. 247.

has gone back upon his conclusion as a result of new experiments, made upon a set of scholars. But he has shown that the raising of the threshold by fatigue does not take place with all the pupils taken individually: thus 21 boys out of 45, and 18 girls out of 38, were found to be unaffected by this test of fatigue. It is only in considering *the mass* of the results of a whole class that one observes the answers " one point " are as a whole more numerous, for the same separation of the compasses, when the pupils are fatigued than when they are not. Thus Binet holds that the æsthesiometric method makes possible the measuring of the scholars' intellectual fatigue, but it informs us only about the collective fatigue, and not about the individual fatigue.[1]

If this is so, the æsthesiometric method loses a great part of the practical value which we had anticipated, namely, the permitting of a rapid diagnosis, settled in one or two minutes. If it is necessary, so as to obtain an estimate of the fatigue of a class, to test the sensibility of *all* the pupils, this complicates matters, for the examination, naturally, can only be individual, and it ought to be made by the same experimenter—inasmuch as the manner of placing the compasses upon the skin of the subject, &c., plays a certain part, it is best that this manipulation should be done by the same operator for the same series of experiments.

On the other hand, Schuyten[2] has found that the æsthesiometric method is less dependent than others upon the interest of the moment, or the other contingencies of the experiment. This should be a great advantage.

Another objection to the æsthesiometric method is that it is not a method of " measure," since we do not know if the variations of the threshold are proportional

[1] Binet, An. ps. XI., 1905, p. 1.
[2] Schuyten. Ar. de. Psy. IV., 1904, p. 126.

to the variations of the state of fatigue. This is true, but the criticism applies quite as much to the other ponometric[1] methods, and one cannot deny that—if it were established that there exists a parallelism between the variation of these phenomena, however gross and approximate this parallelism might be—the æsthesiometric method would be very useful for estimating whether the fatigue increases or decreases in given circumstances.

Whatever may be its advantages and disadvantages, the æsthesiometric method is a very delicate one to make use of, in that the manipulation of the æsthesiometer demands great experience. It ought not, therefore, to be applied by untrained persons. It is most difficult for the teacher to use. I do not suppose, however, that he will lose his time in undertaking, by way of a trial, a certain number of experiments upon the threshold of Weber. Nothing will better show him what delicacy and steadiness are required in the carrying out of a psychological experiment. He will certainly make, during the experience, a large number of interesting notes, however little he may have of the ingenious and inquiring mind. Binet,[2] for example, has shown how very differently children react to the Weber compasses, according to the type of their intelligence—a fact which ought to be taken into account when we make use of this instrument to estimate fatigue.

2. **The Algesimetric Method.**—Vannod (1896) had the idea of measuring fatigue by the variations in sensibility to pain which were produced by the state of fatigue. Intellectual fatigue, at least when moderate, aggravates the sensibility to pain. To measure this

[1] It seems useful to create this adjective (from *ponos*, fatigue) to designate that which relates to the measure of fatigue.

[2] Binet, *La mesure de la sensibilité ; les simplistes, les distraits*, &c., An. psy. IX., 1903, pp. 78–245. Compare also Schuyten, Report of Sixth Internat. Congress on Psy., Geneva, 1909, p 781.

sensibility to pain we employ the algesimeter, an instrument consisting of a point fixed to a spring in such a manner that the intensity of the pressure exerted may be read (expressed in grammes or in millimetres) on a graduated scale.

This method is much simpler than the preceding one, and appears to be more practical. The differences due to fatigue are quite clear, as is shown by the results obtained by Vannod in the schools at Berne. For example, the pressure which it is necessary to exert on the front or inner side of one of the fingers of a certain scholar to cause pain is, at 8 A.M., 45 grammes; at 10 A.M., 39 gr.; and at noon, only 29 gr.

This method was employed by Swift in 1900, and he obtained analogous results from it in American schools. It was re-invented by Binet in 1905, to whom it has given, much to every one's surprise, results diametrically opposite; for, according to Binet, intellectual fatigue *diminishes* the sensibility to pain! This is a point to be restudied with care.[1]

3. **Dynamometric Methods.**—Intellectual and muscular fatigue are not so distinct as is generally believed. They react on each other. This is a very important fact for pedagogy, to which we shall have to return. The psychognostic has used it as a means of measuring fatigue. In fact, if to intellectual fatigue there corresponds a certain degree of muscular fatigue, we shall be able to measure the first by the same apparatus as that which we use to determine the second. The most convenient of these instruments is the hand *dynamometer*—well known to everybody—which consists of a steel ellipse that has to be pressed by the hand: the force exerted is indicated upon a dial-plate (see fig. 9, F). Certain precautions are necessary in the handling of

[1] Swift, Am J. Psy. 1900; Binet, An. Psy. XI, p. 32

the instrument: we should take care not to hurt the hand of the subject, as this would result in stopping him before he had reached his maximum. The steel ellipse ought always to be held in a uniform manner, and pressed exactly in the middle. It would be well to require on each occasion many successive pressures, for example, ten, and to take the average of them. These pressures should follow at strictly equal intervals, say one every five seconds.

Clavière did some researches in a philosophy class, in Paris, with this method. By comparing the force of pressure that he obtained from the students before and after two hours' lesson, he showed that: "1st, With intense and prolonged intellectual work lasting for two hours, there is a corresponding proportional diminution of muscular force as measured by the dynamometer; 2nd, With a moderate intellectual effort there is no appreciable diminution of muscular force; 3rd, With no intellectual effort there is a corresponding augmentation of the muscular force. This last proposition means that if we pass two hours in talking, smoking, singing, and laughing, without having made any definite effort, this simple intellectual activity acts as a stimulus to the organic forces.

Here is an example of some figures obtained by Clavière (pupils from 15 to 18 years): [1]—

AVERAGE OF THE PRESSURES OBTAINED

Pupils	*Before* intellectual effort.	*After* intellectual effort.
A	43.2 kilos.	36.2 kilos.
B	33.4 "	27.3 "
C	45.6 "	39.9 "
D	42.9 "	37.7 "
E	46.5 "	42 "
F	50 "	46.2 "

[1] Clavière, *Le travail intellectuel dans ses rapports avec la force musculaire*, An. Psy. VII., 1901.

The differences between the values taken before and after the effort are very clear. It is necessary to add that the pupils from whom the measurements were taken were well used to the handling of the dynamometer. Among subjects not familiar with the instrument the differences are less marked, being in part hidden by the irregularities in the manner of working the pressure.

There have been but few researches in schools with the dynamometer, an instrument which deserves more attention. Its price is comparatively moderate—about twenty-five shillings. Those who wish to undertake experiments with it would do well to carry out a number of *preliminary trials* so that they may clearly understand the sources of error which arise in the handling of the apparatus ; and they will profit much by reading the remarks and directions drawn up by Binet in his essays on the use of the dynamometer in schools.[1]

Various new models of dynamometers have recently been devised, with arrangements which allow of a much greater steadiness in the manner of operating the pressure with the hand. They are very much to be recommended, but they are more costly.[2]

Though the dynamometer has some small difficulties in application, it has as a set-off a great advantage which is not to be disdained in experiments with children : it interests them. Children are delighted to test their strength, and we may be sure that they press

[1] Binet and Vaschide, *Expériences de force musculaire et de fond chez les jeunes garçons*, A. psy. IV., 1898 ; *La mesure de la force musculaire chez les jeunes garçons ; Critique du dynamomètre*, same volume.

[2] Amongst others, the dynamometer (*Arbeitsschreiber*) of Weiler, which has, in addition, an arrangement by means of which successive pressures register themselves on a paper disc : Weiler, Psy. Arb. V., 1910, p. 538.

the apparatus with all the energy of which they are capable.

Another apparatus for measuring muscular fatigue, and, by its medium, mental fatigue, is the *ergograph*, invented by the celebrated Italian physiologist Mosso.[1] This instrument has the advantage of allowing the registering, upon a cylinder covered with smoke black and slowly revolving, of the work done until complete exhaustion is reached. The work consists in holding with one finger a weight of from 6½ to 11 pounds,

Fig. 10.

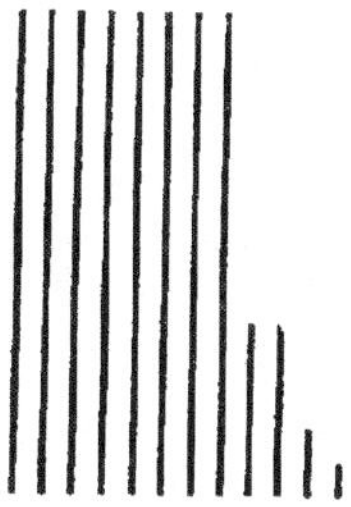

Fig. 11.

attached to a string which turns upon a pulley. The ergograph is, however, open to a certain amount of criticism of a technical kind, into the details of which we cannot enter.[2]

Its principal advantage is that it gives immediately, in a visible manner, the way in which fatigue occurs, and the character of the fatigue curve ; and this curve varies from one person to another. Here, for example, schematically presented, is the appearance of two of these ergographic curves, the one showing fatigue

[1] Mosso, *La fatigue*, Paris, 1894.

[2] See, amongst others, Binet, *Critique de l'ergographe*, An. psy. IV., 1898 ; Treves, *Le travail, la fatigue, l'effort*, An. psy. XII., 1906 ; Hirschlaff, Z. päd. psy., 1901, p. 184.

regularly developed, and the other an abruptly supervening fatigue.

Dubois (of Berne) has constructed a very convenient

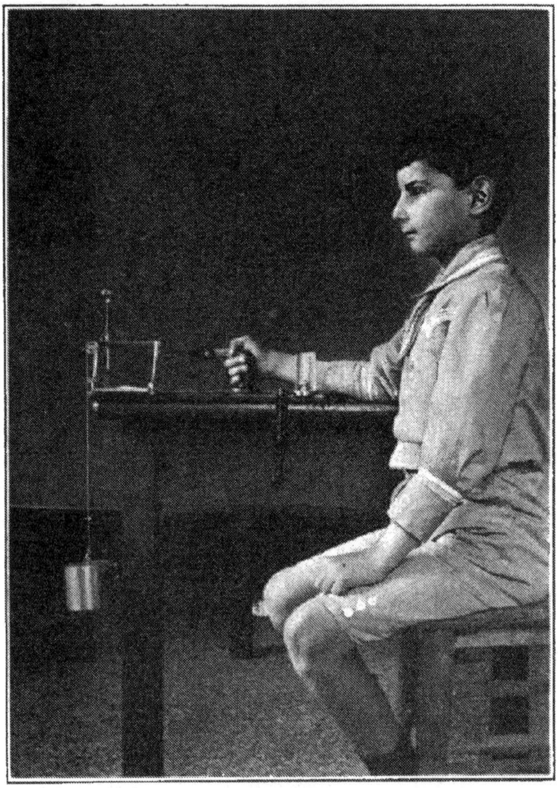

FIG. 12.

form of ergograph, which does not involve the use of a registering cylinder : the given work recording itself directly upon a paper band by means of a pencil fixed perpendicularly to the string which the subject holds (see fig. 12).

Philippe has suggested the utilising, in class, of a kind of simplified ergograph, without registering, to which he has given the name of *ergometer*. This ergometer, like the ergograph, includes a weight attached to a thread which turns upon a pulley. The subject pulls in a uniform manner, and we record how many pulls have been made up to the moment when he says that he is tired; or we may require the subject to make the greatest possible number of pulls in a given time, and count the number made.[1]

A still simpler ergographic method, in that it requires hardly any apparatus, has been employed by Weichardt: the subject takes, in each hand, a heavy dumb-bell weighing from 4½ to 11 lbs., raises them, with the arms extended, starting from the horizontal position in such a way as to make them describe a quarter of a circle, then lowers them again. The movements are made rhythmically according to the beats of a metronome. At the end of about twenty seconds it is found that the arms fall down tired. The fatigue is measured by the number of liftings performed.[2]

4. **The Method of Tapping.**—This method brings in and combines physical fatigue with mental fatigue. The subject should tap *as quickly as possible* with the finger the handle of a telegraphic keyboard, or some other transmitter, in such a way that each blow is marked on a registering drum, and so that we are able to count the number of blows made per second.[3] The experiment may be made to last for an indefinite time, for example, 45 seconds. We count how many taps

[1] Philippe, *Un nouvel ergomètre*, Bull. S. psy. E., 1900, p. 60. See also an ergometer of the same kind described by Bourdon in An. psy. VIII., p. 328.

[2] Weichardt, *Ueber Ermüdungsstoffe*, Stuttgart, 1910, p. 40.

[3] Dresslar, *Rapidity of Voluntary Movements*, A. J Psy., 1892.

have been given during the first five seconds, and how many during the last five. The second number is less, and this decrease is due to fatigue. The relative diminution of the taps given in the last five seconds enables us to measure the fatigue, or the susceptibility to fatigue. If 40 taps have been given in the first five seconds, and only 30 in the last five, the relative difference, *i.e.* $\frac{40-30}{40}=25$ per cent., will measure the fatigability. This method, which has been employed by Gilbert in school researches, as we have already said, is very simple ; but it has been too much neglected up to the present. It is true that it necessitates an arrangement for registering which is only found in laboratories.

In a recent work Wells seeks to extend this method of measurement. He shows what advantages it has : the method permits of a precise measurement, and the measurement can be carried out in a time sufficiently short for avoiding the feeling of *ennui* which accompanies the carrying out of tests by the other methods, such as that of additions.

Lastly, it is probable that the act of accelerated tapping is an act involving the intervention of a nervous process, of an organisation already highly developed. It is this last fact, he says, which ought to give the method of tapping preference to the ergographic method. With the ergograph we measure the *force* of movements ; but the *quickness* of movement, says Wells,[1] more deserves to be taken into consideration than force, for it is more dependent upon the nervous centres.

[1] Wells, *A Neglected Measure of Fatigue*, Am. J. of Psy., July 1908. See also *Normal Performance in the Tapping Test*, ibid., Oct. 1908 ; and *Sex Differences in the Tapping Test*, ibid., 1909.

5. **The Rhythmometric Method.**—We must not confound quick tapping with "rhythmic" tapping (*Taktklopfen*), which Stern used for estimating what he called *psychic tempo* (psychic rhythm). This method consists in allowing some one to tap *as he pleases* (and not as quickly as possible, as in the preceding method) a rhythm in triple time, in such a way as to show what is the speed which the subject naturally adopts. Stern assumes that this speed expresses the psychic energy of the subject. He has shown, by experimenting on several persons, that the rhythm varies in a characteristic fashion, for the same person, according to the time of day.

Lay repeated these experiments on school children. He asked each pupil to beat with the finger, upon the table, a rhythm in triple time (dactyl) during a minute. By counting the number of strokes made during the minute, the speed of the rhythm is obtained. Like Stern, Lay showed that the rhythm is beaten more *allegro* at certain hours of the day, notably about 10 A.M. and 5 P.M.[1]

These experiments are very interesting, but we do not know what part fatigue plays in the rate of the rhythm. If, as we may infer, the speed is proportional to the intensity of the psychic energy, we must conclude that psychic fatigue ought to slacken it. But fresh experiments are necessary in this matter.

We are certainly able to apply rhythmometry in a collective experiment: if we make all the class beat a rhythm in triple time by tapping upon the desks, we notice that the pupils soon agree among themselves

[1] Stern, *Ueber Psychologie der individuellen Differenzen*, Leipsic, 1900, p. 122, Lay, *Experimentelle Didaktik*, Wiesbaden, 1903, p. 410 (3rd ed 1910, p. 171). See also Lobsien (Pad. psy. Stud. V.), quoted by Lay.

and instinctively choose a certain speed, as do the impatient spectators at a theatre when stamping their feet in cadence to demand the raising of the curtain. We thus obtain the rhythm of the whole class considered *in globo* (in the lump), and we are easily able to follow the variations of the rhythm, and to study especially in what measure it depends upon fatigue.

6. **Reaction Time.**—Reaction time, that is to say, the time necessary for a reaction to a certain excitation, or a certain order—time that we are able to measure very exactly by means of a chronoscope—generally lengthens under the influence of fatigue.[1] I do not lay stress upon this method, which is only applicable in laboratories; besides which, the relation between the lengthening of the reaction time and fatigue is far from being exactly established.

Keller sought to measure fatigue by means of the time taken in reading. The method consists in reading as quickly as possible; the number of syllables read in a given time being counted, or, which amounts to the same thing, the average time for the reading of a syllable.[2] This author found that fatigue due to gymnastic exercises lengthened the reading time about 15 per cent.

7. **Persistence of Visual Sensations.**—P. Janet has shown that in persons with certain psychoasthenic diseases visual impressions persist longer than with normal people. If a disc, having coloured sections, is revolved before their eyes, less speed is required to bring about a uniform sensation (therefore the fusion of retinal impressions) than in the case of normal subjects.[3]

[1] Oehrn, Bettmann, Psy. Arb. I.; Ley, *L'arrieration mentale*, Brussels, 1904, p. 206.

[2] Keller, *Pädagogisch-psychometr. Studien*, Biol. Centralblatt, 1894 and 1897.

[3] Janet, *La durée des sensations visuelles élémentaires*, Bull. Institut. général psy. IV., 1904, p. 540.

The method that Janet employed to measure pathological mental depression may be applied also to ordinary fatigue. Experiments ought to be made in this direction.

8 **The Method of Ocular Accommodation.**—Every one knows that we are unable to see clearly objects which are too close to our eyes. This comes about because we are unable to contract beyond a certain limit the muscle which makes convex our crystalline lens, and permits near sight. This limit is called the *punctum proximum* [near-point]. But the action of the accommodating muscle of the crystalline lens is subject to the influence of fatigue: when we are fatigued we are unable to see clearly objects at the same distance as when we are fresh. Dr. Baur, a school doctor in Germany, had the excellent idea of founding upon this fact a method for measuring fatigue.[1] For this purpose he made use of the arrangement invented by Scheiner, of which we find a description in treatises on physiology, or optics. If we look at a pin through a card pierced by two little holes, we find that the pin appears to be two when it is brought sufficiently near for it to be inside the near-point [the minimum distance for an object so that the eyes can focus for clear vision]. To make more easily appreciable, especially for children, the precise moment when the pin appears as double, Baur replaced the two little holes in Scheiner's card by two coloured glasses, the one red and the other green. When the pin is in focus for the sight it looks white, the two colours (complementary) being fused. But when it is brought inside the near-point it appears as two, one image being red and the other green. Then we measure, by means of a special arrangement, and one easy to

[1] Baur, *Die Ermudung im Spiegel des Auges*, Langensalza, 1910.

devise, the distance of the pin from the eye at the moment when the subject says that he sees it as two —that is to say, at the moment when the accommodating muscle has done all that it is able to do.

Numerous experiments have proved to the author the validity of this method, which recommends itself by the following advantages: by reason of its great resistance the accommodating muscle is more influenced by general than by local fatigue; and it therefore serves well for estimating intellectual fatigue. Suggestion does not have any part in this measurement, the action of the muscle being independent of the will. The arrangement is simple, the experiment rapid; and we are easily able to control the result obtained.

We may recall here that the influence of fatigue upon the accommodating muscle of the crystalline lens had previously been studied by Moore, who had observed that fatigue influenced the perception of depth and caused an over-estimation of distance. This author has shown that fatigue exercises an analogous action upon the apparatus for converging the eyes: the act which consists in moving the gaze from one point to another, since it demands more effort, suggests that the distance travelled over is greater—in the same way as, when one is fatigued, a mile walk appears longer than when one is fresh and active.[1] Moore further remarks, in the same work, how fatiguing it is to the eyes of pupils to copy in the usual way sentences written on the blackboard: in order to carry their gaze from the board to their writing-book, they must continually change the convergence of the eyes.

9. **Other Methods.**—It has also been proposed to measure or estimate fatigue by the determination of

[1] Moore, *Studies of Fatigue*, Stud. Yale Psy. Lab. III., 1895.

the pulse,[1] by the breathing, by the body temperature,[2] by kinæsthetic memory (the repetition of an extension movement of the arms, of which we measure the displacement by the aid of the kinetometer: the movements carried out under the influence of fatigue are generally too short)[3], and by the estimation of the time.[4] Seashore has invented a "psychergograph," and M'Dougall has tried a method consisting, for the subject, in marking in ink points imprinted upon a revolving cylinder,[5] &c.

We cannot enter into details of these. The various methods here spoken of have not been sufficiently tested, or are too complicated, to be applied to the diagnosis of school fatigue.

10. **Average Variation.**—In all the methods which we have passed in review, fatigue was measured by a value expressing the *lowering* of the quantity, quality, or rapidity of a certain psychic function. But there is another value, which varies with fatigue, as Moore showed (in his work quoted above), and which we are able to take as a measure of that phenomenon: that is, the *average variation* of the results, which indicates the *regularity* with which the successive trials constituting the test have been accomplished. The average variation is calculated by taking the average differences which exist between the result of each of the trials and the average of the total results.

[1] Binet and Henri, *La fatigue intellectuelle*, Paris, 1898; Larguier des Bancels, An psy V, 1898, p. 190.

[2] Larguier, as in [1]; Gley, *Etudes de psychologie*, Paris, 1903.

[3] Gineff, *Zur Messung geistiger Ermudung*, Diss. Zurich, 1899, p. 63.

[4] Lobsien, *Ermudung und Zeitshatzungen*, Psy. päd. Stud. IV., 1903

[5] Seashore, Iowa Stud. in psy. III., 1902; M'Dougall, *On a New Method for the Study of Mental Fatigue*, B. J. of Psy. I., 1905.

Suppose, for example, that a subject presses the dynamometer five successive times, before fatigue, and that he gives the following results: 46 (lbs.), 44, 43, 41, 41. The average of these values will be 43, and the average variation is obtained by calculating the average of the differences of each of the five results with the average 43. These differences are 3, 1, 0, 2, 2, and their average (the average variation) is 1.6. Suppose, however, that our subject, being fatigued, gives the five following values on the dynamometer: 42, 36, 40, 32, 30. The average will be 36, and the average variation 4.

Thus we see that we are able to estimate fatigue not only according to the lowering of the work in the second trial, but also according to the augmentation of the irregularity: the average variation which is equal to 4 represents an irregularity stronger than the average variation which is equal to 1.6. I must add that the example I have just given is fictitious, and that it would be interesting to pursue the study of this question experimentally.

General Criticism of Ponometric Methods, and Precautions to be taken

Ponometric methods, which may be either direct or indirect, nearly all assume that the subject executes with the maximum of application, attention, and effort, the trials serving for the test. But this supposition is not always a reality. Also, as Schuyten has clearly shown by striking experiments, the *interest* that the subject takes in the experiment is far from being constant, and varies, from one trial to the other, more than one would think possible.

If we take, for example, a first measure of fatigue

in the morning, and a second measure in the evening, we find—particularly in the case of the æsthesiometer—that the evening results will be less good than those of the morning. But we must not rush to the conclusion that it is because the children are more fatigued in the evening. No; for if we take the first measure in the evening and the second in the morning, we shall find that it is the results of the morning which are inferior. In other words, the first measure is frequently the best, whether it be taken before or after work, because the children are specially interested in the first trial, and this interest stimulates their attention and improves the results.[1] It is necessary, therefore, if we wish to have valuable results, to eliminate this interest factor.

Another factor which interferes with attempts to determine fatigue, and tends to render the results useless, is that of *practice*. Most of the tests which we have reviewed are influenced by practice, by habit; the more one practises the trials involved, the more easily are these trials done: practice has an influence not only upon the direct methods. which involve a certain amount of work, but also upon the indirect methods, such as the æsthesiometric, the dynamometric, &c.

To eliminate these agents which may hide the real influence of fatigue, we have recourse to certain artifices, of which the two principal are *The method of equivalent groups* and *The method of repetitions*.

The method of equivalent groups was recommended for the first time, I believe, by Schuyten, for the pur-

[1] Schuyten, *Sur les methodes de mensuration de la fatigue des écoliers*, Ar. de Psy. II., 1903, p. 321; *Comment doit-on mesurer la fatigue des écoliers*, ibid. IV., 1905. See also a minutely critical section on the various methods of measuring fatigue in Baade's *Exp. u. kritische Beitr. zur Frage nach den sekundaren Wirkungen des Unterrichts*, Diss. Göttingen, 1906.

pose of avoiding the variability of interest; but it is also good for eliminating practice. It is necessary, says this writer, to operate not upon the same pupils, but upon groups of children identical as to age, intelligence, and social position. These groups should be examined *only once,* and in conditions absolutely comparable. If, then, one of the groups is submitted to the test before school and the other after school, we shall obtain results which evidently will be equivalent with regard to the interest which the novelty of an experiment excites among children, and with regard to the absence of practice. But the difficulty is to make up equivalent groups, which is not always possible.

Winch, whose researches in London schools I have already drawn attention to, has got some very interesting results from the method of equivalent groups. The tests which he used to estimate fatigue comprised six complex sums, or little problems, of this sort:—

$$6\tfrac{7}{8}+3\tfrac{4}{5}+1\tfrac{1}{3};$$
$$0.03576 \times 42.75, \text{ \&c.}$$

"If a man is able to row 3 miles an hour against the stream of a river which runs at the rate of $2\frac{1}{2}$ miles per hour, how far will he be able to row in 6 hours with the current?" &c.

A preliminary experiment was made for classifying the subjects, who were arranged in order of merit, according to the marks they obtained for their work. This classification being made, they were subdivided into two groups, A and B, the first on the list (top pupil) being put in the group A, the second in group B, and so on, in such a way that the total of marks obtained by all the pupils in each group was very nearly equal. These two equal groups being formed, they were given an identical task (and analogous to that of the preliminary exercise) to perform; but one group did the work at 8 P.M., and the other at 9 P.M. Here, as an illustration, are the results obtained for some of the subjects :—

Group A.			Group B.		
Subjects.	Marks.		Subjects.	Marks.	
	Prelim. Exper.	At 8 P.M.		Prelim. Exper.	At 9 P.M.
A . .	79	99	B . .	79	79
C . .	63	67	D .	68	57
E . .	57	59	F .	64	43
G . .	53	53	H . .	44	44
I . .	30	42	J . .	43	34

This table shows very clearly the action of fatigue, freed from other factors which might have intervened. The subjects of group A have *all* done better in the second trial (8 P.M.) than in the preliminary trial (this may be due either to practice or to the fact that the second trial was easier). On the other hand, *none* of those in group B have done better in the second trial: for two of them the marks are unaltered, while the marks of three are lower. All other things being equal (the groups having been made equal), it is clearly to fatigue that we must attribute the difference in the results obtained.

The Method of Repetition—employed formerly by Kraepelin to unmask the effects of certain toxics upon the rapidity of psychic processes [1]—consists in annulling the influence of practice by causing a great number of preliminary experiments to be made until practice has developed all its effects: since there is a limit to the results of exercise, for we cannot perfect ourselves indefinitely; and once this limit is attained, the influence of practice is no longer felt.

[1] Kraepelin, *Ueber die Beeinflussung einfacher psych. Vorgange durch einige Arzneimittel*, Jena, 1892.

This method has the inconvenience of needing a very great number of experiments. But it is not necessary to reach the limit of the effect of practice in order to demonstrate the presence of fatigue. It suffices if series of experiments are arranged as follows: if we wish, for example, to study the fatigue produced by a day at school, we shall make an experiment on Monday *morning* before school; on Tuesday *evening*, at the time of dismissal; on Wednesday, at the beginning of the *morning;* on Thursday, in the *evening*, and so on. We shall be able, in this way, to recognise very clearly the presence of fatigue; for if practice produces an acceleration of work from day to day, it is evident that the gain due to this practice will be noticed less on the days when fatigue is shown than on the days without fatigue. We shall also have, from one day to another, unequal progress. This relative decrease of progress, if it coincides with the days when the experiment took place in the evening, will certainly be attributable to fatigue.

It will be well, also, in such series of repetitions, to vary the order of the experiments, so as to eliminate with greater certainty other possible factors which might falsify the results. Thus, if during one week the morning experiment was taken on Monday, then the following week the Monday experiment should be done in the evening, &c. In this way the influence of the order of the tests will be completely annulled, even when operating on the same children.

2. *The Fatigue Curve*

The methods which we have just passed in review have been devised for estimating, or measuring, what is the *state* of fatigue of an individual *at a certain moment*. But most of them also serve, particularly the direct methods, for studying the manner in which fatigue develops, from what it begins, and its progress in a worker. For this it is sufficient to employ a method which allows of the measurement, *at each moment*, of the work done. We thus obtain the variation of work while it is being performed, and we are then able to establish the curve of work, from which we can deduce, with more or less exactness, the fatigue curve. We have already seen that an instrument, the ergograph, automatically gives the outline of such curves; but these principally concern muscular fatigue.

1. **Method.**—The principle of the experiment is very simple: we give a person a continuous piece of work to do, during a certain time, advising him to do it *as rapidly* and *as well* as possible, and we then observe if the speed and the quality of the work varies in the course of the time (*Method of continuous work*).

It was Oehrn who, in 1889, first employed this method. Burgerstein in 1891, Höpfner in 1894, and Holmes in 1895 made use of it to determine the curve of work during an hour of school. Since then Kraepelin and his pupils have applied it to numerous laboratory researches, which have opened out a number of new possibilities.[1]

As to the work to be done, we can take a long dictation, or the counting of letters, &c.; or we can simply have a series of numbers written, *e.g.* from 100 to 999, or beginning from 1000. The best test is the doing of sums, since this is a more intellectual work.

[1] Oehrn, Burgerstein, see articles quoted above; Höpfner, *Ueber geistige Ermudung der Schulkinder*, Z. f. Psy. VI.; Holmes, *The Fatigue of a School Hour*, Ped. S III.; Kraepelin, &c., Psy. Arb. *passim*.

Kraepelin has published books specially for this, in which there are long prepared columns of figures ready to be added.[1] The subject is made to add these figures *two by two*, and to write the total each time at the side of the column, ignoring the figure for the tens so as to gain time. For example (the figures in italics represent those written by the subject) :—

8
3 *1*
5 *8*
7 *2*
9 *6*, &c.

This is added thus :—8+3=11 (only the second 1 of 11 is written) ; 3+5=8 ; 5+7=12 (only the 2 is written) ; &c. This method of writing the sum has been strongly criticised. Binet and Henri condemn it as bringing motor fatigue into the experiment, which finally becomes extremely annoying and very much exceeds the mental fatigue. To avoid this inconvenience, Oker-Blom used columns of ten figures, which had to be added in full.[2] But this system does not permit us to see exactly what is the number of errors committed : we see only the error in the total.

An intermediate method, which I have employed for an experiment, and of which I shall speak presently, consists in adding four figures of Kraepelin's columns each time, and writing down, at the right of the fourth figure, the total of the addition. This method has the advantage, on the one hand, of augmenting the mental effort, since it is necessary to take care not to add too many or too few numbers ;

[1] *Rechenhefte*, Buchdruckerei Hörning, Heidelberg.

[2] Binet and Henri, *La fatigue intellectuelle*, p. 232 ; Oker-Blom, *Ueber die Entwickl. der geistigen Leistungsfähigkeit bezw. der Ermüdung*, Z. exp. Päd. X., 1910, p. 76.

and, on the other hand, of diminishing, and sufficiently separating, the writing actions, so that their intervention becomes negligible. For example :—

8
3
5
7 *23*
9
6
8
5 *28*, &c.

What we can fairly object to in the test of continued addition is that it is very little like school work, which is never so monotonous and exacting. The method of dictations, employed by Höpfner, should have an advantage in this respect. But the method of additions is extremely valuable for exact laboratory researches, by reason of its uniformity.

While the subject is doing his work, the director of the experiment sounds, at regular intervals (for example, every two, three, or five minutes) a signal of some kind (a bell, or blow on the table); the subject should then, without interrupting his work, make a mark at the place where he was when the signal sounded. We can thus find out afterwards how many additions (or other operations) had been done in the unit of time which had been chosen. These signals can also be made by an apparatus, such as a striking clock, or other analogous arrangement.

The method of additions is very well suited for a collective experiment. Fig. 13 shows 8 tracings obtained in a collective experiment made upon the students of my laboratory with the Kraepelin books, additions being made of each group of four figures, as I have pointed out. The work lasted 45 consecutive minutes. Signals were given every three minutes. The curves were then drawn according to the number of additions (of four figures) done in each interval of three minutes.

2. **Results.**—The curves which are obtained by operations of this sort do not in the least resemble what we might have expected. Fatigue, it seems, ought to give regular decreases. But, very much to the contrary, these curves—independently of great individual differences, upon which I cannot dwell here—have a tendency to rise at least in a certain part of their course, and it is only if the work is prolonged beyond an hour that we see them waver.

What are the factors which are opposed to fatigue? It is to the honour of Kraepelin and his school that they have, with much sagacity, discovered these. And, though the last word upon this very complex subject has by no means been said, it seems to me that the most important factors have already been brought to light.

The first of these factors antagonistic to fatigue to which we may direct attention is **practice** (usage). If the curve does not fall, but, on the contrary, presents a tendency to rise at the end of a certain period of work, it is because the subject is habituated to his task; by force of repeating the same task, the operations are done more easily in the brain. We have here a factor really antagonistic to fatigue, for it is not restricted to *masking* the effects, but it really diminishes it during a certain time: in effect, the more an activity is exercised the less trouble it takes, and therefore the less it fatigues. In the long run, however, activities even when practised finish by fatiguing: fatigue gets the best of it, and tends to lower the curve of work.

[1] Kraepelin, *Die Arbeitskurve*, Philos. Stud. XIX., 1902.

Another fact which also immediately strikes us is the zigzags, the oscillations, often very considerable, of the curves. We might say that the subjects, feeling their work waning, make a vigorous effort of application every now and again : they make a "**spurt.**" And it is so in fact. Two of these work impulsions are characteristic : the spurt initial, and the spurt terminal. We have a good illustration of the first in the curves A, E, and F of fig. 13 ; and of the second, in the curves B, D, F, and H. These spurts are due to the will, to interest. We shall speak again of them later (see section 7).

But there is a third factor which can also be seen in certain curves : the **getting up steam** (start, attack). Certain persons are unable to give their maximum at the first start ; it is necessary for them to get their steam up. This short phase of getting up steam, which produces a rise at the beginning of the curve, is characteristic of the curves C, D, and G in fig. 13.

To these three factors yet others have to be added : those which are brought out by the comparison of curves taken under different conditions, notably those curves of work which is interrupted by a pause more or less long. The pause is found to be an excellent instrument of analysis, which the Kraepelin school has ingeniously exploited.

If, at the end of an hour of continued additions, we cause the subject to take a rest for five minutes, we perceive that the rest favourably influences the work. The work which follows the interval is superior to that which preceded it. Such an effect from rest is easily understood. But this is less easily understood : if, instead of stopping the work for five minutes, there is an interruption for fifteen minutes, the interval has an unfavourable influence on the work, which becomes

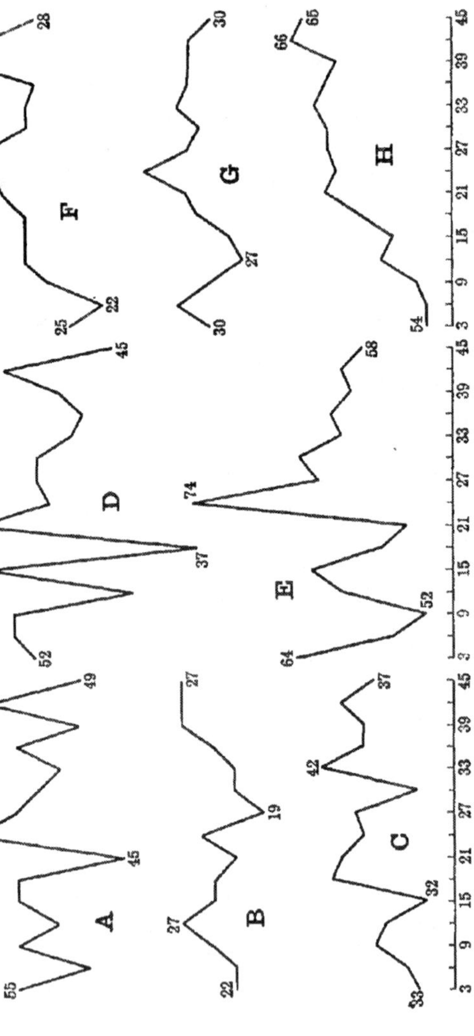

FIG. 13.—Curves of work (continued additions during 45 mins.) of 8 persons; a collective experiment.

less. Does this come from losing the effect of acquired practice? By no means. Practice is a possession which is preserved for a considerable time, even after an interval of one or many weeks, as experiments on the point have shown. After only 15 minutes' arrest this loss is very small and is compensated for, and more than compensated for, by the rest. There is then a new factor in play, and this factor is "**swing**" (animation). The very fact of working stimulates us, excites us, puts us in the mood for work, in a specially favourable humour for activity. Everybody knows how much harm is done by an untimely interruption when one has got into the swing of a piece of work.

We may notice as a final factor **familiarisation**, which acts in the same manner as practice, but is distinguished by the fact that it is more a psychical than a physiological factor. When a certain work has been going on for some moments, we understand it better, we know it better, we perceive the intricacies better, we adapt ourselves to it—in a word, we are familiarised with it. Wundt[1] gives to the *Gewöhnung* (accustoming) of Kraepelin the very characteristic name of *apperceptive*, or *intelligent*, *practice*, opposing it to mechanical practice, which he calls *associative practice*.

Familiarisation includes, to some extent, habituation, understanding by this word resistance to noxious agents, *i.e.* indifference with regard to the painful sensations which accompany forced and fatiguing work.

To examine in detail each of these factors would take up far too much time. They are not recognised by all the psychologists, *e.g.* Schulze and Meumann no longer admit the influence of practice when operating with subjects already practised, and the latter author

[1] Wundt, *Grundzuge der physiologischen Psychologie*, 5th ed., 1903, III., p 622

reduces the various factors of work to two principal ones: the adaptation of attention and fatigue.[1]

We must not forget, when interpreting these different curves, to distinguish between the speed and the quality of work, two properties which, we have seen, do not always go hand in hand. The curve of errors reveals, much better than that of speed, the appearance of fatigue. Burgerstein, for example, had arithmetic done in his class for an hour, with slight pauses every ten minutes, and afterwards counted how many operations had been done, and how many mistakes made in each of these periods of ten minutes. He found that the work had constantly augmented in speed, but that the number of mistakes had also increased: 3 per cent. of mistakes in the first quarter of the hour, and 6 per cent. in the last quarter.

3. *Influence of Various Factors on Fatigability*

Once in possession of the various methods of measurement, it is possible, theoretically at least, to study the influence which the most diverse factors of age, sex, time of the year, &c., have upon the appearance of fatigue.

We propose to give a sketch of some of the researches undertaken up to the present. Of course the results are only provisional, since the methods of investigation are still imperfect. It is also probable that all the methods are not of equal value, and that, in a given research, the result would have been more or less different if another method than that actually made use of had been employed.

Nevertheless, all the investigations are most suggestive, and they are worth repeating and checking.

[1] Schulze, *Aus der Werkstatt der exp. Psy*, Leipsic, 1909, p 255; Meumann, *Vorlesungen*, II. pp. 11 and 133.

1. **Age.**—The variation of fatigue according to age has been investigated in schools, by Gilbert, by the method of taps, of which we have spoken. Fatigability decreases with age, but the curve of this decrease is not regular; it rises abruptly at 8 years, at 13–14 years, and at 16 years. We know what this means: at these epochs there is an acceleration of growth, and the available energy being diminished, fatigability is augmented.

2. **Sex.**—There are hardly any researches in this domain. Schuyten has attempted to compare the fatigability of boys and girls, but he has not obtained definite results.[1] Binet has shown that the diminution of sensibility after a fatiguing lesson was a little greater amongst the girls than amongst the boys.[2]

It is only by the method of tapping that any systematic researches have been done. Miss Thompson, and Wells, found no very marked difference between the sexes: the men, however, better sustain rapidity of movement, and, according to Wells, women are usually more subject to "spurts." [3] According to the figures published by Gilbert,[4] who has worked with the same method, it seems that boys are fatigued more quickly. But we must remember that they have also worked more (that they have given more taps per second); if we take account of all the factors involved, we ought to conclude that they are fatigued *less easily* while appearing to be fatigued *more severely*. We have now got our finger on the real difficulty of such experiments: fatigue depends both upon the quantity of

[1] Schuyten, Paedol Jaarb X, 1906, p. 85.

[2] Binet, Ann. Psy. IX., p. 29.

[3] Thompson, *The Mental Traits of Sex*, Chicago, 1903, p. 14; Wells, *Sex Differences in Tapping*, Amer. J. of Psy., 1909.

[4] Gilbert, Stud. from the Yale Psy. Lab. II., 1894, p. 68.

the work done and its speed. To compare the fatigue of two categories of individuals, it is necessary to make them do the same quantity of work in the same time, a condition which, when it has to do with mental work, can never be obtained except by "groping" or by chance.

One means, which has not yet been tried, and which, I believe, will be very suitable for comparing the fatigability of individuals having a different capacity for work, consists in utilising *the method of pause:* a given pause is introduced at a given moment in the working of the test, and we judge the existing fatigue at the moment when the work had been interrupted, according to the favourable effects of the pause (the more the pause revives the subject, the more was he exhausted).

3. **Intelligence.**—The difficulty of the method to which we have just alluded appears when we try to establish the relation of fatigability to intelligence. If the dullards are less fatigued, is it because they are, by nature, more resistant to fatigue? Might they be perchance of a more robust nervous texture, whereas intelligence would imply, on the contrary, an exaggerated nervous sensibility, of which the highest limit would be a psychopathic state favourable to the production of a genius (whom some think is merely a neurotic person)? Or does this diminution of fatigability arise from the fact that the dullards work less? The second way of looking at it appears, till there is proof to the contrary, much the more probable.

With equal work, on the contrary, the intelligent subjects will be less fatigued—at least that is what Schuyten believes he has established in his æsthesiometric researches.[1] But we do not know if, all allow-

[1] Schuyten, Paedol. Jaarb. X, 1906, p. 89.

ances being made, the intelligent are more fatigued than the unintelligent. This question is almost insoluble, for I assume that if we wished to try to determine what is the amount of work which gives an imbecile exactly as much trouble to do as a certain amount of work done by an intelligent subject, we should be obliged, so as to be able to solve this sort of psychological rule of three, to bring in precisely the amount of time taken and the fatigue occasioned by each of these amounts of work. We should be able, however, also to try in this case the method of pause just suggested.

4. **The Individual Type.**—Individuals are distinguished according to the *degree* of their fatigability, and according to the *manner* in which they become fatigued.

There is nothing in particular to say upon the first of these characteristics: that every one does not offer the same resistance to fatigue is a well-known fact, although we do not know how great, in this respect, are the individual differences. A master assumes *a priori* that all his pupils have the same capacity for work. Up to what point is he justified in believing this?

The manner in which one becomes fatigued is a characteristic still more important for individual psychology. Mosso, at the time of his ergographic experiments, had already noticed that the curves which he obtained did not all have the same outlines, but varied according to the individuals. Certain persons did work which remained at a maximum for a certain time, after which it suddenly fell to zero. Others, on the contrary, showed work decreasing from the commencement in a regular way (see figs. 11 and 12). "I have not been able to explain to myself the reason of this fact," he says, "and I have had to come to the conclusion that this was really a constant fact which indicated the variety which each person presents in the manner in which he is fatigued."

Kraepelin's experiments have also thrown light upon the diversities of fatigue and of work. Unfortunately this most interesting question has given rise, up till now, to but very few systematic researches. We know only a few which can be quoted, as those of Kemsies, and of Blazek, made upon school children, and those of Meumann upon adults.

Kemsies worked, in a communal school in Berlin, upon 55 children of 10 to 11 years. At different hours of the day they were set to do a dozen sums mentally, *e.g.* $417 + 338$, or 74×8, or $291 \div 7$, &c. They were allowed to take 12 minutes for the work. Then the percentage of mistakes was reckoned. These experiments have revealed the existence of four different types of work :—

In the 1st type, which we may call the type of *increasing work*, the number of mistakes goes on decreasing, from the first to the last experiment of the day ; for example, 40 per cent. mistakes at 8 A.M., 29 at 9 A.M., 27 at 10 A.M., 28 at 11 A.M., and 23 at noon.

In the 2nd type, or *decreasing work*, the number of mistakes increases with the range of the experiments; for example, 54 mistakes at 8 A.M., and 77 at noon.

In the 3rd type, which we will call the *convex curve work*, at the beginning the work shows a rising phase, to which succeeds a descending phase.

In the 4th type, the *concave curve work*, the work begins to decrease from the very beginning, and then, after having attained its minimum, increases.

We may conclude from experiments of this kind that each pupil shows his "best work" at a certain time of the day. Amongst a third of Kemsies's pupils this optimum was found to be before 10 A.M.

Blazek took the curve of fatigue with the æsthesiometer, during 5 successive hours of morning school. He found 3 different types: a type of *crescendo* work found in about 20 per cent. of the cases (among the industrious pupils), an *ascensional with relapses* type (the relapses in the middle of the curve) found amongst two-thirds of the pupils—children less gifted, who, at the end of a certain time of work, relaxed so as to rest themselves—and finally a *horizontal* type amongst the best pupils. According to Blazek, there are no pupils who work 5 consecutive hours: 17 per cent. would work 4 hours consecutively, 55 per cent. 3 hours, 17 per cent. 2 hours, and 11 per cent. 1 hour.

Meumann has described 3 types: *increasing*, *decreasing*, and an *intermediate* type in which the maximum of work is not found either at the beginning or at the end of the curve.

How shall we interpret these diverse facts? Is it a question of types of *fatigue* or types of *work?* Does the increase or the decrease of the yield of work result from organic diversities—*e.g.* in some people fatigue is produced and accumulates more quickly, whilst among others, on the contrary, a sort of habituation is created which renders the organism more resistant to the phenomenon—or, again, is it a question of differences in the nature of the voluntary reaction, of excitement, or of the aptitude to profit by practice?

These two circumstances have to be taken equally into account. Beside the *net* fatigability, which depends entirely upon physiological causes, and which varies from one individual to another, there is *gross* fatigability, that which we actually observe in the complexity of life. Now, this gross fatigability depends upon all the factors which constitute personality. Certain of them specially concur with fatigability in impressing their particular mark upon the curve of work. These factors, which were pointed out by Kraepelin, are: the aptitude to profit by practice, the aptitude to retain the good effects of practice, to become "worked up," to profit by repose, to be distracted, and to become familiarised.

The general forms of character also modify, in a large measure, the rate of fatigue. Tissié has made some judicious and excellent remarks about this. "Each subject," he says, "is fatigued or not, according to his will. The *passive* ones are not fatigued very much, because it is necessary to urge them into activity; the *sensitive* ones are timid and afraid of fatigue, but they become emboldened as soon as they become aware of their own value. The *assertive* ones rise above fatigue, they overwork themselves; it is necessary to calm them, for they are always ready to commit excesses. An obstacle is always vanquished by the assertive, more especially if the obstacle seems to say to them: 'You shall not pass.'" [1]

5. **The Seasons.**—The cycle of the seasons and the changes of temperature, or other things which accompany them, act upon the organic life. It is therefore probable that it also influences fatigability, which is an organic function. But the determination of this influence is a very delicate matter. Schuyten, and afterwards Lobsien, in experimenting upon children found that the curve of fatigue is subject to periodic oscillations from September to July; but, on the whole, the curve would rise. If this is the case, if fatigability

[1] Tissié, Bull. off. de l'instr. primaire, Dép. des Basses-Pyrénées, Oct. 1903. See also *La fatigue et l'entraînement physique*, Paris, 1897, by the same author.

only increases from the commencement to the end of the school year, this augmentation must be put to the account of the school work, or else to some other factor outside the work itself, such as growth in height or weight ? Schuyten, who has given much attention to this subject, considers that the child exhausts himself almost without cessation from the beginning to the end of the school year,[1] and he throws the responsibility for this sad fact upon our existing school system. It is to be noted that the curves of fatigue, rising during the months of work, show during the holidays a descending movement. There is need here for an entire study to be made, which is as yet only sketched out.[2]

6. **The Time of the Day.**—Is fatigability greatest in the morning, afternoon, or evening ? This is a very complex question, for, as we have seen, fatigue does not solely depend upon the work accomplished, but upon the general disposition of the worker, and the state of the nervous system. But it is not evident that this disposition should be better in the morning than at other times.

[1] Schuyten, article quoted (p. 250), p. 83. See also his observations on the variation of attention and of muscular force in the course of the year, and under the influence of temperature, Bull. Acad. roy. de Belgique, vols. 32 and 34, 1896–7, and Paedol. Jaarb., 1900, 1904; Lobsien, *Schwankungen der psychischen Kapazitat*, Berlin, 1902, and *Ueber Schulversaumnisse und Schwankungen physischer Energie*, Z. päd. Psy., 1909.

[2] After a series of experiments, Lehmann and Pedersen (*Das Wetter und unsere Arbeit.*, Ar. f. ges. Psy. X., 1907) have shown that meteorological conditions have a very marked influence upon physical and mental work ; thus the memory and muscular force vary in accordance with barometric pressure, a rise of temperature is prejudicial to the work of additions, &c. These authors consider that it is to meteorological variations that we must attribute the oscillations of physical capactiy during the course of the year. See also Dexter, *Conduct and the Weather*, Psy. R. Monog. Suppl. 1898, and Paidologist, 1906, p. 11.

It seems, on the contrary, according to experimental researches made in recent years, that the aptitude for work undergoes, during the course of the day, various oscillations. Stern and Lay, we remember, have found that psychic energy culminates towards the end of the morning, and towards 5 P.M. Other writers, Dresslar,[1] Bergström, Baade, Marsh, having studied, by various methods, the "diurnal rhythm" of the aptitude for work, have all found very marked differences according to the time of the day. There is not complete agreement upon all points, but most of the observations show that the first hours of the morning and of the afternoon are the most unfavourable for work:[2] the end of the morning and of the afternoon, or even the latest hours in the evening, give the best results.

It appears very probable that meals, with the digestive activity which succeeds them, interfere, in a large measure, with the play of cerebral activity. "Under no pretext," says Dr. Doléris, with good reason, "ought the child to work immediately after the evening meal."[3]

[1] Dresslar, Am. J. Psy., 1892, p. 519; Bergström, ibid., 1894; Baade, work quoted, p. 65; Marsh, *The Diurnal Course of Efficiency*, New York, 1906.

[2] Kemsies, however, considers that it is the first two hours of the school day which should be the most favourable for work (*Arbeitshygiene der Schule*, 1898).

[3] Doléris, *Valeur du travail du matin et de l'après-midi.* Report to the first congress on School Hygiene (Paris, 1903). At Geneva we rejoice in a deplorable system; the morning classes (including those of the College) finish at ten minutes to 12, and recommence at 1.30 P.M. I have still before my mind the sweet sleep, which was not long before it benumbed the class, master and pupils, during the first hour, especially in the summer. By not commencing before 2, or 2.15, we should have made up for it, and gone beyond (even without finishing later); and, besides, the work of this first half-hour was nil. This would be an excellent investment, since we should gain without risking the loss of anything.

If, side by side with this objective study, we take into account the feeling of the workers and ask them which is the time of the day which is most favourable for their work, we obtain answers which corroborate the results indicated above. Below is a brief summary showing, in percentages, the votes received by Heerwagen (392 answers to a questionnaire); by Barnes (answers from 111 American students); by the review *L'Enseignement mathématique*, in its inquiry about mathematicians (64 answers); and by Marsh, who has, for this purpose, ransacked the biographies of 157 writers: [1]—

	Percentage of Votes					
Authors	Morning	Afternoon	Evening	Night	Morning and Evening.	Indifferent (all day)
Heerwagen,	46.5	1 5	34	—	11	7
Barnes,	60	5	35	—	—	—
Ens. Math,	47	4.5	37.5	—	11	—
Marsh,	34	1	12	6	21	23

These statistics show us that, though the morning is generally preferred, the individual divergences are rather considerable. Beside the *morning* type, we notice an *evening* type very strongly represented, and a mixed *morning-evening* type; the *afternoon* type includes only a very few representatives. It still remains to be known whether the fatigue produced is necessarily less when one works at the time he prefers. This is a question difficult to decide. Many of the mathematicians, in their reply to the inquiry, declared that evening work, though preferred by all of them from the point of view of the quality, had the disadvantage of being injurious to health, since it has a bad effect on sleep.

[1] Heerwagen, Philos. Stud. V. 1889, p. 304; Barnes, quoted by Bergstrom, see above; Fehr, Flournoy, and Claparède, *Enquête sur la méthode de travail des mathématiciens*, Paris and Geneva, 1908, p. 110; Marsh, see above (book named)

The measurements of fatigue taken during school by Schuyten and others[1] generally show a stronger fatigability in the afternoon (independently of individual differences such as those indicated above, p. 253); and this confirms the general opinion. As to the fatigue produced by evening courses there is disagreement between Schuyten and Winch. Whilst the latter found that evening work was much more tiring (see above, p. 240), Schuyten found, on the contrary, that a two hours' course produced no appreciable fatigue.[2]

7. **The Days of the Week.**—Does fatigability vary with the days of the week? This can only be the case if the fatigability of a certain day is dependent upon the fatigue contracted during preceding days. In normal circumstances—that is to say, when the fatigue of a day is entirely dissipated by a night's rest—every day ought, it would seem, to be equal in relation to fatigability.

In fact, the aptitude for work on the various days of the week is subject to variations; but this is probably connected with other causes than a greater or lesser degree of fatigue. The variations are due, above all, to lassitude, ennui, excitement, impatience—not to mention the arrangement of the time-table—factors which, themselves, certainly vary in the course of the week. On Monday the pupils generally have some difficulty in recovering their ardour; by Tuesday this has become much better. But on Wednesday lassitude commences. Then comes the holiday on Thursday—or, in certain countries, on Wednesday afternoon. On Friday and Saturday the children are often more active, because they rejoice at the approach of Sunday: it is the making of the spurt terminal.

[1] Griesbach, Vannod, Wagner, Sakaki, Abelson, &c.

[2] Schuyten, Paedol. Jaarb., 1908, p. 32.

Up to the present experimental researches have been few, and I can find none to quote except those of Kemsies, carried out in a class, by the method of calculation and of ergography. This author found that the best days were Monday and Tuesday.[1] Kemsies did not perhaps sufficiently protect himself from the source of error pointed out subsequently by Schuyten (see above, p. 237).

8. **Habit, Swing, Interest.**—We have already considered these various factors, as antagonistic to fatigue. The question whether they really diminish the state of fatigue, or whether they only conceal it, is undecided. As to habit, we shall see later that a physiologist, Weichardt, believes that the production of fatigue may even directly diminish fatigability. We shall have occasion to speak of interest in sections 6, 7, and 8.

9. **Change of Work.**—What is the influence of change of work upon fatigue? Is one fatigued less quickly by changing his work? It does not appear that such is the case. Schulze, at Leipsic, made some instructive experiments on this point, upon some young girls of 12 years of age. These young girls were made one day to do additions for 25 minutes, then to copy letters for 25 minutes, then to do fresh additions for 25 minutes, and lastly to copy again for 25 minutes. Another day they had to do analogous work but distributed differently: the additions for 50 consecutive minutes, and then, immediately following, copying for 50 minutes. The second group of tests gave better results than the first, in which change of work had taken place three times.[2]

The laboratory experiments long pursued by Wey-

[1] Kemsies, *Arbeitshygiene der Schule*, Berlin, 1898.

[2] Kraepelin, *Zur Ueberbürdungsfrage*, Jena, 1897, p. 20.

gandt show analogous results. This was how this author proceeded: on the days of continued work, the subject pursued his work (for example, additions) for an hour and a quarter; on the days of varied work, the subject did additions for half-an-hour, then changed to other work (for example, crossing out certain letters in a text), during the following half-hour; and lastly he returned, during the last quarter of an hour, to the original work of additions. In comparing the work done during the last quarter of an hour of the days of continued work with that of the last quarter of an hour of the days of varied work, we are able to determine the influence of change of work. The author has shown that change of work is sometimes slightly advantageous, sometimes harmful, and generally it is without appreciable effect.[1]

What we know of the physiology of fatigue enables us to understand why change of work is not restful. Fatigue is, in fact, a general phenomenon: it corresponds, amongst other things, with an accumulation in the blood of toxic waste resulting from nervous and muscular work. But the blood also irrigates those parts of the brain which work as well as those which do not work, and as it is toxic it does as much harm to the activity of the cerebral regions which do not function as to those centres whose work has been the origin of the fatigue.[2] Besides, the change of work risks destroying the good effects of practice and of swing.

It is, however, an ordinary observation that change

[1] Weygandt, *Ueber den Einfluss der Arbeitswechsels auf fortlaufende geistige Arbeit*, Psy Arb. II, 1897.

[2] The well-known experiment of Mosso proves that this is so: if we transfuse the blood of a fatigued dog to a rested one, the latter shows all the symptoms of fatigue; and *vice versâ* we can defatigue a dog by transfusing in him the blood of a rested one.

of work (if it is not too frequent) favours work. This is true. But from the fact that it favours work, it does not necessarily follow that it *dissipates* the state of fatigue. Change of work has the effect of reviving the interest of the worker wearied by the sameness of an occupation; and the new work, if it is subjectively more agreeable, has the effect of augmenting the fatigue capital of the organism. It is true that when the new work is interesting it is effected under less exhausting conditions (see later, section 7).

10. **Body Position.**—Is work easier in certain attitudes than in others? Very probably it is. Mental activity intimately depends upon the cerebral circulation, and this is strongly influenced by the position of the body. According as an individual is lying down or standing up, the blood flows in greater or lesser quantity to his brain, and the blood pressure undergoes diverse variations. Münsterberg once showed that the association of ideas is more rapid in the lying on the back position, which favours cerebral irrigation.[1]

An American writer, Elm. Jones, has recently published some experiments concerning the influence of the position of the body on various psychical processes.[2] He has specially shown that the horizontal position improves tactile discrimination, visual memory, and the act of adding; whereas auditive discrimination, quickness of tapping, and strength as measured by the dynamometer, were, on the contrary, favoured by the vertical position. Muscular fatigue (estimated by means of the digital dynamometer) is found to be augmented by the horizontal position. Not much information is to be gained from these first

[1] Münsterberg, Beitr. z. exp. Psy., vol. iv., 1893.

[2] E. Jones, *The Influence of Bodily Posture on Mental Activities*, New York, 1907.

experiments, the chief advantage of which is to draw attention to a new question. More interesting are the answers to an inquiry which Jones has made among intellectual people, relative to the position in which they work best. The favourite attitudes are the horizontal position, and, above all, the semi-horizontal position. In the latter "the feet of the worker are placed on a table, or some other raised object, the chair being tilted backwards" (the inquiry was made in America !).

We are not told whether fatigability diminishes in these attitudes; but the facts have, nevertheless, a certain importance from the school point of view. We often grumble at pupils who "carry themselves badly"; but may not the tendency which scholars have to lie down at times upon their desks sometimes be a reflex attitude set up by the need of irrigating the fatigued brain ? Lauder Brunton (quoted by Jones) relates that one day, being fatigued and having an essay to write, he was unable to find a single idea. He then thought to himself, being a good physiologist, that since the blood was not able to rise to his brain, it was necessary that he should "bring the brain down to the blood"; so he placed his head upon the table. At once ideas began to come and his pen to go of itself over the paper. Having then raised his head, his mind became instantly blank, and he was obliged to write his article with his head upon the table.

11. **Orientation.**—Is it necessary to speak of the influence which, according to some writers, orientation with regard to the cardinal points may exercise upon the aptitude for work ? Nothing appears to me to be less demonstrated, but, after all, we cannot regret *a priori* the possibility of such an influence of

the magnetic earth currents, and it would be worth while to take up the question again.

In 1844, von Reichenbach, the celebrated chemist who discovered creosote and paraffin, the author of a work upon *Phénomènes odiques*, observed that persons who sleep when lying in the direction north-south (head to the north and feet to the south) had a more profound and refreshing sleep than those who slept in the other direction. Some years ago, Féré, when studying, with the ergograph, the influence of orientation upon work, found that the subject, when facing towards the west or the east, did twice as much work as when he turned towards the south or the north (this should be an indirect confirmation of "Reichenbach's law"). But Féré, having only experimented upon himself, may have been the victim of an auto-suggestion. Bertoldi, however, who has repeated the experiments, declares that he has obtained analogous results.[1]

It goes without saying that if these facts are confirmed, pedagogy should derive profit therefrom; and it would be necessary to begin to orientate schoolrooms towards the west!

12. **Dietary: Alcohol.**—Vegetarians affirm that they are able to get through a greater amount of work than flesh-eaters, and that they are less subject to fatigue than the latter. Mlle. Ioteyko has made some ergographic experiments which bear this out.

[1] Féré, *Influence de l'orientation sur l'activité*, C. R. Soc. de Biol. LVII., 1904, p. 244, and LIX., 1905; Bertoldi, *L'Orientazione ha influenza sul lavoro?* Riv. Ital. di neuropat., Dec. 1909. See also Duchatel and Warcollier, *L'art du travail et l'art du repos*, Paris, 1909 (experiments made with the *sthenometer* of Joire, a kind of mariner's compass consisting of a straw turning upon a needle which is displaced when the hand approaches it; the displacements should be more considerable if the operator is made to face the south).

"Vegetarians," she concludes, "are able to work two or three times longer than flesh-eaters before becoming tired." [1] The cause of this endurance should be the lesser quantity of toxine produced by vegetable foods. It is probable that this way of looking at it contains a good deal of truth. Though, to go on to say, with our learned colleague at Brussels (Mlle. Ioteyko), that "meat ought, like alcohol, to be considered as a medicament," is perhaps to force the note.

The problem of food is so complex, and still so little elucidated, that it seems to me very risky to lay down very precise rules. To be able to judge of the value of a régime, it is necessary to include not only the immediate effects but also the remoter consequences.

As to alcohol, its case is settled. Though it is capable of momentarily concealing the consciousness of fatigue, it does not in the least retard the real effects. In the long run it diminishes the amount of work done.[2]

4. *The Ponogenic Coefficient of Various Subjects*

Do all the branches of study fatigue in the same degree? Ordinary observation says no. But in what measure does each tire the learner? What is the coefficient of fatigue—the *ponogenic coefficient*, shall we call it—of each of them? This is what some authors have tried to determine approximately.

[1] Ioteyko, *Enquête sur les Végétariens de Bruxelles*, Brussels, 1907.

[2] See, among others, the works of Kraepelin, Smith, *Die Alkoholfrage*, Tubingen, 1895; Schnyder, *Alcool et Alpinisme*, Ar. de Psy. VI, 1907. The latter work contains the answers to an inquiry upon the use of alcohol made among Alpine climbers. There also we shall find, pp. 241 and 243, the ergographic curves obtained with and without ingestion of alcohol.

By the use of the æsthesiometric method, Dr. Wagner [1] (by researches made in the Gymnasium of Darmstadt) has compiled the following table in which the number 100, which represents the fatigue coefficient produced by mathematics, has been taken as the maximum of comparison :—

Mathematics	100	History and Geography	85
Latin	91	French and German	82
Greek	90	Natural History	80
Gymnastics	90	Drawing and Religion	77

Sakaki,[2] after researches pursued in four Japanese schools, also by the æsthesiometric method, has laid down the following coefficients (as before, the point of maximum comparison is equal to 100) :—

PRIMARY SCHOOL

Arithmetic	50	Play, Gymnastics, and Singing	19
Reading and Dictation (Japanese)	50	Geography	13
Composition	44	English	9
Morals	44	Drawing	0
History	37	Physics	−18
Caligraphy	31	Natural History	−25
Needlework	25		

The two last negative coefficients signify that the branches to which they belong not only did not fatigue, but rested the pupils. The fact that the highest coefficient is 50, and not 100, arises from the fact that the author has related the values obtained in the different schools to the same maximum. We find, in fact, that Sakaki found the coefficients higher for the upper classes of a young girls' school :—

[1] Wagner, *Unterricht und Ermüdung*, Berlin, 1898, p. 131.

[2] Sakaki, *Ermüdungsmessungen an vier japanischen Schulen*, Ar. int. hyg. scol. I., 1905, p. 93.

Arithmetic	100	Gymnastics	25
Japanese	100	Geography	13
History	56	Singing and Drawing	6
English	50		

By a totally different method (dynamometry), another teacher, a very experienced experimenter, Kemsies,[1] arrived at the following classification :—

Gymnastics (the most fatiguing branch).	Mother-tongue.
Mathematics.	Natural History and Geography.
Foreign Languages.	History.
Religion.	Singing and Drawing (the least fatiguing subjects).

Though the various experiments have been undertaken with different methods and upon different pupils, by different experimenters, and in spite of the diversity of circumstances, yet the results show a great similitude, which proves that the school measurement of fatigue is not a chimera. It goes without saying that the effort exacted by a given branch will be more or less great according to the professor who teaches it: a master who knows how to interest his pupils will fatigue them much less. It seems nevertheless that, leaving out of account these causes of variation, each branch has its own ponogenic value.[2]

[1] Kemsies, *Arbeitshygiene der Schule*, Berlin, 1898, p. 54.

[2] Lehmann and Pedersen (quoted above) have been led to distinguish two kinds of mental growth . *works of production*, and *works of precision*. The works of production require concentration of attention ; in this group come memorisation, and the innervation of voluntary movements. On the other hand, the discrimination of impressions and the reproduction of recollections will be among the works of precision : they depend upon the intensity of the states of consciousness, not upon attention [?]. It seems to me preferable to consider, with V. Henri, the various psychic works as forming a continuous line, from the most automatic to those which are being done for the first time and which necessitate a strong concentration of attention (Henri, *Travail psychique et physique*, An. Psy. III., 234).

Assuredly these results require to be carefully checked: it would be interesting to find out whether the order of the coefficients varies according to the age of the children. That might indicate at what age the brain is best suited for a certain branch of study, and consequently at what moment it is necessary to make it dominant in the curricula. It would be useful also to take into account these data in the drawing up of the daily time-table: the most tiring lessons ought to be placed, if possible, at the beginning of the day.

5. *Influence of Physical Work upon Mental Fatigue*

The inspection of the foregoing tables reveals to us another very interesting fact, which has been verified by numerous experiments, viz. the high ponogenic coefficient of physical work. Just when the traditional pedagogy considers gymnastics as an occasion of intellectual relaxation, experiment shows us that—quite as much intellectual work, and perhaps even more—muscular work, has for its effect the momentary lowering of mental energy.[1]

The pedagogical consequences following from this statement are easy to perceive: we must no longer, as has so often been done, place the gymnastic lessons at the beginning of school, for they fatigue the organism for all the rest of the day. Neither must recreation time be used for gymnastic or military exercises requiring much attention.

When I one day submitted these reflections to the professor of gymnastics at the Geneva College, he

[1] Also, recently, Oker-Blom (Z. exp Päd. X., p. 187) has shown that if the gymnastic lesson produces a psychometric excitation which stimulates mental activity, this favourable influence is only very passing, and very soon gives place to a marked enfeeblement.

pointed out to me that if the whole time given to gymnastics was placed at the end of the day, it would no longer be possible to get any serious work done. "In those of my lessons which come after school," he said to me, "the pupils are fatigued, and it is impossible to get them to do anything well; they do not pay attention to new movements which are taught them, and they are no longer able to exercise with uniformity."

This remark shows us, which is perfectly reasonable, that intellectual work also has as a result the lowering of the physical functions.

What, then, is to be done? If we place gymnastics at the beginning of school, it is injurious to the teaching which follows it, and if we place it at the end, the teaching which precedes it does harm to it. The dilemma in which we find ourselves comes from this: that school gymnastics has not a well-defined end, but is trying to do two things at the same time. On the one hand, it has for its end the development of attention, promptitude of movement, courage, and will: which is its strictly educative rôle. On the other hand, it is supposed to serve for relaxing and correcting the body which has to remain immobile all day upon a school form, to quicken the slackened circulation, and to relieve the congested brain. This is its hygienic rôle. But it is obvious that these two ends are partly incompatible, and cannot both be pursued at once, since the first demands an organism fresh and alert, and the second has no *raison d'être* unless, on the contrary, the organism is tired. It is necessary, therefore, to divide gymnastic lessons into two categories according to their aim: *pedagogic* gymnastics should be placed in the morning, and *hygienic* gymnastics at the end of school.

6. *The Problems of Fatigue*

We have so far considered fatigue in a wholly empirical manner, without inquiring into its nature, its exact causes, and the mechanism of its production. The time has come for asking ourselves these questions. I say asking, not solving, them.

The nature of fatigue is a subject which is still very obscure. The numerous researches, both physiological and psychological, which have taken place concerning this phenomenon, have so far had the effect of giving rise to new points of interrogation rather than of suppressing those which presented themselves at the outset. They have resulted, in fact, in this: that fatigue is a problem infinitely more complex than it was originally believed to be, and that it depends upon a number of factors some of which themselves would need to be analysed.

What is fatigue?

We give the name fatigue to a subjective impression united with an objective impotence: "the feeling of pain with difficulty in taking action," says Littré. But this definition as it stands raises some difficulties, for if it is true that in physical fatigue we nearly always encounter this duality of phenomena, it is not the same in mental fatigue. In the latter, the parallelism between the interior feeling and the incapacity for work frequently does not show itself. It is possible to have the feeling of fatigue without diminution of the capacity for work, and inversely, diminution of capacity without conscious fatigue.[1]

[1] This is a fact of ordinary observation; it has also been shown by the systematic experiments made by Thorndike (*Mental Fatigue*, Psy Rev., 1900). Mosso had already drawn attention to it (*La*

We are obliged, therefore, to make here a first subdivision of the concept of fatigue into subjective fatigue and objective fatigue. And this subdividing raises

The First Problem: *What is the reciprocal relation of these two aspects of fatigue?* Why are they not always on an equality? If the feeling of fatigue is not the correlative of an objective state of fatigue, whence comes it, and what does it mean?

To answer this first question it is necessary to know in what this objective state of fatigue consists. Unfortunately the concept of objective fatigue is not itself very clear even in its entirely empirical acceptation. I have noted above (p. 217) that the measurement of fatigue by work done was liable to grave errors, arising from the fact that fatigue can be counterbalanced by voluntary efforts. It is necessary to dwell for a moment upon this fact, which is essential. Essential both because it puts us on our guard against the causes of colossal errors which might vitiate the results of experimental researches, and because it partly discloses to us that which conceals the psychophysiological nature of fatigue.

The first conclusion which can be drawn from this statement is that fatigue is not uniformly revealed by the decrease of work done. This decrease may be masked by other factors which momentarily prevail over fatigue, without however preventing the fatigue from being continually increased. But we also see at the same time that the objective concept of fatigue is no longer precise, and that it conveys two meanings

Fatigue, p. 131). Wells (Am. J. Psy., 1909, p. 356) has shown that, in the tapping test, the parallelism between the feeling of fatigue and objective fatigue is closer among women than among men.

itself: fatigue may signify "the decrease of the capacity to work," or again it may signify "the physiological state of one who has done work" (even if the power of work has not, in fact, diminished).

Let us take as an example two individuals who are carrying out the experiment of continued additions. They have worked for sixty minutes. In the case of one, A, the curve of work is descending: at first he made eighty additions per minute, at the end he does no more than forty. In the case of the second, B, the curve remains horizontal: the rate of work has not varied through the whole course of the experiment. Which is the more fatigued at the moment when the experiment comes to an end?

It appears evident that the results drawn from the work done do not suffice for judging of the fatigue of each of the subjects. A behaves as if he were the more fatigued. But it may well be that B is in reality the more tired; only, as he has struggled against fatigue, the effect of it is not seen in the work done. If we were able to examine the nervous system or the blood of A and B, or if, at the end of the experiment of additions, we could measure the fatigue of each by the æsthesiometer (assuming this method to be valid), we should probably ascertain that it is the latter who, in spite of appearances, is the more "worn out."

And so we are obliged to subdivide, in its turn, the concept of objective fatigue: it is necessary to distinguish the gross incapacity for work from the internal physiological state engendered by work. This distinction lays down

The Second Problem; *What is the relation between the physiological state of fatigue and effective capacity for work?*

That the dynamic effects of fatigue may be attenuated or retarded by an effort of will, is corroborated by everyday observation. We are able not only voluntarily to overcome the fatigue which we experience, but we can see the fatigue suddenly eclipsed in consequence of a circumstance which interests us. If you are fatigued by a long day's work, and, just when you are rejoicing at the thought of going to bed, some one comes to announce the visit of a dear friend, your fatigue is dissipated as though by enchantment. At the moment when the striking of the clock announces the time for going out of school, the scholars who were somnolent on their seats, depressed and yawning, suddenly recover an unbounded amount of energy, rush out of class, shouting uproariously, capering, jumping, and displaying an activity which in no way resembles that of a fatigued organism. This constitutes

The Third Problem: *The influence of the will, or of interest, on fatigue.*

The Fourth Problem concerns *the physiological nature of fatigue.* Apropos of the re-echoing, so to say, of physical fatigue by mental fatigue, we have said that fatigue is a general phenomenon due to the accumulation in the blood of certain particular toxins. This is, without doubt, only one of the factors of fatigue. It also consists, possibly, in a diminution in the reserve energy of the organism. Beside this general fatigue we may assume that there exists a local fatigue due to the wear and tear of certain special regions of the nervous system of other organs.

Some physiologists clearly distinguish between these two kinds of fatigue. Verworn, for example, calls *fatigue* that which is due to the circulation in the blood of ponogenic substances, and *exhaustion* that which is due to the wear of local nerve cells characterised by a deficiency of oxygen.[1]

The Fifth Problem: *What is the seat of mental fatigue?* That is to say, what are the regions which suffer the wear and tear: the nervous system, or other organs? This important question is far from being solved. It seems at first sight that if it is the brain that works, it is that which should be the seat of the wear and tear which is produced. But we must not forget that the organism is not a simple machine, but a machine which is endowed with the faculty of adaptation. It may very well be that, in proportion to the amount of cerebral wear and tear, this wear and tear might be compensated for by a bringing in of reserve material. This is the idea, and a very interesting one, of Mosso: mental fatigue is repaired at the expense of the muscles; when the brain works, the blood stream would be able to carry off from the muscles substances useful for supporting the brain, which demands a strong provision of chemical energy. In fatigue as in inanition, the less important tissues would be destroyed to conserve those which are more important. Muscle, beside its own special functions, would also act as a reserve of energy.

The Sixth Problem is that of the *habit of fatigue.* Can we become habituated to fatigue? If a fatiguing piece of work is carried out every day, shall we end by becoming more resistant to exhaustion?

It is well known that, if there be an enthusiasm for

[1] Verworn, *Ermudung, Erschopfung,* Pfluger's Archiv., 1900 Most writers have made the difference between fatigue and exhaustion depend upon the fact that fatigue is dissipated by normal rest, while exhaustion is chronic, indeed even pathologic. This way of looking at it would agree with that of Verworn, if it were demonstrated that there is no local wear and tear in normal fatigue.

physical or mental work, it is possible to accomplish a constantly increasing amount before fatigue is felt. But in this case it is not the fatigability which diminishes, but the effort which the work demands that becomes less. Through practice, in fact, the nervous connections which maintain the work become more numerous and more perfect, and the resistance opposed to the work diminishes. If one is less fatigued it is because he is accustomed to the work, not because he has become accustomed to fatigue.

A physiologist, Weichardt, claims, however, that the organism subjected to the action of fatigue toxins makes an antitoxin capable of annihilating the pernicious influence of the fatigue-poisons. This author, having been successful in experimentally obtaining some of this antitoxin, affirms that he has been able to render some mice immune to fatigue by injecting a dose into them.[1]

These experiments have not, so far as I know, been sufficiently repeated and checked to have positive value. They have, however, the merit of opening the way to some suggestive and very useful researches. A serum against fatigue! That would certainly be most valuable.

The Seventh Problem: *Is fatigue a normal or abnormal circumstance?* I mean, *does fatigue necessarily accompany all work, or, on the contrary, ought work to be suspended when fatigue supervenes?*

This is an equivocal question. For many writers fatigue is an inevitable phenomenon, and even useful. "Fatigue is the base of all creation in science, as in the fine arts," says Mosso. "It is only by fatiguing oneself that one manages to develop oneself, alike from

[1] Weichardt, *Ueber Ermüdungstoxin und Antitoxin*, Münch. med. Woch., 1904, and Med. Klinik, 1906.

the physical point of view as well as intellectually," affirm Binet and Henri. "It is not a question, I imagine, of avoiding all fatigue, but only the excess of fatigue. And quite possibly it is the duty of the school to let the child learn what it is to be fatigued, to bring on fatigue, and to resist it; that it is destined to teach him not slackness but effort, that it ought to give him the habit not of ease but of work," declares Malapert; and Offner defends an analogous thesis.[1]

But, on the other hand, it is undeniable that the work of a fatigued person is inferior in quality; and it can be maintained also that success comes to him who knows how to manage his strength, who knows how to organise his work in such a way as never to be tired.

These contradictions arise from the fact that the term fatigue is equivocal: if we call expenditure of energy by the organism fatigue, it is quite evident that we are not able to work without being fatigued, since all work absorbs energy; but if we call fatigue a degree of diminution of energy, or of intoxication, such that it entails a decrease of the capacity for work, it is certain that there is an advantage in not defying fatigue. We shall return later on (see p. 293) to this question, which is so important to pedagogy.

Lastly, **The Eighth Problem** is that of *overpressure*, of chronic exhaustion: in what way is overpressure to be distinguished from ordinary fatigue? To this problem, most particularly interesting to pedagogy, we will devote a special paragraph a little later on. Besides, it is not possible to consider it before having tried to clear up, a little, the problem of normal fatigue.

[1] Malapert, *Rech. exp. sur la mesure de la fatigue intell*, Bull. S. psy E, 1905, p. 47; Offner, *Die geistige Ermudung*, Berlin, 1910, p. 79.

The solution of the problems which we have just formulated is very complex and delicate. Most of them can only be elucidated by minute experiments done in physiological or psychological laboratories. It appears to me, however, that it may be useful to investigate so as to obtain for oneself, provisionally, while awaiting the verdict of science, a rough conception of the phenomenon of fatigue, a conception which synthetises the most marked characteristics of the phenomenon as it appears in everyday life.

7. *The Reservoir of Energy*

The most salient fact which we shall use as a starting-point for outlining this general conception is the following: when we work we do not get fatigued at once, but only at the end of a longer or shorter time during which the work remains perceptibly equal. Sometimes the keeping up of the high level of the work produced is due to a voluntary effort which combats the nascent fatigue: more often, however, the maintaining of this steadiness of work is spontaneous, and the subject is not conscious of making an effort, nor of being fatigued. This is what takes place when we do work which interests us.

Here we again find the factor of "interest," of which we have already often spoken. And we see that it also comes in to reinforce the energy of the individual, to the extent of very much augmenting his period of resistance of fatigue.

The hypothesis of a reservoir of energy, to which we have already had recourse (p. 167), permits us, not to explain, but to represent in a concrete form by what mechanism interest is able to maintain steadiness of work and to retard or prevent manifestations of fatigue.

The reservoir of energy, as its name implies, contains a *reserve* of energy. This energy it accumulates little by little, but in a continuous manner, during rest and during sleep, in such a way that it always contains sufficient for it to be able to furnish at certain moments a great quantity at once, and to allow of a steadiness in work which only a reserve is able to furnish.

With this hypothesis it is easy for us to understand that the wear and tear does not commence from the beginning of the work, but that the organism is able to function during a considerable length of time before its capacity for work decreases.

This fact is analogous to that which is produced if we draw electric energy from an accumulator (instead of getting it from a battery).

This hypothesis seems to me to have the advantage of accounting for the following facts :—

1. *The Dynamogenic Action of certain Stimuli.*—Thus, as the works of Féré have shown, certain stimuli have the power of dynamogenising the organism, that is to say, of raising its faculty for work. Everybody also knows by experience the influence of certain representations upon work: if we think about the pleasure that we shall procure by the achievement of any work, this gives us strength to work at it. These stimuli do not create any new energy, but probably they liberate or put at our disposal some latent energy. According to our hypothesis the stimuli called dynamogenic are those which (by virtue of biological causes which we have not to scrutinise here) have the property of opening certain taps of the reservoir of energy.

2. *The Oscillations of Work.*—If a work is not of very great interest, nor very easy, we generally accomplish it by fits and starts. We enter on the work with

enthusiasm, then, in a moment, we have a tendency to think of something else—we look out of the window, or scribble a caricature: but the interest which we attach to the end of the work stimulates us afresh, and we return to the work with ardour. Then comes a new slackening and a new spurt. I strongly believe that the slackenings are in general due rather to *ennui* than to fatigue. We are diverted from our work when a more interesting thought crosses our mind and turns to its own use the current of energy coming from the reservoir.

We have previously seen that these intermittent impulses stamp themselves very clearly upon the curve of work. These it is which constitute the "spurts" which have been spoken of. In our experiment in continued additions (fig. 13) the work was maintained at a very constant total among all the subjects, and the oscillations due to the repeated impulses of the will can be clearly noted. Having myself taken part in the experiment, I took particular account of the periodicity of the effort.

This periodicity seems also to be characteristic of all mental work. Seashore, who has devoted a study to it, has found in every case that this is so whatever may be the nature of the tests worked. If we follow it far enough the curve of work appears like a succession of broad waves which are broken up into very small undulations.[1]

This rhythmic behaviour of cerebral activity has doubtless a cause for its existence, a biological signification. If mental tension were always maximal, we should probably be exhausted much too quickly, and there is an advantage, upon the whole, in our effort

[1] Seashore and Kent, *Periodicity and Progressive Change in Continuous Mental Work*, Iowa Stud. in Psy. IV., 1905.

being thus constantly interrupted by semi-rests, which permit a fresh access of energy. These short periods of mental concentration are, without doubt, also most favourable to thinking, and make it more fruitful than would a sustained but mediocre attention. For making a voyage of discovery at night, in an unknown country, the intermittent but powerful flashes of an electric lighthouse are more useful than the continuous illumination of a paltry lantern, and to ripen fruit some bright rays of sunshine are worth more than a long series of dull and cold days.[1]

We may remark in passing that the school takes no account whatsoever of the intermediate character of intellectual work; that which it demands of the pupils above all is continuity of attention, constantly to "pay attention"; but we concern ourselves very little to know whether this continuity is not brought about at the expense of the quality of the mental adaptation, the lucidity of thought, and the originality of the work done.

3. *The Difference between Fatigue and Lassitude.*—Many writers, with Kraepelin, rightly distinguish between *lassitude* and *fatigue*. Lassitude is the weariness caused by work which is monotonous or uninteresting. We may tire, at the end of a minute or two, of a tedious occupation. We may even tire of doing nothing.

[1] I do not forget that it is often in the penumbra of the subconscious that the solution of certain problems is prepared; but the concentration of conscious thought is indispensable for directing, verifying, and improving the products of "inspiration." M. Henri Poincaré, in whom subconscious work is highly developed, attests that this kind of work "is only possible, and in any case is only fruitful, when one part of it precedes and the other part follows a period of conscious work" (Poincaré, *L'invention mathématique*, Bull. Inst. gén. psy., 1908, p. 182).

Lassitude may, however, have as a consequence a lowering of work. This lowering must not be confused with that of fatigue. That which causes it is the *closing* of the taps of energy, not the *diminution* of the provision of energy. Lassitude is generally neglected as not appertaining to the problem of fatigue. I think this is a mistake. Lassitude, it is true, is not a sufficient sign of fatigue, but if one is obliged to accomplish a piece of work which is wearisome, this work brings on fatigue much more quickly, as we shall see in the following paragraph.

4. That *change of work* does not, as a matter of fact, suffice of itself as rest, but that this change may indirectly increase energy, by reviving interest, is comprehensible by the hypothesis of a reservoir.

If, in fact, there is a great reservoir, sole and central, to which the various activities come to draw the energy which is necessary for them, it is comprehensible that the lowering in the potential of the reservoir produced by a certain work may also make itself felt in subsequent work.

On the other hand, we can conceive also that if, in the long run, a work becomes sufficiently wearying or monotonous to close the taps of the reservoir, a new and interesting work, by suddenly reopening the taps, momentarily increases the energy of the worker.

5. *Unexpected Activity.*—The presence of a reservoir of energy enables us also to understand the unexpected activity which may be displayed by persons who think themselves exhausted or neurasthenic, if they are touched on the right spot, if they are encouraged, or if there be revealed to their eyes an ideal which inflames them all at once. All who are concerned in the treatment of psychasthenics know how much a word happily placed, the removal of a prejudice, or the self-

confidence that is given to an invalid, may cause the almost instantaneous vanishing of chronic fatigue of long standing.

Professor Dubois, of Berne, who has taken up ergographic researches on neurasthenics, relates that certain among them, who were in a complete amyosthenic condition, and incapable of using their arms, "suddenly interested by an experiment, recovered unsuspected powers and furnished an ergographic curve above the average." [1]

6. *The Lowering of Psychological Tension.*—M. Pierre Janet has explained, by a depression of mental tone, which he calls "the lowering of psychological tension," the incapacity which we find in psychasthenics, and also in people normally fatigued, for executing the higher mental operations. In our hypothesis this decline corresponds to the decline of the potential of the reservoir of energy.[2] Our scheme has the advantage of taking account of two categories which we meet among psychasthenics: those who are truly fatigued, suffering from troubles of nutrition, and those who are simply nervous, with obsessions, &c. These two classes correspond to two possible causes of want of dynamogenisation of our actions: (1) Asthenia (debility) *through deficiency in the formation of energy* (slackening of nutrition, &c.); (2) Asthenia *through the closing of the taps of energy* (defect of interest, psychic inhibitions, &c.). These two forms may also combine and unite with one another. Treatments on a physical basis (rest, a generous diet, &c.) succeed best of all in

[1] Dubois, *Les psychonévroses*, 1904, p. 146.

[2] This decline of the potential also takes into account the effects of fatigue upon ideation: the lowering of the value of the association of ideas. Compare the experiments of Aschaffenburg, Psy. Arb. II., 1899, upon the associations in fatigue, and Claparède, *L'Association des Idées*, p. 241.

the cases of the first kind; and those on a moral basis (suggestion, persuasion, &c.) in cases of the second sort. The great differences which are found in the efficacy of the same mode of treatment arise, no doubt, from the fact that the origin of asthenia varies from one patient to another.

The hypothesis of a central reservoir accounts for still other facts; we need not mention more than one, the examination of which will be the subject of the following paragraph: the difference between fatigue and overpressure.

It only remains, for the moment, to ask what normal fatigue is. This includes in reality three different phenomena, which it is necessary clearly to distinguish: *the fatigue-capacity, the fatigue-function*, and *the fatigue-state*. Let us see what part each of them takes in our hypothesis.

Fatigue-capacity is the external aspect of fatigue: that which the physiologists take into account when they define fatigue as "a diminution of the capacity to work," or "a paralysis," or, again, "a diminution of irritability" [*i.e.* susceptibility to stimuli which usually arouse action]. This fatigue-capacity is an essentially relative fact: thus, in a laboratory, a muscle of a frog, to which a certain weight has been attached, is made to contract through stimulation induced by electric current:—it is found that the muscle, though it is fatigued for a weight of 50 grams, may not be so for a less weight; and it may still be able to lift the weight of 50 grams if the stimulation becomes more intense. In the complex circumstances of life, fatigue-capacity depends at the same time upon the difficulty of the work to be done, on the amount of reserve energy, and on the greatness of the causes (interest, stimuli) which make energy available. For the same work, and for the same provision of energy, we shall be more or less quickly fatigued (from the point of view of effective work) according as the work happens to be wearisome or interesting. When fatigue-capacity depends wholly upon *ennui*, it is confused with lassitude.

What is the mechanism of this lowering of capacity? It is twofold: sometimes the lowering is the result of an active and inhibitive process, and sometimes of a passive process of paralysis. Let us first consider the former of these cases.

Fatigue, as most biologists admit, with Mosso and Mlle. Ioteyko, is a defensive function. In working our organism tends to become exhaustion, and it is necessary that when the organism approaches the moment when exhaustion will begin, it should be warned and urged to stop. Fatigue has for its precise function to bring about the arrest of activities which are about to bring on exhaustion. Things go on as if this function of arrest, at any rate in intellectual fatigue, were started in a reflex manner by the lowering of the potential in our reservoir of energy.[1] We may suppose that the reservoir (which is, like all living machines, a machine endowed with the power of adaptation) tends to limit its output in proportion as its level falls. This limitation is generally accompanied subjectively by a feeling of difficulty in keeping up attention,

[1] This fatigue would otherwise supervene long before the reservoir was completely empty; it would be a signal indicating only that it *is beginning* to empty itself. All our defence functions, as we know, are anticipative, that is to say, they put themselves into motion *before* there is great urgency; thus hunger supervenes many days, or even many weeks, before we are at the point of death through inanition, so fatigue, which whispers in our ear that we are able to work no more, supervenes a good time before we really are able to work no more.

of being uninterested. We have here the *fatigue-function* in a pure state, since it is not mixed up with the slightest element of poisoning. This explains to us how it may be dissipated or diverted by means of interest, when this is sufficiently strong to hold in check the reflex of defence.

If we resist the appeals of this first fatigue, there will doubtless soon be added the poisoning due to the waste materials proceeding from the functioning of the organs brought into play by the work. These waste products clog the machinery of our activity; and, in order to work, a larger and larger amount of energy becomes necessary. The ponetic phenomena quickly appear, and constantly increase; the more the machinery is clogged, the more energy is necessary, and the more the level of the reservoir is lowered. This is the *fatigue-state*. It is probable, however, that as long as the work is done at the expense of the energy in the reservoir, the poisoning is of little importance. The dangerous poisons are only formed when, the reservoir being dry, energy must be created on the spot, in the centres which work, and at the cost of the albuminoid substances.[1] Then overpressure begins.

8. *Overpressure*

It is generally admitted that overpressure is a chronic or pathological state of fatigue, which shows itself by symptoms more or less definite: giddiness, headache, sight troubles, want of appetite, bleedings at the nose, &c.

[1] "Normal activity would result from the use of carbon hydrates, whilst the other would imply the using of albuminoids. In the course of the latter chemical destruction of numerous wastes more or less abnormal, and in every case relatively poisonous, arise" (Demoor, *Rapport sur la fatigue* at the 11th Hygiene Congress, Brussels, 1903).

Binet and Henri consider that it is not in these symptoms in persons that we should try to find the distinction between ordinary fatigue and overpressure, for they may be absent, and be present, on the contrary, amongst persons who are not overworked. For these writers the distinctive character of overpressure is in the mode of the recovering from fatigue: normal fatigue is that in which there is self-recovery, without any special precautions being taken; on the contrary, there would be overpressure whenever the fatigue which is experienced requires exceptional conditions for recovery.

This definition seems to me very suitable. It has, from the practical point of view, only the inconvenience of completely subordinating the diagnosis of overpressure to the methods of measuring fatigue; for, to know if the day's fatigue has been entirely dissipated by the night's repose, it is necessary to be able to determine whether, on waking in the morning, any signs of the fatigue of the day before still exist. On the other hand, it neither informs us as to the physiological nature of overpressure nor of the producing causes. Doubtless overpressure results from too much work; but at what point, when it is a question of scholars, do we enter the domains of excess? Here is the great question which pedagogues and doctors discuss without coming to an agreement. Finally, what are the natural limits of overpressure, which separate it on the one side from great fatigue (normal), and on the other from neurasthenia?

Until further researches adduce some decisive elements in this debate, I wish to submit two or three remarks, the results of ordinary observations.

It is undeniable that certain children or adolescents are abnormally tired by the school system. It is said that these cases are rare. This is true. But, if they are rare, is it because the modern school system is only capable of overpressing specially weak individuals, or because most children defend themselves against the system by their indolence, and escape from its dangers? This is a delicate question, for the number of factors at work is very considerable: curricula, school methods, pedagogical capacity of the masters on the one hand, and the individual health, intelligence, zeal, or laziness on the other.

If we examine what goes on around us, we notice that sometimes some individuals are able to complete a very considerable piece of work without being overworked, whilst at other times the same individuals are overworked by a very moderate piece of work.

The idea which is forced upon us—and which confirms the observation of what happens to oneself—is that *it is not so much the amount, nor even the difficulty, of the work which overtires us, as its nature*, its psychological nature: generally the work which interests us does not overtire us, whereas tedious work, work without interest, and drudgery, overtires.[1]

In fact, we infinitely prefer difficult and interesting work to easy and tedious work. The scientist who freely follows up a problem will be able to work many consecutive days without fatigue, whereas he would be exhausted if he were compelled, without reason, to make additions for a few hours. Do children overtire themselves with playing? Certainly not; play rather rests, even if it demands sustained attention, because it is fed by interest.

[1] Thorndike (*Mental Fatigue*, Psy. Rev., 1900, p. 571) has already remarked that the overpressure of scholars arises above all "from a maladroit inhibition of agreeable activities." See also Wagner, book cited above, p. 116.

The problem comes back, therefore, to considering what distinguishes, from the psycho-physiological point of view, difficult and interesting work from easy and tedious work. The kind of fatigue is assuredly different in these two cases. In tedious work there is a struggle to be maintained, and we have the impression that the forces which are absorbed in the struggle against disgust or tedium are lost for the work itself.

Let us examine each of the four typical cases which present themselves in everyday life: (1) *Easy and interesting work*, which does not fatigue; (2) *Difficult and interesting work*, which does not fatigue, or only a very little; (3) *Easy and tedious work*, which fatigues in a manner disproportionate to its importance; and (4) *Difficult and tedious work*, which fatigues to a maximum.

If we accept the hypothesis, mentioned above, of two different sources of energy, the central reservoir and the local manufacture in the nervous centres, we are able broadly to schematise what happens in the various cases. Interesting work is done at the expense of the reservoir, but tedious work—which has not the power of opening the taps[1]—is done at the expense of the energy produced locally in the nervous centres presiding over the elaboration of the work. And such local production uses up the neurons infinitely more quickly than the simple transmission by their fibrils of an energy coming from somewhere else. Here is a first cause of the more exhausting effect of tedious work.

But there is also, in my opinion, a second, of which I have already made mention: in tedious work[1] the organism defends itself, it makes use of those reflexes of defence of which we have spoken (p. 155–7). This

[1] By the definition, in fact, a tedious work is a work which does not call forth interest (see above, p. 156).

is a fresh obstacle to vanquish, which is added to the resistance of the work to be done.[1] And this is not yet all: we recall that, in the local production of energy, the wear and tear produces poisons which are more harmful than in the utilisation of the reserve.

Finally, we may point out a last circumstance which makes tedious work a cause of overpressure: that is, that it is not educative. When work is normal, interesting, each step in advance taken, each piece of knowledge assimilated, facilitates subsequent acquisitions. If, on the contrary, the work is tedious, assimilation does not take place, and the pupil is not able to help himself by past lessons to learn the new ones. Each step forward becomes, therefore, so much the more troublesome as it loses the assistance of the preceding step; the pupil feels swamped and, so as not to be completely engulfed, he makes efforts which need to be more considerable every day.

Local production of energy necessitated by the closing of the reservoir, increased poisoning by the waste products, reflexes of defence to overcome, greater expenditure of energy, absence of normal progress facilitating subsequent work—such are the causes which make tedious work exhausting work.

The following table sums up and schematises the differences between the four cases which we have reviewed. Let us express by the number 10 the greatest resistance to be overcome in a difficult work, and by the number 1 the resistance in an easy work. These resistances will be overcome, respectively, by 10 units of energy for the difficult work, and by 1 unit of energy for the easy work. If it is a question of in-

[1] It is for this reason, doubtless, that easy and tedious work tires; the resistance of the work itself is not great, but the resistance offered by the reflexes of defence enters into the account.

teresting work, it is the energy of the reservoir which is employed to oppose the resistance; there is then no need in this case for the production of local energy.

Work.	Resistance.		Expenditure of Energy.		Toxins.
	Of the work itself.	Of the reflexes of defence.	From the reservoir.	From local production.	
1. Easy and interesting	1	0	1	0	Few
2. Difficult and interesting	10	0	10	0	"
Over pressure. 3. Easy and tedious	1	10	0	11	Many
Over pressure. 4. Difficult and tedious	10	10	0	20	"

In tedious work, to the resistance of the work itself there is added the resistance of the reflexes of defence. Let 10 be the magnitude of this resistance when the tedium is maximum. The sum of resistance will be the equivalent to 11 for the easy and tedious work (1+10), and to 20 for the difficult and tedious work (10+10). As the taps of the reservoir remain closed during tedious work, it devolves on the local production to furnish the energy necessary to triumph over the resistances, hence the wear and tear and the abundance of toxins.

According to this way of looking at the matter, the psycho-physiology of overpressure is wholly different from that of ordinary fatigue. *Overpressure does not result only from too great a work; it is due above all to work of a psychologically inferior nature.*[1]

[1] I do not here wish to consider whether, side by side with overpressure due to defect of interest, there also exists an overpressure

If the work of an inferior nature is very common in schools, the fault is in a great measure due to the system of examination. Examination! It is useless to arraign the system here. The teaching body know better than any one else all the evil for which it is responsible. What makes it so formidable for the intellectual hygiene of children is that, little by little, it has deviated from its original aim, which was to estimate the capacity of scholars. To-day it serves, more often, to judge *the master*: "the pupils are the accusers, the master the accused."[1] We know the fine results of the system!

I cannot resist the pleasure of quoting, apropos of this, the following passage from a communication presented to the first Congress of School Hygiene by M. Gory: "If the chief preoccupation of pedagogues were to enlighten the consciousness of children, to develop their reason, to mature their judgment, and to strengthen their energy, they would have a perfect understanding with the doctors; for they would not be able to obtain these ends by overpressure and excessive work, nor by violating the rules of hygiene. But often the only end which they propose to themselves is to make their pupils win prizes for algebra, or a Latin theme, and it is according to successes of this kind that the value of the teaching given in the Lycées and in private schools is judged. It is for this that we overwork children, and so, by hindering their

due to excess of interest, which occurs among artists, merchants, &c., carried away by the love of art or by love of money. It would be necessary to consider further what is the rôle of the emotions in the pathogeny (origin and growth of disease) of overpressure: competition, ambition, the desire to rise in the world, or the fear of being shipwrecked on the way, are certainly factors of great importance.

[1] L. Zbinden, Report on *L'Examen* to the 17th Congress of the Soc. péd. romande, Geneva, 1907.

physical development, we hinder the development of their will, of their heart, and of their intelligence also. For I refuse to call this senseless heating of young brains an education of the intelligence!"[1]

The great examinations—final, bachelor's degree, leaving—which terminate the secondary studies are above all an occasion of overpressure, because of their foolishly encyclopædic programme. Professor Ostwald has earnestly protested against these examinations, apropos of which he scoffs at our school system. "That the school," he says, "after having followed a pupil's career for *nine* years, is not even capable, at the end of that lapse of time, of judging if the pupil is fit to leave secondary teaching, is an absurdity such as only an arch-antiscientific organisation of teaching could render possible."[2]

There are, of course, still other causes which are able to influence overpressure, to accelerate its advance, as, for example, growth which in supplying its own needs lowers the reserves of organic energy, and thus obliges the pupil to work all the more quickly at the expense of the local production of energy, or again alcohol, tobacco, bad habits, and other agents of nervous enfeeblement, to which it is necessary to add bad hygiene, immobility, insufficient respiration, all which, in a word, Dr. Matthieu rightly calls "school maltreatment."

To school maltreatment may, alas, often be added home maltreatment. Many children are exploited by their parents who, after school, when the hour of detention ought to have sounded for them, are obliged to run errands to the town, to light the fire for the

[1] Gory, *Nécessité du repos*, Reports of the 1st Congress of School Hygiene, Paris, 1903.

[2] Ostwald, *Wider das Schulelend*, Leipsic, 1909.

evening meal, and to clean the room. For them it is the school which is the place of rest, and it should surprise nobody that they are sleepy there.[1] A master who is anxious about the health of the pupils ought not to preoccupy himself only about the causes of fatigue during school-time, but he should also take account of the overwork which may be undergone in the home, if only that he may not punish them wrongfully. Indolence, the deficiency of zeal of a pupil, may often depend upon causes which we do not suspect. A teacher of Wurzbourg, having remarked the extraordinary apathy of his pupils, aged from 10 to 12, had the idea of making an inquiry into the conditions of their sleep. He learnt that most of them (34 out of 54) shared their bed with another person (brother, parents), which led to disturbed sleep, and many did not sleep a sufficient number of hours.[2]

9. *Rest*

When we are fatigued it is necessary to rest. This is certainly so. But this very simple truth raises, nevertheless, certain problems. We may ask in the first place *at what moment* it is proper to rest oneself; next, *for how long a time;* and finally, *how* to rest.

[1] One reads in *L'Educateur,* 1908, p. 574: "In our Vaudois country districts hand-work has become so dear that children are obliged to take the place of workmen who cannot be found. Nearly all, boys and girls, rise at 5 o'clock in the morning, if not before, having to attend to the work of the house or the stable. They have only just time after a hasty breakfast to run to school. . . . The two hours passed at school are a rest for the body, but a torture to the mind. These children, half worn out, depressed, and indifferent to everything, trouble themselves very little about the glorious deeds of William Tell, the agreement of participles, or proof by casting out nines."

[2] Friedrich, *Ueber die Schlafverhältnisse meiner Schüler,* Kf. IV., 1699.

There is, then, a science of rest. It is because they have ignored this that so many people are overtired and worn out, in a manner quite disproportionate with the work which they have done.

1. **When to Rest.**—We may rest when fatigue is present; or, again, we may rest before fatigue comes upon us; or, finally, we may not rest, but persist in working a certain time in spite of fatigue. Let us first consider the last of these circumstances.

Some authors, we have seen (p. 276), and amongst others Malapert and Offner, have maintained that the duty of the school is to teach the child to be fatigued. Offner goes so far as to affirm that it is necessary to make children who are under the influence of fatigue go on working for an appreciable time longer. What are we to think of a pedagogical principle such as this?

I consider, for my part, that it is very dangerous. It reflects the gloomy and anti-psychological conception of education by coercion, a conception of Catholic origin which we have already had occasion to stigmatise.[1] I certainly recognise that there is a very correct idea in the doctrine of education by fatigue, and the intention of its defenders is excellent: it is to habituate the child to rising superior to disagreeable sensations, and not to believe himself done for when he feels tired. It is certain that there are times when it is necessary to work while under the influence of fatigue, when the work ought absolutely to be finished by a certain date. In addition to this it may be

[1] "Our system of education," says Payot (Rev philos XLVIII., p. 601), "is in great part a heritage from the Catholic doctrine that human nature is fundamentally bad and corrupt; and that it follows that education ought to be a *constraint*, and founded upon fear." And, he ought to add, upon fatigue

useful, on the score of exercise of the will, and for teaching the child to measure his forces and to know what is his reserve of energy, to cause him now and again to do forced work. But those are only exceptional or special cases, and we could not set up M. Offner's principle as a pedagogical maxim.

It is a grave error to think, with M. Malapert, that "the duty of the school is to teach a child to fatigue itself." What a singular idea! How can we believe that we are rendering the child a service by teaching it to work with a tired brain, that is to say, with a defective instrument? But is not the first duty of a good workman to take care of his tool, and to keep it in good condition? What should we say of a teacher of the violin who should teach his pupil to go on playing till "an appreciable time" after his strings are slack, or when his bow has lost its resin? Or of a peasant who would persist in mowing when his blunted scythe was no longer able to do more than ruffle the grass which he ought to cut down?

To teach the child to fatigue itself? No; quite the contrary! In our civilisation, with life so hurried and intense, where precocious wearing-out and neurasthenia are often the only recompense for those who work, what it is above all advisable to teach the child is *to work* **without** *fatiguing itself.* And it is not by fatiguing it that we attain this result, but by making it contract good habits of work.

Ask those who work with their head and you will find what they think of work done under the pressure of fatigue; they will tell you, for the most part, that it is wrong, when fatigue is present, to force ourselves in spite of it, because intellectual work produced under conditions of nascent fatigue is generally inferior. It is much better, when one feels that he "is not getting on well," to abandon his work, and to take it up again a little later.

Darwin is an illustrious example of the amount of work which may be done by a man of feeble health, not able to work many hours a day, but knowing how to take rest as soon as he felt tired. M. Beaunis states that as soon as his work no longer goes of itself "he does not worry about it": "As soon as I feel (and it is a thing which can be distinctly felt) that *it does not go*, I do not wait for cerebral fatigue to come on; I stop, and go on with something else. Thanks to this method of work I have never suffered either cerebral fatigue or intellectual overpressure." M. Henri Poincaré, the famous contemporary mathematician—whose output, we are assured, is more considerable than has been known since Gauss and Cauchy—works in an automatic and spontaneous manner, but "when speculation is not easy, voluntary effort is of little use, and M. H. Poincaré abandons the work." [1] "The worker," says Mosso, "who persists in working when he is fatigued, produces only feeble work of little utility, at the expense of his organism," &c., &c.

There are besides, as everywhere in psychology, marked individual variations. With some, work continues productive even under the depressing constraint of fatigue—witness Zola, who "became relentless over an obstacle, and did not breathe till he had overcome it." [2] With others, fatigue supervenes immediately, and not to be fatigued would for them be not to work.[3] It is

[1] Darwin, *Life and Correspondence*, and Mosso, work quoted, p. 163; Beaunis, *Comment fonctionne mon cerveau*, Rev. Philos., Jan 1909, p. 40, Toulouse, *Henri Poincaré*, Paris, 1910, p. 177.

[2] Toulouse, *Emile Zola*, Paris, 1896, p. 262

[3] Other individuals always feel ready for work. We may compare, as an example of the two types, the two following replies, furnished by two young mathematicians, about the same age, to our inquiry

not less true that to compel some scholars to work under the pressure of fatigue is a deplorable system, were it only that work done in these conditions is nearly always of inferior quality, and that we must not under any pretext habituate the pupil to do bad work, when with another system he is able to do good.

To make him like work, it is necessary to place the pupil in such conditions that he arrives at the best possible results with the least possible trouble. The method of constraint and fatigue only succeeds in making work detested or despised; for it engenders results which are not proportionate to the trouble which they cost; and however little intelligence the pupil may have, he concludes, and not without reason, that "the game is not worth the candle." [1]

It is therefore necessary to interrupt intellectual work when fatigue supervenes.

already quoted: "Yes [it is necessary to interrupt work], the work of continued mathematics being very fatiguing to mind and body," and "It seems to me that mathematics never fatigues"!

[1] Perhaps M.M. Offner and Malapert meant to speak simply of lassitude, or of the first obstacles which give to work what I have called "the fatigue-function in a pure state" (see p. 285). In that case, these authors are right, to a certain extent, in engaging the pupil to struggle against these reflexes of defence. But, then, it is not at all a question of teaching the child "to work a considerable time under the influence of fatigue"; in fact, in order that the struggle against this nascent fatigue may turn to the worker's profit, it is necessary to stimulate the interests capable of overcoming these inhibition reflexes (see above, p. 154); the awakening of these interests has for its consequence the *suppression* of lassitude and the feeling of nascent fatigue. It is no longer, therefore, a matter of "teaching the child to fatigue itself"; but, on the contrary, of teaching him to make his fatigue to vanish. If this is what the two authors quoted above intended to say, then I am in entire accord with them—and I beg them to forgive me for having joined issue with them in regard to their conception, of which the formula appears to me very dangerous, and calculated to encourage the partisans of constraint.

It is important for the teacher to be able to diagnose from without the *signs of fatigue* in his audience. These signs—of which Galton has drawn up a list by means of an inquiry addressed to some professors—are, for the most part, well known to all: agitation, twitchings, grimaces, yawning, inattention, blunders, memory or speech troubles, stammering, &c. Some masters have mentioned a change in the normal colour of the skin, or the movements of the eyes.[1]

Among the signs of school fatigue we must mention that of *play* during lessons, which is a thing too severely condemned by traditional discipline. Physiology teaches us that the suspension of the higher cerebration has for its correlative the activity of the lower reflex and automatic centres. The play of tired scholars is only a particular case of this general law. As soon as mental fatigue supervenes, instinctive acts and impulses—and the need of play is, as we have seen, the impulse *par excellence* of the child—gain the upper hand. Of course, it does not follow that it would do to allow free course to the scholars' tendency to play during lessons; but the teacher should always bear in mind that play is one of the symptoms of school fatigue.[2]

When the signs of fatigue appear, it is certainly necessary to rest. But we may ask ourselves whether, from the point of view of the amount of work to be done, there is not, in many cases, an advantage in resting *before* fatigue appears. Experience shows that this is so.

Physiologists have long since proved that if we prevent a muscle from reaching a certain degree of exhaustion by resting it now and again, we may, in a

[1] Galton, *La fatigue mentale*, Rev. scient, vol 17, 1889.
[2] Boubier, *Les jeux pendant la classe*, Ar. de Psy. I., p. 64.

given time, make it accomplish a very much greater number of contractions than if it had worked without relaxation. In such a case the intervals devoted to rest are not time lost, but time gained: for example, we exhaust a muscle by making it perform thirty contractions; it needs two hours of rest for complete recovery; but if we had interpolated rest in the middle of the work, that is to say, after fifteen contractions, half-an-hour would have sufficed to repair the fatigue produced, in place of an hour (as it would have been if the time for the rest necessary for reparation was proportional to the duration of the work). And the work done in the second case would be superior to that which was done in the first experiment.[1]

Here, then, is a new practical problem: after what time from the beginning of work is it necessary to make a pause so that it may be most advantageous? This problem is intimately bound up with that of the duration of the pause, and it is necessary to consider them together.

2. **Duration of Rest.**—During what length of time is it necessary to rest in order to dissipate the effects of the fatigue produced by a certain work? That depends upon the moment when the pause takes place. As we have just said, these two problems, that of the moment and that of the duration of rest, are connected and dependent: according to the length of the rest

[1] Féré has proved, by the ergograph, that if we stop to take rest at the moment when the first sensation of fatigue arises, the work accomplished in the course of a series of twenty ergographic experiments is very much superior to that furnished by an analogous series in which each ergogram has been continued until exhaustion. The series interrupted by rest is a little longer than the other, but the gain to the work is relatively much more important than the lost time: for example, for a gain of 50 per cent. the increase of time is only 15 per cent. (Féré, *L'économie de l'effort et le travail attrayant*, C. R. Soc. biol., vol. 59, 1905, p. 611.)

allowed, there will be an advantage in placing it at such or such a moment; and according to the moment at which the work ought to be interrupted, there will be an advantage in making a shorter or a longer pause.

Many studies have been devoted, during the last twelve years, to this question of the place and the duration of *the most favourable* pause. All these studies have been carried out in laboratories, and we may take exception to them for not having realised the conditions of school work. They have, however, had the advantage of bringing certain facts very clearly to light. When an individual does a piece of work, many factors, we have seen, influence the quality and rapidity of the work: besides fatigue, there are "*swing*" and *skill*, which are capable of completely counterbalancing fatigue for a certain time. But an untimely rest is as harmful to "swing" as to the skill obtained from practice. We can understand, therefore, that a rest coming too soon after the beginning of the work may be more harmful than useful, since it has for effect the interruption of the "swing," and prevents the worker from reaping the advantage of acquired skill, at a period when the fatigue is still insignificant.

It has been shown, for example, that in a task of addition, a pause of fifteen minutes after an hour of work has no favourable effect: it is long enough to destroy the "swing" and to dissipate the good effects of acquired skill, and too short to repair completely the fatigue. On the other hand, a pause of fifteen minutes after two hours of additions is proved to be very favourable, &c. There are otherwise some rather considerable individual variations.[1]

Useful as may be the laboratory experiments, one

[1] See the works of Amberg, Rivers and Kraepelin, Lindley, Heuman, in the Psy. Arb. I.–IV., and Wimms, work quoted above.

would not know how to draw direct conclusions from them as to the length of time necessary to give, in a school, to *recreations*, so that they might have the greatest possible restorative value, for the exercises which serve as tests in laboratories are often more irksome than the work done in class. It would be necessary, therefore, to undertake school researches of the kind followed, in a very methodical fashion, by Friedrich.[1] This author, working with the method of dictations, has shown that a recreation of eight minutes, between two hours of lessons, has a very favourable effect. Here, for example, is one of the results that he obtained :

	Number of Faults.	Pupils with no Faults.
After 2 hours of lessons with one recreation .	122	18
2 „ „ without „ . .	158	14
3 „ „ with two recreations	112	18
3 „ „ with one recreation .	172	12
3 „ „ without „ .	183	10

N.B.—In the experiments embracing 2 hours of lessons, the intermediary recreation was 8 minutes ; in those embracing 3 hours of class the interpolated recreations were of 15 minutes. The erasures were counted as mistakes. The last column indicates, for each experiment, how many pupils had not committed any fault.

Friedrich has also shown that the pause at midday (11 to 2 o'clock) is not sufficient to dissipate the morning's fatigue ; at 2 P.M., for example, the number of faults was equal to sixty-two, whereas in the morning before the classes, they amounted to forty-seven (but it may be that there are other influences at

[1] Friedrich. *Untersuch. über den Einfluss der Arbeitsdauer und der Arbeitspausen auf die geistige Leistungsfähigkeit der Schulkinder*, Z. f. Psy. XIII., 1897.

work here: digestion, the daily variation of psychic energy, &c.).

No systematic experiments have been made upon the influence of the duration of recreations. Friedrich has shown that, for three hours of lessons with only one pause, a pause of eight minutes after the first hour is more favourable than a pause of fifteen minutes after the second.

The question of knowing of what length a lesson ought to be so that the pupils may not be fatigued, and how the lessons ought to be distributed over the day, has given rise to numerous studies. There is but little agreement on the subject. Whilst most of the researches made in the schools with the various methods of measurement (dictations, æsthesiometer, &c.) have shown that the scholars were fatigued at the end of an hour's lesson (Sikorsky, Burgerstein, Laser, Holmes, &c.), Thorndike affirms that the pupils "are just as capable" of work after having had a day of school, since the work done by them at the end of the day "has not decreased by an iota," and that it is not the ability which is less but the willingness. According to this writer, it would therefore be rather lassitude than fatigue which would be in evidence.[1]

[1] Thorndike, Psy. Rev, 1900, p 547. We discuss elsewhere the advantage of lessons of two hours or of one hour (see Marcheix, *Durée du travail et du repos des écoliers*, 1st Congress of School Hygiene, Paris, 1904, De Fleury, ibid; Mathieu and Mosny, *Revision de l'horaire du travail et du repos*, 2nd Congress, Paris, 1905). In France, lessons of two hours in length have been the rule Marcheix demanded that they should be reduced to one hour and a half. This is still very long! It is, besides, necessary to distinguish: when the pupil is actively working, doing problems in mathematics, for example, it is an advantage for him to have a long time in front of him, so that he may be able to profit by the "swing" But if the lesson consists of passively listening, fifty minutes appears to me a maximum not to be exceeded.

Pauses of long duration have sometimes for result, strangely enough, the strengthening of the effects of practice instead of diminishing them: Specht, for example, having made experiments in additions with fifteen subjects, remarked that, after two weeks' interruption, nine among them had shown, on again taking up the tests, a clearly augmented capacity for work.[1] Persons who are practising the acquisition of a certain sport, bicycling, horse-riding, &c., have also noticed the progress which was made during a long period of inaction. This influence of rest on the perfecting of acquired activities has caused the physiologist Exner to announce this amusing paradox, that it is in summer much more than in winter that the art of skating is perfected!

3. **How to Rest.**—In general the organism knows quite well how to preserve itself from exhaustion; it possesses a certain number of safety valves which open of themselves when it feels menaced. These valves are inattention, dislike of the work in hand, and the desire to rest, sleep, or play. The importance of these means of defence of the organism is often misunderstood by teachers. The old-time pedagogy, which shut its eyes to the physiological conditions of mental activity and fixed its attention only on the duties of the mind considered by itself, was very severe on inattention and idleness. We must, however, accept the evidence that, in many cases, these faults against "discipline" are nothing but the reactions of defence of the organism against the fatigue which is invading it.

But these spontaneous means, though they are among the most efficacious, have the defect of not being officially admitted as such.

[1] Specht, *Zur Analyse der Arbeitskurve*, Z. päd. Psy., 1910 p. 29.

In the schools we often endeavour to guard the pupils against fatigue by *changing the work*. We have already spoken of this factor (pp. 260, 281), and have seen that by varying the work we may renew the interest of the child, and also reopen the taps of energy which lassitude in the preceding task had closed. By skilful variation in the daily programme, it could be arranged that all the energy required should be derived from the reservoir of energy, and thus prevent overpressure. It must always be clearly understood that the changing of work does not *by itself* suffice for rest; it only has this effect if to difficult work there succeeds work that is easier or more interesting. We ought also to guard ourselves against stopping, by an untimely interruption, the "swing" of the young workers. What we said a moment ago about pauses applies also to the changing of work.

Is it to *gymnastics* that we must apply for rest from intellectual work? No; we have said why (p. 268), and cannot revert to it. *Play* itself, the beneficent and educative action of which I have emphasised so often, and which can be pursued so long without fatigue, would not always constitute, according to certain authors (*e.g.* Wagner), an efficient means of rest.

We must note here the method of treating fatigue by the "antikenotoxin" of Weichardt,[1] the more so because it has recently been made the object of a school experiment, in Berlin: the hygienist Lorenz, having shown by the method of sums that the capacity of scholars for work was greatly diminished after the fifth hour of lessons, sprinkled one day in the class-room, by means of a spray-producer, a solution of 1 per cent. of antikenotoxin, immediately before proceeding to the last test of calculation; then found

[1] Weichardt, *Ueber Ermüdungsstoffe*, Stuttgart, 1910, p. 41.

that this antikenotoxin, which had penetrated the bodies of the pupils by their respiratory channels, had had the effect of augmenting the speed of reckoning by 50 per cent., and had lowered the number of mistakes made. We would naturally desire that fresh experiments of this kind should be undertaken. For the moment it is impossible to pronounce upon the value of the method—it seems too good to be true!

But, certainly, the only means of rest, the efficacy of which admits of no doubt, is that of doing nothing. A means so simple that it has needed centuries to discover it. Is it not, so to say, only from yesterday that we date the method of "the rest cure" for the treatment of neurasthenia, that is to say, of chronic exhaustion?

To do nothing is not always synonymous with loss of time—as the pedagogues believe. Without speaking of the subconscious—which constantly works—and without ever being fatigued[1]—we may recall that pure loafing is often very educative. Listen to Toepffer, who knew what he was talking about:[2] "Looking out of the window is the true pastime of a student: I mean, of an industrious student. . . . I pass my days there, and if I dared to say it . . . No, my professors, Grotius and Puffendorf, never gave me a hundredth part of the instruction that I imbibe there, doing nothing but looking out on the street. . . .

"Yes, loafing is a necessary thing, at least once in a lifetime, but above all at eighteen, on leaving school. It is then that the soul, parched with worthless old books, refreshes itself; it takes a halt to get to know itself; and it finishes its borrowed life to commence

[1] Beaunis, work quoted above, Rev. philos. XXXIV., p. 40.

[2] Toepffer, *La bibliothèque de mon oncle* (*Nouvelles genevoises*), Geneva, 1832.

U

its very own. Thus an entire summer passed in this state does not appear to me to be too much in a proper education. It is probable that only one summer would not suffice to make a great man: Socrates loafed some years, Rousseau until he was forty, and La Fontaine all his life.

"And yet I have not seen this precept incorporated in any work on education."

It is difficult to obtain complete repose for children during the day, and in normal conditions it is from sleep that we should seek restoration from fatigue.

10. *Sleep*

What is *sleep?* It does not much matter by what theories we seek to account for this phenomenon of which the physiology is still obscure. It seems to me to be, like fatigue, a function of defence having for its end, by overwhelming the animal with inertia, to prevent the arrival of the stage of exhaustion.[1] When we sleep, hardly any toxins are formed, since motor and mental activity have ceased; the toxins are therefore eliminated more quickly than they are formed, and consequently the blood is soon cleared. On the other hand, the functions of attention and relation being suspended, the nervous force not utilised for the needs of mental adaptation is employed in the work of restoring the tissues which have been used up during wakefulness.

The importance of the restorative process of sleep has been proved in a very suggestive fashion by Weygandt.[2] This writer took, late at night, certain

[1] Ed. Claparède, *Esquisse d'une théorie biologique du sommeil*, Ar. de Psy. IV., 1905, and Rivista di Scienza II., 1909.

[2] Weygandt, *Exp. Beitr. z. Psy. des Schlafes*, Z. f. P., vol. 39, 1905. See also the communication of Roemer to the Congress of Psy. at Munich, 1896.

tests of work with a subject (*e.g.* by the method of additions). Afterwards the subject slept, and at the end of a certain time, half-an-hour, an hour, &c., was awakened and took up a new test. The results are curious. They show that the restorative influence of sleep is not the same for all kinds of work. Half-an-hour of sleep suffices to repair the fatigue due to a test of additions, while it is necessary to sleep five or six hours to repair the fatigue due to a test of memorisation. Learning by heart, without appearing so, is one of the most exhausting of mental exercises.

It is, then, necessary that children should sleep. But how long ought we to allow them to sleep? This is a much-debated question.

> "Sex horas dormire sat est juvenique senique
> Septem do pigris, nulli concedimus octo,"

taught the school of Salerne. Six hours, seven hours to the idle, and never eight! The good doctors of old were a little stingy; but doubtless life was then more tranquil. To-day the workers require more. Of the sixty-five mathematicians who have responded to the inquiry quoted above, forty-five sleep eight hours or more, and eleven alone need from six to seven hours. And these are adults.[1]

Children need much more. Why? Because they have to grow. Sleep is favourable to development. A remarkable parallelism is shown between the need of sleep and the intensity of growth (above all, of the growth of the cerebral hemispheres); in the periods of great growth (early infancy and puberty) the need of sleep increases.[2]

[1] See also the inquiry inaugurated by *La Revue* (Paris), Oct. 15, 1908.

[2] Trömner, *Zur Biologie u. Psy. des Schlafes*, Berl. klin. Woch, 1910.

How is this creative action of sleep to be explained? We are probably justified in assuming that, during this state, the disposable organic energy is utilised not only to repair the deficiencies occasioned by the day's activities, but also for the needs of the growth of the organism. *It is during sleep that the child builds itself up;* sleep is for him a primordial need.

The schoolmaster who scolds the unfortunate scholar who comes late to class, through having remained asleep a little longer than usual, never dreams of this. To be punctual to the minute in the morning is one of the dogmas of school pedagogy, about which perhaps our masters are most high-handed—doubtless because its strict application exacts the least ability: it is not necessary to be very versed in the art of educating to be able to put a bad mark against the little late-comers who arrive after the last stroke of the clock has sounded.

Nevertheless, to punish a child who arrives late because he has slept too long or too soundly amounts to punishing him because he is busy with growing, which is, every one will agree, incomparably foolish.

Nothing should be more sacred than the sleep of a child! Parents ought to take as a rule of conduct *never to wake a child who is sleeping soundly,* even if the hour for school has struck. For if the child sleeps so profoundly—I mean, if the usual sounds of the house do not suffice to wake him, and it is necessary to pull him out of bed, to tug him forcibly, to sprinkle cold water—then he still needs sleep; and in these circumstances a quarter of an hour of sleep is worth a hundred times more for his development than an hour of the most admirable lesson.

On the other hand, the experiments which have been undertaken, in the course of the last twenty years, upon the profoundness of sleep at various times of the night, have revealed the existence of various types of sleepers: whilst amongst some (*the vesperal type*, much the most common) the profoundness of sleep attains its maximum at the end of about an hour, and afterwards decreases, among others (*the matinal type*) sleep gets profound slowly, and is comparatively more profound in the last hours of the night.[1] And these two types are also found among children. Michelson claims that the matinal type is a sign of nervousness; but Aschaffenburg affirms that he has frequently met it amongst individuals possessing a nervous system as strong as it is possible to conceive.[2] These types of sleep appear to depend on the constitution of the individual. Two brothers may each belong to a different type.

By taking no account of these facts, which it ignores as it ignores many others, the school shows how remote it keeps itself from life, and how vain are its pretensions of wishing to develop the child by a knowledge of causes.

But I hear the outraged protestations of our masters at this: "Not punish late-comers! But that would be to allow the reign of indiscipline, disorder, and anarchy; and it would open the door to every abuse, for if we did not oblige the scholars to be punctual they would not come at all!"

Abuses! The children would no longer come if they were not compelled to come! Your confession is valuable: you recognise, then, that they do not like

[1] The profoundness of sleep is measured by the intensity of the excitation (noise, pricking, &c.) necessary to waken the sleeper (method invented by Kohlschütter, in 1862, *Messungen der Festigkeit des Schlafes*, Diss., Leipsic).

[2] Michelson, Psy. Arb. II.; Aschaffenburg, *Der Schlaf im Kindesalter*, Wiesbaden, 1909.

your school. Well, they are right! if they feel that it is a prison, hostile to their natural bent, in which reigns suspicion, and where everything is an agency for catching them out in a fault, instead of being a hospitable and pleasing house with open arms to welcome them, and ready to trust them.

What! Here is a poor little chap, who has been kept in bed by sound sleep a little longer than usual; hardly are his eyes open before he is conscious of his misdeed, which he has done nothing to bring about. But the school has already so falsified his sense of reality that he quite believes he is guilty—he who has done nothing more than live a little bit of healthy life. And see how he hurries, rushing away at a gallop without waiting to take food. In the street he runs as hard as his little legs will go, and arrives exhausted and breathless, but triumphant, at the school gate. Alas! he is too late. The fatal hour has just struck, and it is by a rebuff that he will be welcomed. Of the cause of his lateness, of his efforts to repair his appalling fault (almost a crime), no account whatever will be taken. Just think of it! Is the school made for the children? But surely we are trifling with ourselves by entering into all those "details"! For having slept a little too long, that is to say, for having, last night, grown a little more than usual, made a little more than usual of the bodily frame and cerebral substance, our little friend has to be kept in, and is made to copy twenty times the verb "I sleep too much," and on his weekly report book a bad mark will be entered under the heading of "indiscipline," just as though he had been late through having played about in the street!

And you wish that he should love your school!

Only make it attractive, and you need no longer

fear that by not punishing the late-comers there will be abuses. Make your arrangements such that your pupils may be punctual not through fear of some punishment, but for the reasons which render punctuality desirable, because they will understand the confusion which a late-comer causes, and you will thus do truly educative work. For later, in real life, there will not always be "bad marks" in view to oblige them to be punctual.

The school, however, is not alone to be blamed. Parents are also often blameworthy. How many there are who not only do not take any trouble to see that their children go to bed early, but who even make them stay up late, by taking them to the café or to some entertainment. By sleeping late in the morning the children are only repairing, and this is the best way in which they are able to make up for, the fault of their parents. To do otherwise would be to arrive in school with a brain unfit for work. That is what the school, which punishes them, does not understand.[1]

I have just criticised the school. The criticism is easy; but it is less easy to discover how we may be able, without falling into disorder, to take account of the various requirements in the way of sleep of all our little disciples. The difficulty arises mainly from the fact that the school, as it actually is, is not adapted to the real needs of the child. The child whom the

[1] In many cases also, as every one knows, there are home tasks to be done by the scholars, which keeps them up late. We ought not, in fact, to require from children, who have been shut up in school all day, that they should set to work again immediately they return home. A walk, and many indispensable occupations (though not scholastic) find a place between the return home and supper-time. Evening tasks ought therefore to be abolished. In his researches on scholars, Axel Key has arrived at the conclusion that it is these school tasks which, above all, oblige the child to curtail his sleep (A. Key, see Burgerstein's *Handbuch d. Schulhygiene*, 1902, p. 680).

"regulations" have in mind is a sort of average and schematic being who does not exist in reality. The school is not, therefore, in a position to take account of particular cases and of individual diversities, because it has never been organised for this; and this is so true that, when its eyes are opened to the pedagogic importance of these individual diversities, it is as dumbfounded and unable to move as a night-bird which opens its eyes in an intense light.[1]

Nevertheless, these individual differences exist, and if the aim of the school is to develop individuals, and not to satisfy regulations and curricula, it is very necessary to take account of them, if only so as not to violate the *primo non nocere* which we have regarded (p. 55) as the first duty of education. How, then, can we arrange for children who are not to be awakened by force in order to go to school?

[1] Do I exaggerate? Alas! I believe not. Here, amongst many others, is a fact which has been brought to my knowledge while I am writing this paragraph: A boy of 13, whom it was necessary to wake by force every morning to go to college (although he went to bed in good time), at last fell ill; he grew thin and pale, and was inattentive, in spite of his efforts, at school. A doctor was consulted, who naturally demanded that his desire for sleep should be respected, and that he should be allowed to sleep at least an extra hour. The child's mother then went to the director of the college and asked him if her son might not, for a certain time, go to school at 9 P.M. instead of 8 P.M. The director replied that it was a very complicated matter, not foreseen in the regulations, that he was unable to give an immediate answer, that it would be necessary to consult the Council, and that he would let her know its decision later. Many weeks passed, but the answer of the director had not arrived. During this time the child continued to overwork himself, although that had not been "foreseen by the regulations." Meeting the director in the street one day, the mother of the scholar asked him for a reply. This being in the negative, it was necessary to keep the boy away from college for two months; this was the only way "according to regulations" of allowing him to satisfy his need of sleep.

The simplest way would be to make the time for entering school later, say 8.30 or 9 A.M. (in place of 8) in winter, and 8 (instead of 7) in summer. Or better, if we wish not to lose the first hour, to make it optional for children to arrive at what time they like between 8 and 9 A M. It would be necessary, of course, to put on the time-table, for the first lesson, a subject of secondary importance, such as singing, drawing, manual work, and various revisions. This would be a question to be studied.

There is in all cases one day of the week when lessons ought to begin later, viz. Monday, because of the excursions which the children often make on Sunday. Nothing so disposes one to sleep as these days in the fresh air, without mentioning the fatigue due to walking.[1]

We may, however, ask ourselves whether it is worth while to take account at this point of individual needs, and if there is not, on the contrary, an advantage for the education of character in habituating the child to complying with certain rules, and sometimes to do itself violence.

Doubtless, but on condition that the rules and the

[1] It would be interesting and useful to make an inquiry into the difficulty children have in getting up in the morning This inquiry could be easily carried out by teachers. It would be sufficient to question the children themselves when they came to school. Each might be asked the following questions. "Did you wake *yourself* this morning; or, better, was it necessary to wake you (alarum, call, &c.), and, in this case, were you awakened *easily* or *with difficulty* (was it necessary to call you many times), or *with great difficulty* (was it necessary to pull you out by force, &c)?" By repeating this questionnaire a certain number of consecutive days, we should find out individual differences, we should see how the waking was affected by the days, the seasons, &c. It would be necessary to note separately the wakings due to accidental causes (loud noises in the street, claps of thunder, nightmare, &c.).

violence may not be to the detriment of its health. Doubtless we ought to fight against greediness, and to accustom the child to eat everything that is given it—except, however, indigestible or unsuitable food, which would only upset his stomach.

From what we know of sleep we do not exactly know how far it is expedient to repress its excess—or that which appears to us excess—because we do not yet well know its cause. When the child sleeps very much, is it greedy of sleep, or is it from pure need? I decidedly believe that it sleeps only because it needs sleep, and while there is any doubt on this point, one should not hesitate to act as if it were so.

But is not sleep educable? Are we not able to teach waking up at a certain time, and even how to sleep only a short time?

If sleep is, as my biological theory assumes, a positive function, an instinct, nothing prevents us from considering such education as possible (within certain limits, of course). It is the property of instinctive functions—as opposed to reflexes, which are entirely mechanical—to be, up to a certain point, plastic, adaptable, and modifiable by habit.[1] And our everyday observation shows us how much waking is subject to *habit*. But it is also precisely because of this that when we see some one, and especially a child, not waking at the usual time, we are entitled to assume that the organism claims, for that day, more sleep than ordinarily. To habituate a child to wake itself at a certain fixed hour is therefore an excellent rule, on condition that it is not an inflexible rule, since sleep depends in a large measure upon the processes of growth, phenomena with whose irregular behaviour we ought not to dream of interfering.

[1] Claparède, *Théorie biologique du Sommeil*, Geneva, 1905.

Waking is not only under the influence of habit, it is also under that of *interest.* When we have an interesting day in view, we wake much more easily, and more spontaneously, than when this is not the case. Children do not remain asleep on Christmas morning, when the night before they have put their little stockings on the bed-rail. And perhaps they would remain asleep less often on other days if the school had more attraction for them. It is quite possible, in fact, that when it is to their interest to get up early, they will sleep a *sounder* and therefore more rapidly recuperative sleep. I have noticed in my own case that in mountain climbing, on a tour, on military service, &c., if I sleep only four hours at a time, *knowing beforehand that I could not sleep more,* this short sleep is very much more recuperative than if I am suddenly awakened at the end of a four hours' sleep, *when I believed, on going to sleep, that I should be likely to sleep eight.* It is as though my organism, knowing that my sleep was bound to be short, had crowded it into a few hours, had made it gain in soundness what it was bound to lose in duration.

Is education capable of thus shortening sleep without causing the loss of any of its recuperative value, in other words, of augmenting its *speed?* In the absence of observations and experiments it is impossible to answer this question. We do not know if the rhythm of sleep is sufficiently independent of inborn temperament for us to be able to modify it to an appreciable degree. We see intelligent and strong-willed people who have never been able to bring themselves to get up early or to do with little sleep; and if they force themselves, they are good for nothing for the whole day.

What ought to be the normal duration of sleep for

children? Doctors are agreed upon the following figures:—

Children from	5 to 8	years of age:	11 to 12 hours.
„ „	9 to 10	„ „	10 to 11 „
„ „	11 to 13	„ „	9 to 10 „
„ „	14 to 15	„ „	9 „

These are average values. Certain children need more; perhaps there are some who are able without any inconvenience to content themselves with less (it would be interesting to have returns of observation by teachers or parents on this point). Finally, let us remember that the child, like the man, has greater need of sleep in winter than in summer.

With children for whom the night's sleep does not suffice, a short sleep of fifteen minutes, after the midday meal, may have very beneficial effects.[1]

If we inform ourselves about the conditions of the sleep of children, we find that for the greater part they are defective. We have quoted above the inquiry of Friedrich. We are able to add the observations of Dr. Bernhard on 6651 Berlin scholars from 6 to 14 years of age, and of Miss Ravenhill on 6180 English scholars.[2] Bernhard found that the deficiency in the hours of sleep amounted to one and a half hours, and Miss Ravenhill to two hours and three-quarters on the average. Bernhard has further shown that only a third of the children sleep by themselves in their bed, and that most share their room with numerous other persons (44 per cent. with four persons or more), the consequence of which is a vitiation of the

[1] Seashore, *The Mid-day Nap*, J. of Ed. Psy, May 1910, Heller, *Ermudungsmessungen*, Wien. med. Presse, 1899

[2] Bernhard, *Zur Kenntniss d Schlafverhaltnisse Berliner Gemeindeschuler*, Bericht Kongross f. Kinderforschung, Berlin, 1906; Ravenhill, *Investig. into Hours of Sleep*, Ar. int. hyg scol. V, 1908.

breathable air, without taking account of the other inconveniences of a cohabitation so little hygienic.

To inquire into the manner in which the child behaves with regard to deprivation of sleep is therefore one of the first duties of pedagogy. We should laugh at a "chauffeur" who started out on his automobile without being assured that his accumulators were sufficiently charged. But, I do not know why, we find it quite natural that an educator should go on his way without ever having a care for the cerebral accumulator upon which depends the intellectual work and the moral strength of the children entrusted to his guidance.

BIBLIOGRAPHY

General Works.—In the first place we must mention the admirable book of Mosso, *La Fatigue*, 1891 (Fr. trans., Paris, 1894). The work of Binet and Henri, *La Fatigue intellectuelle*, Paris, 1898, is an exposition of the methods of measuring fatigue, and of the chief experiments made up to the time of its publication. Ioteyko's article on *Fatigue* in Richet's Dictionary of Physiology, 1903, gives a general view of the question, with bibliographies. Offner (good bibliography). Tissié (quoted above). Burgerstein and Netolitzky, *Handbuch der Schulhygiene*, second edition, Jena, 1902, p. 454.

Measurement of Fatigue and School Investigation.—Sikorsky, *Sur les effets de la lassitude provoquée par les travaux intellectuels chez les enfants*, Ann. d'hygiène, publ. 1879. Laser, *Ueber geistige Ermüdung beim Schulunterricht*, Z. f. Schulgesundheitsflege, 1894. Holmes, *The Fatigue of a School Hour*, Ped. S., 1895. Vannod, C. R., Congrès de Nuremberg, II., 1904. Adsersen, *Eine ästhesiometrische Untersuchung*, ibid. (the author has ascertained some periodical oscillations of Weber's threshold, and believes them to be dependent on the oscillations of the temperature of the body). Abelson, *Mental Fatigue*, Ar. int. hyg. scol. V., 1908. Bonoff, Noikow, ibid. IV., 1908. Quirsfeld, Prag. med. Woch., 1908. Freeman, *Fatigue in School Children as tested by the Ergograph*, Am. Journ. Med. Sc., 1908 (no results). A very complete bibliography will be found in the thesis of Baade, quoted p. 238.

Ergography.—LARGUIER DES BANCELS, *Revue des derniers travaux sur la technique de l'ergographe*, An. ps. VII, 1902. TREVES, *L'énergie de contraction volontaire et la fatigue nerveuse*, Arch. di Fisiologia, 1904, *Contr. allo studio dei fenomeni soggettivi di fatica*, Giorn della Soc. ital. d'Igiene, 1905. BERGSTROM, *A New Type of Ergograph*, Am. J. Ps., 1903. ATHANASIU, *Ergographe double à bille*, C. R Soc. Biol., 1908, t. 64, p 79, and 65, p. 691.

Comparison of the Different Methods.—GINEFF, *Prufung der Methoden zur Messung geistiger Ermudung*, Diss. Zurich, 1899 (according to this author, it is the time taken in carrying out a piece of work which constitutes the best measure of fatigue; he rejects the æsthesiometric method). LARGUIER DES BANCELS, *Comparaison des différentes méthodes de mesure de la fatigue intellectuelle*, An ps. V., 1899. ELLIS and SHIPE, *Present Methods of testing Fatigue*, Am J. Ps., 1903. BAADE, quoted above.

Criticism of the Various Methods (specially of æsthesiometry).—LEUBA, GERMAN, Ps. Rev, 1899. THORNDIKE, ibid., 1900. RITTER, quoted above. KRAEPELIN, *Ueber Ermudungsmessungen*, Ar. f. g. Ps I., 1903. BOLTON, *Ueber die Beziehungen zwischen Ermudung, Raumsinn der Haut und Muskelleistung*, Ps. Arb. IV., 1904. ALTSCHUL, *Wert der Experim. bei Schuleruntersuchungen*, C. R. Congrès de Nuremberg, 1904, II. CHABOT, *Les nouvelles rech. esthésiométr.*, Rev. Pédag., 1905 MALAPERT, *Les rech exp. sur la mesure de la fatigue et les conclusions pédag qu'on en peut tirer*, Bull. S. po. E, 1905 ALEXANDER, *Die Methoden z. Messung der geist. Ermudung der Schulkinder*, Diss. med. Breslau, 1908 (conclusions: æsthesiometry has no value, ergography scarcely more, but ergography would be useful for detecting neuropathic pupils See the reply of Griesbach in Pflug. Arch., vol. 131, 1910, p. 126) Mlle. MOTCHOULSKY, Thèse de Berne, 1900, has noted the variations of the sensibility of the skin under the influence of temperature, of health, &c.

Curves of Work, and Various Investigations—KRAEPELIN, *Ueber geistige Arbeit*, Jena, 1897. MIESEMER, *Psych. Wirkungen Korperlicher u. geistiger Arbeit*, Ps. Arb. IV. RÜDIN, *Ueber die Dauer der psychischen Alkoholwirkung*, ibid. WIMMS, *A Method of estimating Fatigability*, B. J. of Psy. II., 1907, p. 193. GRIESBACH, *Hirnlokalisation und Ermudung*, Pfluger's Arch., 1910, Bd. 131 (the plan of the author was to determine by the aid of the æsthesiometer the fatigue of each of the hemispheres · in the state of repose Weber's threshold is equal on the right and on the left of the body during the repose; but at the end of a piece of intellectual work, especially of memorisation, the threshold is higher on the right, which indicates that the left hemisphere works more than the right). SCRIPTURE, *Researches on Reaction-time*, Stud. Yale Ps. Lab. IV., 1896 (fatigue prolongs the time of reaction); *Researches on Voluntary Effort*, ibid. (experiments with the dynamometer: fatigue increases the average variation). On *the method of tapping*, see BRYAN, Am. J. Psy., 1892. On *the periodicity of effort*, see LOMBARD, Am. J. Psy., 1891. PILLSBURY, *Attention Waves as a means of measuring Fatigue*, Am. J. Psy., 1903. Descriptions are given of the periodical oscillations of the vital energy of man, comprising periods of about twenty-eight days: see SWOBODA, *Die Perioden des menschlichen Organismus*, Vienna, 1904, and *Die kritischen Tage des Menschen*, Vienna, 1909.

Dynamometry.—Féré, *Sensation et mouvement*, Paris, 1887, and *Travail et plaisir*, Paris, 1904. Mention may here be made of the suggestive discourse of W. JAMES on *The Energies of Man* (delivered in Dec. 1906). James thinks that every man possesses treasures of energy, "reservoirs of energy," but that he does not make use of them because he does not know how to remove the obstacles which block the way. His idea seems to have exercised a certain influence on two quite recent works devoted to the problem of fatigue, viz. that of M'DOUGALL, *Fatigue*, communicated to the British Association, Dublin, 1908, and BRAIN, 1909, and that of BURNHAM, *The Problem of Fatigue*, Am. J. of Psy., July 1908. M'DOUGALL admits that the organism considered as a whole constitutes a "great common reservoir of free energy," and he shows how this way of looking at it throws light upon the problem of fatigue. I was very glad to find in this author views analogous to those which I have developed in the preceding chapter, views at which I had arrived before I had any knowledge of his work (in a bibliographic notice, Ar. de Psy. V., 1905, p. 56, I had already alluded to the presence of a reservoir of energy on which the dynamogenisation of adapted reactions would depend).

Overpressure.—MATHIEU, *La question du surmenage scolaire*, Ar. int. hyg. scol. IV. HERGEL, *Die Schülerüberbürdungsklage*, C. R. Congrès de Nuremberg, 1904, II. SCHUYTEN, *Qu'est-ce que le surmenage?* Rev. Psych., 1908. IMBERT, *Le surmenage professionel*, An. ps. XIV., 1908. TREVES, *Le surmenage par suite du travail professionel*, Congrès int. d'hygiène, Berlin, 1907. H. SCHULTZE, *Zur Frage der Erschöpfungszustände der Schuljugend*, Diss. med. Rostock, 1909 (inquiry into the subject of the backward or feeble children in the schools; not a psychological study).

Time-tables.—SEMERAD, *Ueber die Notwendigkeit und die Vorteile des ungeteilten Unterrichts*, C. R. Congrès de Nuremberg, II. (lessons should only take place in the morning; this result could be achieved if the wholly useless subjects were banished from the curricula, and if actual life were considered). MARTIN, *Contribution à l'étude du travail scolaire*, Bull. S. ps. E., March 1910 (the influence of habit on work is very great: it is important to commence work at the hour at which one is in the habit of working; it is therefore not of great importance to place the most fatiguing lessons at one hour rather than another).

Histological Alterations.—The nervous cells undergo certain alterations under the influence of exhaustion; these have been studied by HODGE, Am. J. Psy., 1888, 1892; STEFANOWSKA, Congrès de Psychol., 1900, Arch. des sc. phys. et nat., 1897, 1901; PUGNAT, Journ. de physiol., 1901; DEMOOR, Arch. de Biol., 1896, &c. See bibliography in IOTEYKO.

Pathological Fatigue.—REVILLIOD, *La fatigue*, Bull. Soc. méd. de la Suisse romande, 1880 (in this remarkable work the author sets forth the symptomatology of the fatigue disease, to which he gives the name of "*ponose*"). See, finally, the various and innumerable works on neurasthenia—we will here mention only JANET, *Les obsessions et la psychasténie*, Paris, 1903; HARTENBERG, *Psychologie des neurasthéniques*, Paris, 1908; WATERMAN, *Treatment of the Fatigue States*, Journ. of abnorm. Psy., July 1909. The curves of fatigue in different pathological states have been undertaken by GROSS, Psy. Arb. II.; BALLET and PHILIPPE, Rev. neurol., 1903; SPECHT, Ar. f. g. Ps. III., 1904; BREUKINK, Journ. f. Psychol. IV., 1904.

Sleep.—NETSCHAJEFF, Z. f. Schulgesundheitspfl., 1900 (quoted by BURGERSTEIN, *Handbuch der Schulhyg.*, p. 679: the author states that as a student he needed more than eight hours' sleep). CZERNY, *Beobachtungen über den Schlaf im Kindesalter*, Jahrbuch f. *Kinderheilkunde*, vol. 33. BEVAN-LEWIS, *Fatigue, Rest, and Sleep*, Journ. of Mental Science, October 1906. CRAMAUSSEL, *Le sommeil d'un petit enfant*, Ar. de Psy. (vol. x., 1911). That pedagogues still take little account of the importance of sleep may be seen, among other things, from the fact that in the great *Encyklop. Handbuch der Pädagogik* of Rein, 10 vols. (1903–1910), there is no article on sleep.

ADDENDA

P. 21. From 1911, the *Zeitsch. f. pädag. Psychol.* and *Zeitsch. f. exp. Pädag.* will be amalgated in the *Zeitsch. f. päd. Psych. und Päd.*, under the editorship of Messrs. Meumann and Scheibner.

P. 27. Add for Italy the name of Mme. Dr. MONTESSORI, of Rome, the authoress of an interesting method of teaching young children (*cf.* Educ., Sept. 1910, p. 360).

P. 34. A new periodical of popular pedagogy has just been brought out in Switzerland, entitled *Zeitsch. f. Jugenderziehung* (Zurich).

P. 37. For pedagogy in France, see GHIDIONESCU, *Moderne pädag. Stromungen in Frankreich*, Langensalza, 1910.

P. 100. To methods of research add ERN. JONES, *Psycho analysis and Education*, J. ed. Ps., Nov. 1910. On the service that animal psychology may render to pedagogy, CLAPARÈDE, *Die Bedeutung der Tierpsychologie f. die Pädagogik*, Z. f. päd. Ps. and exp. Päd. (to appear in 1911).

P. 206. Add APPLETON, *Comparative Study of the Play Activities of Adult Savages and Civilised Children*, Chicago, 1910. COLVIN, *The Educational Value of Humour*, Ped. S., 1907. BARAT, *La joie et la santé dans l'école*, C. R. Congrès de Nuremberg, 1901, vol. ii.

P. 251. On work and rest, see LINDLEY, *Arbeit u. Ruhe*, Psy. Arb. III., p. 499; WIMMS, *Fatigue and Practice*, B. J. of Psy. II., 1907, pp. 173, 193.

P. 253. On work and fatigue, see KEMSIES, *Arbeitshygiene der Schule*, Berlin, 1898; *Arbeitstypen bei Schülern*, Z. päd. Psy. III., 1901, p. 362; BLAZEK, *ibid.*, 1899; MEUMANN, *Vorlesungen*, II., p. 10.

GENERAL INDEX

INDEX OF NAMES

THE END

Printed by Ballantyne, Hanson & Co.
Edinburgh & London

CPSIA information can be obtained
at www.ICGtesting.com
Printed in the USA
BVHW041639280320
576252BV00006B/19

9 781341 153600